Political Community and the North Atlantic Area

INTERNATIONAL ORGANIZATION IN THE LIGHT OF HISTORICAL EXPERIENCE

BY

Karl W. Deutsch · Sidney A. Burrell
Robert A. Kann · Maurice Lee, Jr.
Martin Lichterman · Raymond E. Lindgren
Francis L. Loewenheim · Richard W. Van Wagenen

GREENWOOD PRESS, PUBLISHERS
NEW YORK

To the Memory of

John Parker Compton

killed in action in Italy, 1945

PREFACE

◇◇◇

This is the first report of a large-scale interdisciplinary study designed to throw new light on an old problem. The old problem is the elimination of war. The new light comes from historical evidence gathered within a framework of concepts that has not, to the best of our knowledge, been previously explored by historians. Our study concerns the problem of building a wider political community.

The Center for Research on World Political Institutions, ever since it was founded in 1950, has devoted its efforts to the study of international organization. Its special concern has been the central problem of international organization—the elimination of war. The authors of the present volume hoped, by examining the past experience of Germany, the Habsburg Empire, Italy, Norway–Sweden, Switzerland, the United Kingdom, and the United States, to learn what history might tell us about this problem.

The methods and techniques used in this study are explained in Chapter I. Here, the authors express the hope that their work will be of interest to historians as well as to scholars in the fields of international organization and international politics, and also to the well-informed public.

A second volume, considerably longer, will present our final conclusions and a much greater body of supporting historical detail. Therefore the historical evidence prepared for this longer study is barely reflected in the documentation of Chapters II and III of the present book. In addition, the Center expects to publish, in the near future, two monographs based upon manuscripts prepared for the present book: Professor Robert A. Kann's study of the Habsburg Empire and Professor Raymond E. Lindgren's study of Norway–Sweden. The first is being published early in 1957 by Frederick A. Praeger under the title *The Habsburg Empire: A Study in Integration and Disintegration*, and the latter is being published late in 1958 by Princeton University

Press under the tentative title, *Union, Disunion, Reunion: A Study of the Dissolution of the Union of Norway and Sweden and Scandinavian Integration.* Some of the other authors of the present volume are also preparing their own separate studies for publication.

This is an interdisciplinary study in the sense that historians and political scientists collaborated closely at all stages, and also in the sense that one of the political scientists (Professor Deutsch) has had considerable experience in other social sciences. The eight co-authors met frequently as a group, and each resided in Princeton for periods up to two years, as members of the Center's staff. Although all members do not necessarily subscribe to every statement in the book, the group collectively accepts responsibility for the work as a whole.

The historical material in this volume and the later one was prepared by the following: German case, Francis L. Loewenheim (College of William and Mary); case of the Habsburg Empire, Robert A. Kann (Rutgers University); Italian case, Maurice Lee, Jr. (Princeton University); case of Norway–Sweden, Raymond E. Lindgren (Occidental College); United Kingdom cases (England–Wales, England–Scotland, and United Kingdom–Ireland), Sidney A. Burrell (Barnard College); and case of the United States, Martin Lichterman (Massachusetts Institute of Technology.)

The comparative generalizations are mainly the work of Karl W. Deutsch, of the Massachusetts Institute of Technology, and are based on his analysis of all the detailed historical studies. The contemporary application of the historical findings is mainly the work of Richard W. Van Wagenen, of Princeton University, who also originated the project and directed it throughout. The draft of the entire book has been worked over by all collaborating authors and revised in the light of their comments.

Several other persons helped us substantially. Foremost among them was Dr. Hermann Weilenmann, of the University of Zurich, who came to Princeton in the summer of 1953 to prepare for the Center a summary of the Swiss case as seen within the framework of this project. Parts of his work have been incorporated in this volume. Dr. Weilenmann and Dr. Deutsch plan to issue a fuller study of their own on the development of the Swiss political community.

Consultants outside the Princeton faculty who helped us on particular occasions included the late Edward Mead Earle and Nicholas Mansergh. Consultants among the faculty and graduate students at Princeton are too numerous to name, but the members of the Faculty Committee of the Center would be high on any list: Professors Frederick S. Dunn, Dana Gardner Munro, Frank W. Notestein, Whitney J. Oates, Harold Sprout, Joseph R. Strayer, and John B. Whitton.

Of the Center's staff, the two Assistants in Research who devoted the most time to this project at various stages were Mrs. Yvette E. Gurley and Mrs. Johanna M. Lederer. Others who helped from time to time were Julien Engel, Samuel Krislov, Sol Rosenthal, and George Rudisill. Editorial assistance was provided by Dr. Harry T. Moore.

As we have never done in public before, we wish to thank the A. W. Mellon Charitable and Educational Trust for the grant in 1951 which enabled us to undertake this study. We are grateful that the officers of the Trust saw the importance of research on this problem and agreed to do something about it.

Our gratitude to Randolph and Dorothy Compton and their friends and family is expressed here once again. They founded the Center as a living memorial to John Parker Compton (Princeton Class of 1947), to whom this volume is dedicated.

Individual authors wish to acknowledge their gratitude for support they received in pursuing research related directly or indirectly to this work: Sidney Burrell to the American Philosophical Society, the Barnard College Research Fund, and the Columbia University Council for Research in the Social Sciences; Karl Deutsch to the John Simon Guggenheim Memorial Foundation; Robert Kann also to the Guggenheim Foundation, and to the Research Council of Rutgers University; Raymond Lindgren to the Fulbright Program of the United States Government; and Francis Loewenheim to the Institute for Advanced Study at Princeton.

Only the co-authors, however, have any responsibility for the results of our study as presented in this volume. We realize that these results are neither conclusive nor all-inclusive. Yet we hope, with Stephen Vincent Benét, that at the very least "the dry bones littered by the way/ May still point giants toward their golden prey."

R. W. VAN WAGENEN
Director, Center for Research
on World Political Institutions

June 1956

POSTSCRIPT TO THE PREFACE

Since the Preface was written, two events of outstanding relevance to the inquiry have occurred. Both are well known to the most general reader: the invasion of Egypt by Israel, Britain and France, in October-November, and the adoption by the North Atlantic Council in December of the policy proposed by the Committee of Three calling for greater consultation among the members and greater powers for the Secretary-General of NATO. The first event showed a startling lack of mutual responsiveness among some of the leading members of NATO. The second event showed a determination to increase that responsiveness and to institutionalize it to some degree in the making of future foreign policy decisions. At the present time it seems clear that this is a serious resolve and not a routine resolution. In line with our conclusions, it seems to us that this resolve is precisely the kind of plan that should be put into effect if integration is considered the ultimate object within the North Atlantic area.

R.W.V.W.

January 1957

CONTENTS

◇◇

POLITICAL COMMUNITY AND THE
NORTH ATLANTIC AREA

◇◇

CHAPTER I

Introduction

◇◇

A ◇ *THE PROBLEM*

We undertook this inquiry as a contribution to the study of possible ways in which men some day might abolish war.

From the outset, we realized the complexity of the problem. It is difficult to relate "peace" clearly to other prime values such as "justice" and "freedom." There is little common agreement on acceptable alternatives to war, and there is much ambiguity in the use of the terms "war" and "peace." Yet we can start with the assumption that war is now so dangerous that mankind must eliminate it, must put it beyond serious possibility. The attempt to do this may fail. But in a civilization that wishes to survive, the central problem in the study of international organization is this: How can men learn to act together to eliminate war as a social institution?

This is in one sense a smaller, and in another sense a larger, question than the one which occupies so many of the best minds today: how can we either prevent or avoid losing "the next war"? It is smaller because there will, of course, be no chance to solve the long-run problem if we do not survive the short-run crisis. It is larger because it concerns not only the confrontation of the nations of East and West in the twentieth century, but the whole underlying question of relations between political units at any time. We are not, therefore, trying to add to the many words that have been written directly concerning the East-West struggle of the 1940-1950's. Rather, we are seeking new light with which to look at the conditions and processes of long-range or permanent peace, applying our findings to one contemporary problem which, though not so difficult as the East-West problem, is by no means simple: peace *within* the North Atlantic area.

Whenever a difficult political problem arises, men turn to history for clues to its solution. They do this knowing they will not find the whole answer there. Every political problem is unique, of course, for history does not "repeat itself." But often the reflective mind will discover situations in the past that are essentially similar to the one being considered. Usually, with these rough parallels or suggestive analogies, the problem is not so much to find the facts as it is to decide what is essentially the same and what is essentially different between the historical facts and those of the present.

When most people discuss war and history in the same breath, they are likely to adopt one of two extreme positions. Some say that because history shows a continuous record of war, it indicates nothing but more of the same for the future. Others say that history shows a persistent growth in the size of the communities into which men organize themselves, and that this trend will continue until the world is living peacefully in a single community. Neither of these conclusions seems warranted on its face, though both contain some truth.

There is plenty of room between such extreme interpretations of history. Yet we know of no thorough investigation into the ways in which certain areas of the world have, in the past, "permanently" eliminated war. Historians, especially diplomatic historians, have covered a great deal of ground in explaining how wars were avoided for long and short periods of time, but they have not gone into detail in explaining how and why certain groups have permanently stopped warring. Those who believe that international war is here to stay may be correct. But we may point out that war *has* been eliminated permanently, for all practical purposes, over large areas. If we could be sure of results, we would find it worth our while to spend many millions of man-hours and many millions of dollars in studying how this condition came about and how it might be extended over larger and larger areas of the globe. Thus far no such effort has been made, and no techniques for it have been perfected. In the course of our study, therefore, we had to develop our own techniques. This book is the first result of a limited but somewhat novel inquiry.

We are dealing here with political communities. These we regard as social groups with a process of political communication, some machinery for enforcement, and some popular habits of compliance. A political community is not necessarily able to prevent war within the area it covers: the United States was unable to do so at the time of the Civil War. Some political communities do, however, eliminate war and the expectation of war within their boundaries. It is these that call for intensive study.

We have concentrated, therefore, upon the formation of "security-communities" in certain historical cases. The use of this term starts a chain of definitions, and we must break in here to introduce the other main links needed for a fuller understanding of our findings.

A SECURITY-COMMUNITY is a group of people which has become "integrated."

By INTEGRATION we mean the attainment, within a territory, of a "sense of community" and of institutions and practices strong enough and widespread enough to assure, for a "long" time, dependable expectations of "peaceful change" among its population.

By SENSE OF COMMUNITY we mean a belief on the part of individuals in a group that they have come to agreement on at least this one point: that common social problems must and can be resolved by processes of "peaceful change."

By PEACEFUL CHANGE we mean the resolution of social problems, normally by institutionalized procedures, without resort to large-scale physical force.

A security-community, therefore, is one in which there is real assurance that the members of that community will not fight each other physically, but will settle their disputes in some other way. If the entire world were integrated as a security-community, wars would be automatically eliminated. But there is apt to be confusion about the term "integration."

In our usage, the term "integration" does not necessarily mean only the merging of peoples or governmental units into a single unit. Rather, we divide security-communities into two types: "amalgamated" and "pluralistic."

By AMALGAMATION we mean the formal merger of two or more previously independent units into a single larger unit, with some type of common government after amalgamation. This common government may be unitary or federal. The United States today is an example of the amalgamated type. It became a single governmental unit by the formal merger of several formerly independent units. It has one supreme decision-making center.

The PLURALISTIC security-community, on the other hand, retains the legal independence of separate governments. The combined territory of the United States and Canada is an example of the pluralistic type. Its two separate governmental units form a security-community without being merged. It has two supreme decision-making centers. Where amalgamation occurs without integration, of course a security-community does not exist.

Since our study deals with the problem of ensuring peace, we shall say that any political community, be it amalgamated or pluralistic, was eventually SUCCESSFUL if it became a security-community—that is, if it achieved integration—and that it was UNSUCCESSFUL if it ended eventually in secession or civil war.

Perhaps we should point out here that both types of integration require, at the international level, some kind of organization, even though it may be very loose. We put no credence in the old aphorism that among friends a constitution is not necessary and among enemies it is of no avail. The area of practicability lies in between.

Integration is a matter of fact, not of time. If people on both sides do not fear war and do not prepare for it, it matters little how long it took them to reach this stage. But once integration has been reached, the length of time over which it persists may contribute to its consolidation.

It should be noted that integration and amalgamation over-lap, but not completely. This means that there can be amal-gamation without integration, and that there can be integration without amalgamation. When we use the term "integration or amalgamation" in this book, we are taking a short form to ex-press an alternative between integration (by the route of either pluralism or amalgamation) and amalgamation short of inte-gration. We have done this because unification movements in the past have often aimed at both of these goals, with some of

	NON-AMALGAMATION	AMALGAMATION
INTEGRATION	Pluralistic Security-Community EXAMPLE (Norway-Sweden today)	Amalgamated Security-Community EXAMPLE (U.S.A. today)
	....................INTEGRATION	THRESHOLD..................
NON-INTEGRATION	Not Amalgamated Not Security-Community EXAMPLE (U.S.A.-U.S.S.R. today)	Amalgamated but not Security-Community EXAMPLE (Habsburg Empire 1914)

(vertical label between columns: AMALGAMATION THRESHOLD)

the supporters of the movements preferring one or the other goal at different times.[1] To encourage this profitable ambiguity, leaders of such movements have often used broader symbols such as "union," which would cover both possibilities and could be made to mean different things to different men.

One of our basic premises is that whatever we can learn about the process of forming security-communities should be helpful in an indirect way not only to planners, but also to existing international organizations. If the way to integration, domestic or international, is through the achievement of a sense of com-

[1] This point is discussed more fully in Chapter III, Section D.

munity that undergirds institutions, then it seems likely that an increased sense of community would help to strengthen whatever institutions—supranational or international—are already operating. When these institutions are agencies for enforcement of the public will, we encounter that ancient and tantalizing puzzle: who polices the police? Can we make certain that agreements, freely entered into, will be reliably enforced or peacefully changed? Until we can do this, war may be called upon to do the job, liquidating the disputing parties instead of the dispute.

Everyone knows that political machinery already exists for reaching international decisions, and that these decisions cannot always be enforced after they are decided upon. Likewise, judicial machinery also exists which could be used for settling any international dispute without force; but states cannot be brought before a court against their will, nor made to abide by its judgment. It is equally true that enforcement or compliance can be achieved for a time without willing acceptance, as in the case of a strong state against a weak one. But without steady acceptance by large numbers of people, compliance is bound to be ineffective or temporary.

A situation of compliance, then, presupposes general agreement about something. Perhaps the "something" has to be the substance of the matter being complied with, or perhaps merely the legitimacy of the enforcing agent, or even the rightfulness of the procedure being used. Once men have attained this condition of agreement with regard to a social institution for enforcement of the public will, and have stabilized this condition, that institution would seem to be reliably supported: the police are effectively policed. This kind of institution—perhaps the most crucial of all—represents the force organized on behalf of the community. In our terms, a sense of community would have been achieved to a high degree—perhaps high enough to be considered as integration.

It is the object of our inquiry to learn as much as possible about how such a condition has been reached under various circumstances at various times. Through this study, we hope to learn how that condition could be approached more closely in the present world.

B ◈ THE AREA

Although the North Atlantic area has often been called a "community," it may not actually be one. Nor is it necessarily a security-community.

It has been suggested that the United States should support the calling of a conference of democratic countries to consider forming a North Atlantic union; this would presumably be an amalgamated security-community. Certainly there is considerable support for the tightening of one existing international organization—NATO[1a]—until it becomes at least a pluralistic security-community. Indeed, the North Atlantic area contains subareas of integration, some of them already partly equipped with institutions that may or may not have the capacity to develop. Space, however, permits us to deal with these subareas only in the most summary way.

We chose the North Atlantic area for our focus because it includes all major powers of the free world; it is the leading alternative to Western European integration; and it includes Western Europe.

Our first problem here is to decide what we mean by "the North Atlantic area." Three main alternatives appear, once it has been granted that for the time being we would be politically unrealistic if we included the countries now dominated by the Soviet Union. Those countries are not free agents; and, except for East Germany, they are not usually taken into most calculations about possible integration of the North Atlantic area.

One alternative would be to include all countries geographically situated on the North Atlantic Ocean or the North Sea or in the immediate hinterland of that area.

Another would be to equate "North Atlantic area" with "NATO membership." This would mean the inclusion of Greece and Turkey, far from the North Atlantic geographically, and

[1a] The North Atlantic Treaty Organization.

the exclusion of Austria, Finland, Ireland, Spain, Sweden, and Switzerland. Further, this selection would tie us to a consideration of one existing international organization only.

A third alternative would be to confine ourselves to the democracies located in whatever we consider to be the North Atlantic area. This choice, however, would tend to prejudge the question, slanting the answer toward democracy as a requirement for integration. This would also ignore the fact that one of the two nondemocracies in the area (Portugal) has been active in some European international organizations as well as in NATO. Since we are, above all, studying problems of international organization, we would not be fair in excluding at the outset active members of international organizations for any reason except geographic location.

The first alternative seems to us the best because it is both simple and familiar. Geography is the positive test of inclusion; the negative test is membership in a power bloc ideologically and politically incompatible with the West. This means that we shall include all the countries bordering upon the North Atlantic Ocean or the North Sea, along with their immediate land-neighbors in Europe, except the Soviet-dominated countries. The United States, Canada, and what is usually considered Western and Southern Europe make up this area. The following 19 countries conform to the definition: Austria, Belgium, Canada, Denmark, Finland, France, West Germany, Iceland, Ireland, Italy, Luxembourg, Netherlands, Norway, Portugal, Spain, Sweden, Switzerland, the United Kingdom, and the United States. Whether, and by what means, these countries could form a security-community is the immediate object of our inquiry.

C ◈ THE METHOD: APPLYING PAST EXPERIENCE TO PRESENT NEEDS

To reason that historical cases have something to teach us about the contemporary problem of integration is to reason by analogy. This is what most people do when they try to guide present actions by past experience. But intelligent use of experience need not rely completely upon parallels. Past examples are suggestive, not conclusive. They point in a general direction, but not toward a specific destination.

With what assurance can we apply knowledge about one historical period to the situation in another? We are using past experience to find out what arrangements appear possible, which appear probable, and which appear more probable than others. We are dealing not only with possibilities, but with priorities of probabilities. In effect, we are looking for the minimum requirements for a peaceful political community. We are trying to see what is *not* needed for integration. We can therefore subtract, so to speak, from any hypothetical list of present-day requirements, those conditions that did not have to occur during the course of successful integration in the past.

We could have attacked the problem of integration in abstract terms, by means of a purely analytical and deductive approach within the social sciences, especially political science. But we felt that any such analytical schemes were in danger of remaining too narrow, too shallow, and too unrealistic if we did not pay very serious attention to historical data. The record of what happened in history is richer and deeper than any single scheme of deduction or analysis, and we would ignore it at our peril.

But the difficulties of applying any historical findings to the present world are of the kind that have plagued historiography from the beginning. The time-gap is perhaps the most serious of these. We cannot assume that because conditions in one century led to certain effects, even roughly parallel conditions in another century would lead to similar effects. Neither can we be sure, of course, that the conditions were even roughly parallel. Most of our cases came to a climax after the industrial revolution, but not all of them. And some of the most important developments in various cases took place several generations earlier.

One of the questions that must remain in the realm of interesting speculation is this: Did change take place more slowly in earlier times than it does now? The quick answer would seem to be "yes," if we consider the vastly greater speed of travel and of the transmission of messages. But the fact that messages can be delivered more quickly to a person does not mean that he can read and understand them any faster. The speedup of transportation has not been paralleled by a comparable speedup in the human learning process. Our spans of memory and attention have not changed drastically. An hour is still an hour in the crowded schedule of the statesman, and a generation is still a generation in politics. While vicarious experience has been tremendously broadened for many people, what a person can directly experience and remember is nearly the same in one century as in another. Finally, the actual speed of travel and communication may not be so important as the image of that actual situation in the minds of decision-makers. If a place seems close or far away, for practical political purposes it *is* close or far away.

After we made allowances for the relatively small change in the speed of human learning, we found that several of our historical cases showed that large numbers of people changed their political outlook, and acquired new political loyalties, in a very short time.

This difference is perhaps compensated, or even overcompensated, when we consider that from the standpoint of our problem—integration—the relevant areas to be covered are now much greater than they were in the historical cases we investigated. We would have to prepare a series of maps showing many things—equal transportation cost by various means of transport, for example—and covering many areas, before we could say that in travel terms the North Atlantic area had by 1956 shrunk to the size of England, Wales, and Scotland in 1700, or to that of Italy in 1855. But in any event, the comparison does not seem very far out of line.

Apart from whatever degree of uncertainty must occur in our findings, they do not—it is worth remembering—exhaust the subject of our study. Even if all our findings were entirely certain, and all were applied in a particular case, they would not guarantee success. When we call certain conditions "essential," we mean that success seems to us extremely improbable in their absence. Though essential, they also seem to us insufficient: even if all of them were present, we do not know whether any other conditions might be required which we may well have over-looked.

A similar consideration applies to those conditions that we called helpful but not essential: we found that integration oc-curred in their absence, and might well recur in this way in future cases. There might be more of these conditions than we identified; and we do not know whether several of them added together might not form an ensemble or quorum which was itself an essential condition for success, though every one of its members might be replaced by some other condition. This is one of the many fascinating questions that will have to await further research.

In the end, we had to rely most of the time on nothing more scientific than the use of analogy, occasional insight, and judg-ment. It is true that "events are not affected by analogies; they are determined by the combination of circumstances."[2] But analysis of events is certainly affected by analogies. To throw analogies away would be prodigal, in the absence of any better source of clues.

The problem of uniqueness and comparability has always be-set historians. One of the scholar's hardest tasks is "to find a pattern in, or impose a pattern upon, a multitude of individual facts. There are always more facts available than any historian can master; he can deal with them only by arranging them in categories, and by generalizing from the classifications which he has made. Yet he knows that no one historical event is exactly like another, and that a single difference may be more significant than many resemblances."[3]

While the student of history should become as nearly as pos-sible the "universal man," he would need decades before he could approach the breadth of understanding in the other social sciences that he would like to achieve. As an academic discipline, International Organization is chiefly in the domain of political

[2] Harold Nicolson, *The Congress of Vienna*, Harcourt, Brace, New York, 1946, p. viii.

[3] Joseph R. Strayer, ed., in Introduction to *The Interpretation of History*, Princeton University Press, 1943, pp. 7-8.

scientists. Since a few of them have spread their training into some of the social sciences other than history, we felt that in addition to the historians a social scientist of this type was indispensable to our study. He would specialize in comparing the historical data as interpreted by the historians in each case, and in leading his associates toward the discovery of uniformities upon which he could generalize. Perhaps most important, he would provide working concepts and hypotheses.

The need for such a combination has been very well stated by a leading historian: "The Historian thus becomes doubly useful to the disciplines engaged in the effort to understand society. He is not merely a purveyor of data to the social scientist; he also provides a check upon the validity of social science concepts for the past. Social scientists, impatient with the historian who rejects their most favored concepts because he knows exceptions, would do well to remember that the health of a science depends upon its ability to withstand challenge to its laws and to reject or revise those successfully challenged. And, on the other hand, historians should bear in mind that one cannot even issue a proper challenge if one does not appreciate the concept that is under examination. It is taken for granted that the historian ought not to write about the history of theology or of physics, for example, without knowing theology or physics. Too often, however, historians have written about markets, business, and prices or about personality and social behavior or about racial and cultural attributes either without knowing the findings of the relevant social scientists in those areas of study or without making a choice among the frequently baffling conflicts of thought among them."[4] Much may be gained by using analytical concepts to guide our historical inquiry, and by using the results of historical inquiry to modify our concepts regarding present-day problems. "Without adequate use of theory historical study cannot attain its full potential."[5]

[4] Louis Gottschalk, *Understanding History*, Knopf, 1950, p. 255.
[5] *The Social Sciences in Historical Study: A Report of the Committee on Historiography*, Bulletin 64 of the Social Science Research Council, New York, 1954, p. 25.

D ◈ THE CASES

Since historical cases can at best be compared in only some of their aspects, and practically never in all of them, any comparison means the sacrifice of a great deal of detail, much of it important information. Yet to draw limited comparisons from only partly comparable cases is of the essence of human thought. Throughout our lives we all apply selected memories from the past to our decisions in the present and to our expectations for the future. If we elaborate this time-honored practice into a research project and call it the "case method," we can hope to be more explicit in the techniques we use, in the assumptions we make, and in the data we leave out. At any rate, our present study will be of no interest to those who believe that men cannot learn from historical experience.

This brings us to the special problems of the case method. On a rough count, we find about three dozen historical cases which have the characteristics that make them worth investigating with the problem of integration in mind. Other students might add or subtract a few, but since there are only about 110 states in the world (independent or quasi-independent), and since many of them are not involved at present in any major problem of federation or secession, the order of magnitude would not change greatly.

Eleven of these cases are in western and central Europe: Austria–Hungary and its successors, the British Isles, Denmark–Iceland, Finland (the union with Sweden and the union with Russia), France (including the absorption of Languedoc and parts of Burgundy), Germany, the Iberian Peninsula, Italy, the Low Countries, Norway–Sweden, and Switzerland. Six cases are in the western hemisphere: Canada, the United States, Brazil, Gran Colombia and its present-day successors (Colombia, Ecuador, Panama, and Venezuela), the Central American Federation, and the countries of the former Spanish viceroyalty of the River Plate (Argentina, Paraguay, and Uruguay). Five other cases are in eastern Europe: Poland (unions with Lithuania and Ukraine), Russia, Rumania (Moldavia, Wallachia, and Transylvania), Yugoslavia, and in part the Ottoman Empire. Eight cases are in Asia: India, Pakistan, China, Burma, Indonesia, Viet Nam, the Malay Federation, and the political fragmentation of the Arabian Peninsula (particularly the breakup of Palestine). We find three additional cases within the British Commonwealth: Australia, the Union of South Africa, and the new Central African Federation. Twenty of these thirty-three cases are countries of western culture located either in western Europe, the western hemisphere, or the British Commonwealth.

In selecting a limited number of cases for intensive investigation, we concentrated on the area of Western European and North Atlantic civilization. There are obviously other cases that we should have liked to include. Considerations of time, resources, availability of data, or apparent comparability with contemporary problems, excluded some of the earliest cases as well as all of those located in Asia, native Africa (south of the Sahara), and most of eastern Europe.

A much more important consideration than geographic or cultural area was the selection of cases that would show both successful and unsuccessful experience with integration. First, we had to limit ourselves to "closed" as contrasted to "open" cases—that is, those whose outcome is definitely settled, as contrasted with those whose outcome is not. For example, we feel sure that the United States is integrated; Yugoslavia, on the other hand, may or may not be. Second, we had to be certain that two kinds of cases were included: those where a security-community was successfully established and those where a security-community was established for a time but dissolved in the long run. Third, we had to include both types of security-community: the amalgamated and the pluralistic.

We selected ten cases, eight of them for intensive study: (1) the union of the American colonies into the United States in 1789, its breakup in the Civil War, and the reunion that followed; (2) the gradual development of union between England and Scotland and its consummation in 1707; (3) the breakup of the union between Ireland (including Ulster) and the United Kingdom in 1921; (4) the struggle for German unity since the

Middle Ages, culminating in the unification of Germany in 1871;
(5) the problem of Italian unity since the end of the eighteenth
century, culminating in the unification of Italy in 1859-1860;
(6) the long preservation and final dissolution in 1918 of the
Habsburg Empire; (7) the union of Norway and Sweden in 1814
and their separation in 1905; and (8) the gradual integration of
Switzerland that was completed in 1848. Two other cases we
studied less intensively: (9) the union of England with Wales
after 1485; and (10) the formation of England itself in the Middle Ages.

This collection of cases provides at least one of each type
needed. It also supplies reasonably good samples of most of the
important cultural traditions and institutional patterns of western Europe and the North Atlantic area. Although the origins of
their integration go back to widely different times, most of the
cases went through comparable stages, regardless of actual dates.
The cases have enough in common so that the findings from
each are reasonably comparable with the findings from the
others. And we hope the findings from all of them, taken together, will throw new light upon present-day problems of political integration and plans for its attainment.

We know, of course, that every selection of cases involves the
possibility of sampling error, especially when the number of cases
is small. It is possible that if some additional cases were investigated, the results would not conform to our findings. Therefore,
we must point out again that we have stated them in terms of
probabilities. Where we found one set of circumstances occurring
far more frequently than others, we have been inclined to infer
that they are more likely to recur under certain conditions, particularly if other considerations seem to support this judgment.
If contradictory findings from an additional case in a Western
culture should turn up, they would reduce this inference of
probability, but it would ordinarily take more than one case
to invalidate it altogether.

What kinds of question did we ask about these cases? Having
as yet no orderly theory to be tested, we began by asking many
commonsense questions of a descriptive nature. We of course

knew that these would lead to other questions of a less obvious and perhaps more illuminating kind. Clearly we had to know the relative sizes, power positions, and economic levels of the various units that later approached integration. Also we had to know a great deal about their social and political institutions and about the kinds of contact which they had with each other. But as we went into the facts, we began to pay more attention to various aspects of social communication, both within and between the units. We then found that in most cases we had to go back into a much earlier period than we had planned. Despite the difference in time-span of the various cases, we drew up a common outline which we followed as closely as possible in all cases.

In studying the process of amalgamation, we had to break up some of the cases that cover several centuries. We reduced them to shorter-run situations, covering two or at most three generations, in which particular policies might be relevant enough to allow comparisons. As a result, comparisons between sixteen shorter-run situations often proved useful. Identified by their starting dates, these situations were: the increase in the unification of England after 1066; the further increase of English unity after 1215; the unification of England and Wales after 1485; the unification of England and Scotland after 1603; the union of England and Ireland in 1801; the closer identification of Northern Ireland (Ulster) with Britain after 1795; the unification of the American colonies after 1765; the confederation of the original three Swiss Cantons in 1291; the accession of the cities of Zurich and Bern to this Confederation after 1351; the accession of Geneva to the Swiss political community, by means of alliances and joint citizenship arrangements, after 1519; the unification of Italy in 1859-1860; the unification of Germany between 1866 and 1871; the dynastic union between Austria, Bohemia, and Hungary after 1526; the closer amalgamation of Austria and Bohemia after 1620; the increase in amalgamation between Austria and Hungary after 1686 (the conquest of Buda from the Turks); and the dynastic union of Norway and Sweden after 1814.

Five of these situations eventually led to outcomes in which amalgamation failed: England–Ireland, Norway–Sweden, and the three situations involving Austria. In the other eleven, amalgamation has remained successful in that it became integration; and we have sometimes made use of these groupings of "successful" and "unsuccessful" situations in order to ask which characteristics, if any, the situations in each group might have in common.

In all the historical cases we tried to avoid the easy use of some "force of nationalism" as a supposed cause of the political union or separation—or of the integration or disintegration—that followed. Certainly, nationalistic or prenationalistic sentiments—feelings of loyalty to some territory, group, or state—played some role in all our cases. But in the case of any larger community these feelings were themselves the results, not the causes, of the political and historical processes that made for integration or disintegration. Produced by these processes, such feelings and memories then helped to modify the outcome of the developments which earlier had given them birth, but at all times the origin of these sentiments of patriotism or nationalism demanded explanation. Thus, on the eve of the American Revolution some North American colonists considered themselves patriotic British subjects; others spoke of themselves as Americans; still others attached their loyalties to their colony, such as Virginia or Massachusetts, which they considered their "country." Any one of these sentiments could conceivably have prevailed and eventually ousted all the others; and in each case, regardless of the actual outcome, we could have spoken afterwards of the "force of nationalism"—British, American, or Virginian—as accounting for the result. But a concept that would thus explain every possible outcome actually explains none, and this is why despite our very serious interest in the development of nationalism, we have not used the concept of nationalism as a device to explain the success or failure of integration in any particular case. To do so would have been to reason in a circle. Thus we had to try, as best we could, to carry our analysis to a more fundamental level.

E ◆ THE GAPS

We should add a few words here about some of the important problems we are leaving untouched in the present book—problems we expect to deal with in another volume. By concentrating upon the North Atlantic area we put aside the issue of worldwide political community, as well as political community in other regions.

Some readers may feel that we have ignored the overriding problem of the East–West split, and thereby have sidestepped the central problem of war, since this split is the obvious source of the most dangerous international friction today. There are two answers to this. One is that we have no assurance that all the North Atlantic area is already integrated, even though it is frequently called the North Atlantic "community." Many thoughtful people are by no means convinced that France and West Germany, for example, will remain permanently at peace with one another. Even if this were the only example we could cite with assurance, it is one which affects the entire area and indeed the whole world. To reduce the chances of war between any two countries in the North Atlantic area is to reduce the dangers in the East–West split.

The other answer to possible objections to our procedure is that we are studying conditions and processes. We are trying to reach a level of generalization high enough so that findings could eventually be applied to a wide range of situations, including the gap between East and West. While we think that coexistence seems to be the most that can be expected for a matter of decades, we believe that it would be useful to know what conditions will be needed before a pluralistic security-community can be brought about, and to know what processes will have to take place within those conditions in order to achieve this result.

Another range of applications we expect to explore at greater length in the more detailed volume covers more of the leading problems of international organization as a field of study. How much can we say about such questions as these: the extent to which regional integration tends to inhibit or to promote later integration of a still larger area; whether very strong agreement about certain matters has to exist before institutions for preserving order can be set up, or whether certain kinds of order-keeping institutions generate much of the needed agreement by their own operations if they can somehow be set up early; whether the "minimalist" or the "maximalist" view of international organization finds more support in historical experience. That is to say, can a security-community be organized on the basis of agreement on only one point—the necessity for peaceful change—or must agreement be achieved on many other things as well?

In the brief space permitted by this report, however, our findings will have to focus only upon the North Atlantic area. We begin by summarizing the general historical findings.

CHAPTER II

◇◇

Main Findings: Background Conditions

◇◇

A ◈ THE INTEGRATIVE PROCESS: SOME GENERAL CHARACTERISTICS

For purposes of exposition, we have divided our findings into two parts: first, general changes in our way of thinking about political integration; and second, specific findings about the background conditions and the dynamic characteristics of the integrative process. In this chapter, we shall first discuss our general findings. Our more specific findings will follow in later sections of this chapter and in Chapter III.

1. *Reexamining Some Popular Beliefs.* To begin with, our findings have tended to make us increasingly doubtful of several widespread beliefs about political integration. The first of these beliefs is that modern life, with rapid transportation, mass communications, and literacy, tends to be more international than life in past decades or centuries, and hence more conducive to the growth of international or supranational institutions. Neither the study of our cases, nor a survey of more limited data from a larger number of countries, has yielded any clearcut evidence to support this view. Nor do these results suggest that there has been inherent in modern economic and social development any unequivocal trend toward more internationalism and world community.

This is particularly true of political amalgamation. The closer we get to modern conditions and to our own time, the more difficult it is to find any instances of successful amalgamation of two or more previously sovereign states. Thus far we found not a single full-fledged modern social-service state that has successfully federated or otherwise merged with another. (The security-community among the Scandinavian countries has been deepening gradually through limited functional amalgamation, but it has remained essentially pluralistic, since the bulk of its most important functions have not been amalgamated. Its common laws must be adopted by national legislatures, its common parliamentary body can only make recommendations, and it has no common defense forces, police, or controls over the political and economic systems of its members.) There is only a small chance— though it should not be neglected—that there may be such an instance among the cases that we have not studied in detail. The nearest to an exception seems to be Newfoundland, which was not a solidly established social-service state before its union with Canada in 1948. On the whole, however, we find that the increase in the responsibilities of national government for such matters as social welfare and the regulation of economic life has greatly increased the importance of the nation in the lives of its members. This has tended to make nationalism more popular and more intractable than before.

Most countries in the world today devote a larger part of their resources to their domestic economies, and a smaller part to their foreign trade, than they did a half-century ago. Discrepancies between average incomes in different countries, and between national levels of the real wages of labor, do not seem to have become smaller during the last forty or fifty years. Indeed, they may even have increased. Peaceful and voluntary migration across international boundaries, which was still characteristic of the world before 1914, has largely come to an end. In most countries, there has been a considerable decline in the share of foreign mail among the total volume of letters written; and this decline has in general been larger than what would have corresponded merely to the decline in international migration.[1] A large sample count of the share of references to foreign research in major scientific journals in several of the leading countries

[1] This statement is based on calculations carried out at the Center for Research on World Political Institutions, Princeton University, using statistics of the Universal Postal Union, 1887-1951. See also Karl W. Deutsch, "Shifts in the Balance of Communication Flows: A Problem of Measurement in International Relations," *Public Opinion Quarterly*, xx, 1, Spring 1956, pp. 143-160.

of the world between 1894 and 1954 offers no evidence in favor of any clearcut increase in internationalism in the world of science during that period.[1a] The increase in the political and administrative obstacles to the movement of persons, goods, and capital across national boundaries in recent decades is too well known to require documentation. All these data leave us with the impression that men will have to work toward the building of larger security-communities without the benefit of any clearcut automatic trend toward internationalism to help them.

Another popular belief that our findings make more doubtful is that the growth of a state, or the expansion of its territory, resembles a snowballing process, or that it is characterized by some sort of bandwagon effect, such that successful growth in the past would accelerate the rate of growth or expansion of the amalgamated political community in the future. In this view, as villages in the past have joined to make provinces, and provinces to make kingdoms, so contemporary states are expected to join into ever-larger states or federations. If this were true, ever-larger political units would appear to be the necessary result of historical and technological development. Our findings do not support this view. While the successful unification of England facilitated the later amalgamation of England and Wales, and this in turn facilitated the subsequent amalgamation of England and Wales with Scotland in the union of the two kingdoms, the united kingdom of Britain did not succeed in carrying through a successful and lasting amalgamation with Ireland. Nor could it retain its political amalgamation with the American colonies. These seceded from the British Empire in 1776 to form the United States; and Ireland seceded in effect in the course of the Anglo–Irish civil war of 1918-1921. The unity of the Habsburg monarchy became increasingly strained in the course of the Nineteenth Century and was followed by disintegration in the Twentieth; and so was the more limited union of the crowns of Norway and Sweden.

[1a] For the full results, see K. W. Deutsch, George Klein, J. J. Baker, and Associates, *Is American Attention to Foreign Research Results Declining?*, Massachusetts Institute of Technology, 1954, multigraphed.

Generally, we found that successful amalgamation of smaller political units in the past tended to increase both the resources and the integrative skills of the governments of the larger units that resulted. We further found, however, that such amalgamations also may increase the degree of the preoccupation with domestic affairs and reduce the ability of those governments to respond promptly and effectively to the needs and interests of governments and people outside the national borders. This ability of governments to respond to the interests of "outsiders" has always been important, but it has become even more important in our own time.

Our findings suggest that the theoretical possibilities just sketched represent only one part of the process. Consider the successful amalgamations of the United Kingdom, of the United States, of Italy, and of Germany. Here are cases in which adequate responsiveness, as well as power, were developed by the government of the emerging larger political community to make its rule acceptable to its variegated populations. But this does not apply to the disintegration of the Habsburg monarchy, and to the unions between England and Ireland, and Norway and Sweden. Altogether, our findings suggest that greater political capabilities, and in particular greater political responsiveness, cannot be expected to emerge as an automatic by-product of historical evolution, or of earlier stages of the amalgamative process. Rather, these may have to be striven for as distinct and specific political and administrative aims if political integration is to be attained.

Another popular notion is that a principal motive for the political integration of states has been the fear of anarchy, as well as of warfare among them. According to this view, men not only came to look upon war among the units concerned as unpromising and unattractive, but also as highly probable. For they came to fear it acutely while believing it to be all but inevitable in the absence of any strong superior power to restrain all participants. Consequently, according to this theory, one of the first and most important features of a newly-amalgamated security-community was the establishment of strong federal or community-wide laws, courts, police forces, and armies for their enforcement against potentially aggressive member states and member populations. Beliefs of this kind parallel closely the classic reasoning of Thomas Hobbes and John Locke; and some writers on federalism, or on international organization, have implied a stress on legal institutions and on the problem of coercing member states. Our findings suggest strong qualifications for these views. The questions of larger-community police forces and law enforcement, and of the coercion of member states, turned out to be of minor importance in the early stages of most of the amalgamated security-communities we studied.

Thus, at the time of the establishment of the United States, the federal government had next to no means of coercion at its disposal. No federal navy department was established until 1798; at the time of the establishment of the United States War Department in 1789, the federal army numbered under 700 men, and it was not greatly enlarged for a considerable number of years thereafter.[2] For many decades, Americans continued to rely on their militia—and hence on member-state forces—for their defense, and the federal government long remained both unable and unwilling to coerce any member state, even on several critical occasions.

In the evolution of the Swiss political community from the thirteenth to the early nineteenth century, the member cantons retained all means of military power, and no significant role was played by any federal police forces, armies, or courts: the Swiss federal army assumed importance only in a very late stage of the process, during the last decades preceding the adoption of the federal constitution in 1848.[3] The two cases in which problems

[2] An act passed on September 29, 1789, the very last day of the first session of the First Congress, legalized the 840 men authorized by the law of October 3, 1787, which had been passed by the Congress of the Confederation. "Only about 672 of these were actually in the service." In January 1800, when war with France was still threatening, and after much talk of increasing the army, the total army strength was 3,429 regulars. Of these, 1,501 were artillerists and engineers, most of whom were scattered in small detachments along the Atlantic seaboard from Maine to Georgia.—James Ripley Jacobs, *The Beginning of the U.S. Army, 1783-1812*, Princeton University Press, 1947, pp. 43 and 236.

[3] Cf. Hermann Weilenmann, *Pax Helvetica oder die Demokratie der klein-*

of policing and coercion played the largest role were England–
Ireland and the Habsburg monarchy, at times, in its relations
with Bohemia and Hungary. In both these cases, integration
remained precarious for long periods of time, and both ended
in dissolution. On the other hand, there was no national police
or national army covering Norway–Sweden while they were
amalgamated, and they likewise broke apart.

This stress on the supposed importance of the early establishment of common laws, courts, and police forces is related to the
suggestion that it is necessary to maintain a balance of power —
among the member states of a larger union or federation, in
order to prevent any one state from becoming much stronger
than the others.[4] There is much to be said for this point of view:
if a member state is far stronger than all the rest together, its
political elite may well come to neglect or ignore the messages
and needs of the population of the smaller member units, and
the resulting loss of responsiveness may prevent integration or
destroy it.[5] The evidence from our cases suggests, however, that
not merely amalgamation, but also responsiveness and integration can all be achieved and maintained successfully without
any such balance of power among the participating states or

---

en Gruppen, Zurich, Rentsch, 1951, pp. 278-284, 298-300; Hans Kohn, Der
Schweizerische Nationalgedanke: Eine Studie Zum Thema "Nationalismus
und Freiheit," Zurich, Verlag der "Neuen Zürcher Zeitung," 1955, p. 53. For
the predominantly civilian, social and economic character of the liberal
and radical movement that led to the adoption first of many cantonal reforms, and eventually of the Federal Constitution of 1848, see also, E. Bonjour, H. S. Offler, and G. R. Potter, A Short History of Switzerland, Oxford,
Clarendon Press, 1952, pp. 257-273; Edgar Bonjour, "Geschichte der Schweiz
im 19. und 20. Jahrhundert," in Hans Nabholz, Geschichte der Schweiz,
Zurich, Schulthess, 1938, vol. 2, esp. pp. 401-452; Wolfgang von Wartburg,
Geschichte der Schweiz, Munich, Oldenbourg, 1951, pp. 183-251.

4 Cf. Carl J. Friedrich, "Federal Constitutional Theory and Emergent
Proposals," in Arthur W. Macmahon, ed., Federalism: Mature and Emergent,
New York, Doubleday, 1955, p. 515.

5 Prussia's preponderant size and power in Germany, for instance, was both
a source of great strength and great weakness. If Germany were only made up
of "about forty states or cantons of approximately equal size, we would have
been united long ago," the liberal-radical Deutsches Wochenblatt, published
at Mannheim, wrote once in February 1865.—Quoted in Gustav Mayer, "Die
Lösung der deutschen Frage im Jahre 1866 und die deutsche Arbeiterbeweg-
ung," in Festgaben für Wilhelm Lexis, Jena, 1907, p. 254.

political units. Neither England within the United Kingdom, nor Prussia in Germany after 1871, nor Piedmont in Italy for some time after 1860, was balanced in power by any other member or group of members, yet each of the larger political communities achieved integration. In the cases of the American and Swiss federations, no one member state was far stronger than all the rest, even though in the Swiss Confederation Berne could not usually have been coerced even if all other cantons had acted together against her. However, *groups* of member states became clearly preponderant over the rest in the cases of both Switzerland and the United States: the Northeastern states and the older part of the Middle West in the United States between 1865 and 1900, and the liberal and industrial cantons in Switzerland after 1847. In both cases, amalgamation progressed and integration held firmly. In the case of the pluralistic security-communities of Norway and Sweden after 1907, and of the United States and Canada, as well as of the United States and Mexico, integration of the pluralistic security-community was maintained even in periods when Sweden and the United States, respectively, were not balanced in any way by the strength of their partners.

Contrary to the "balance of power" theory, security-communities seem to develop most frequently around cores of strength—a matter about which we shall have to say more below. But military conquest appeared to be the least effective among a large number of methods by which amalgamation was pursued in the cases we studied: amalgamation failed to become integration in more than half of the situations in which military conquest was used to promote it.[6]

A series of negative findings such as those outlined above can at most clear the ground for a better understanding of the positive nature of the integrative process.

2. *General Findings.* Among our positive general findings, the most important seems to us that both amalgamated security-communities and pluralistic security-communities are practicable

6 See Chapter III, Section E, 2, end.

pathways toward integration. In the course of our research, we found ourselves led by the evidence to attribute a greater potential significance to pluralistic security-communities than we had originally expected. Pluralistic security-communities turned out to be somewhat easier to attain and easier to preserve than their amalgamated counterparts. The less stringent requirements for the attainment of a pluralistic security-community in terms of background conditions and of political processes will be commented on below in the appropriate sections of this chapter.

A. THE STRENGTHS OF PLURALISM. The somewhat smaller risk of breakdown in the case of pluralistic security-communities seems indicated by an examination of the relative numbers of successes and failures of each type of security-community. We can readily list a dozen instances of success for each type. Cases of successful amalgamated security-communities would be, for instance: United States since 1877; England since the seventeenth century; England–Wales since 1542; England–Scotland since 1707; Germany since 1871; Italy since 1859; France since at least the late nineteenth century; Canada since 1867; the Netherlands since 1831; Belgium since 1831; Sweden since 1815; and Switzerland since 1848. Cases of successful pluralistic security-communities include: United States between 1781-1789;[7] England–Scotland between the late 1560's and 1707; Prussia and the German states except Austria between 1815 and 1866-1871; Norway–Sweden since 1907; Switzerland between 1291 and 1847; United States–Canada since the 1870's; United States–Mexico since the 1930's; United States–United Kingdom as early as 1871, or certainly since the end of the century;[8] United Kingdom–Netherlands since perhaps 1815; Denmark–Sweden since the late nineteenth or early twentieth century; Denmark–Norway since the same time; and France–

---

[7] The United States between 1781 and 1789 formed a pluralistic security-community in the sense that no state made any serious preparations for fighting or defense against another. This pluralistic security-community was not consolidated, and fears were expressed—and even deliberately exaggerated by promoters of closer union—that this loose community might not endure. But whereas a strong movement for union grew up, no serious movement for secession developed in any state.

[8] Henry C. Allen, *Great Britain and the United States*, New York, 1955, pp. 27-28, 166, 441-442, 507-508, 556-569, 581, 614-615. The security-community

Belgium since some time in the nineteenth century. An example of an emerging pluralistic security-community might be England–Ireland since 1945.

On the other hand, we find a sharp contrast in the number of failures for each type. We have found only one case of a pluralistic security-community which failed in the sense that it was followed by actual warfare between the participants, and it is doubtful whether a pluralistic security-community existed even in that case: this was the relationship of Austria and Prussia within the framework of the German Confederation since 1815. As members of the Confederation, the two countries were not supposed to prepare for war against each other, but appropriate military preparations were made and war between them was considered a serious possibility on several occasions after the 1840's. The actual war between them in 1866, however, lasted only seven weeks. It was followed by an unusually moderate peace as far as Austria was concerned. In 1879 Germany and Austria concluded an alliance which eventually was expected to be permanent, and Austria and Germany thus became a pluralistic security-community. In contrast to this single instance of failure of a pluralistic security-community, we can readily list seven cases of amalgamated security-communities that failed: the United States in 1861; England–Ireland in 1918; Austria–Hungary in 1918; Norway–Sweden in 1905; Metropolitan France with a series of revolutions and wars between 1789 and 1871; Metropolitan France and Algeria in the 1950's; and Spain including the Catalan and Basque populations in the 1930's. A number of these wars were fought with a bitterness that might have proved fatal to both contestants if they had possessed present-day weapons of mass destruction.

On balance, therefore, we found pluralistic security-communities to be a more promising approach to the elimination of war

---

between the United States and Great Britain was seriously threatened by the naval construction race between Great Britain and the United States which broke out in 1919 and continued until halted by the limitation agreement made at the Washington Conference in 1922.—Harold and Margaret Sprout, *Toward a New Order of Sea Power, 1918-1922*, Princeton University Press, 1946, pp. 50-87.

over large areas than we had thought at the outset of our inquiry.

But this relative superiority of a pluralistic security-community as a more easily attainable form of integration has limited applications. It worked only in those situations in which the keeping of the peace among the participating units was the main political goal overshadowing all others. This goal has been the main focus of our study. In our historical cases, however, we found that men have often wanted more: they have wanted a political community that would not merely keep the peace among its members but that would also be capable of acting as a unit in other ways and for other purposes. In respect to this capacity to act—and in particular, to act quickly and effectively for positive goals—amalgamated security-communities have usually been far superior to their pluralistic counterparts. In many historical cases, men have preferred to accept the somewhat greater risk of civil war, or of war among the participating units, in order to insure this greater promise of joint capacity for action. It is only today, in the new age of nuclear weapons, that these risks and gains must be reevaluated. Now a pluralistic security-community may appear a somewhat safer device than amalgamation for dealing with man's new weapons.

B. THE THRESHOLDS OF INTEGRATION. Our second general finding concerns the nature of integration. In our earliest analytical scheme, we had envisaged this as an all-or-none process, analogous to the crossing of a narrow threshold. On the one side of this threshold, populations and policy-makers considered warfare among the states or political units concerned as still a serious possibility, and prepared for it; on the other side of the threshold they were supposed to do so no longer. We expected to apply two broad kinds of tests to the presence or absence of integration—that is, the existence or nonexistence of a security-community—among particular states or territories.

One of these tests was subjective, in terms of the opinions of the political decision-makers, or of the politically relevant strata in each territory. These had to be inferred from many kinds of historical evidence in the past, or from samples or surveys in present-day situations obtained by well-known methods of study-ing public opinion. Did influential people in all parts of the wider area believe that a firm sense of community existed throughout its territories? And did the political elites through-out the wider community believe that peaceful change within this wider group had become assured with reasonable certainty for a long period of time?

The other kind of test was essentially objective and opera-tional. It replaced the recording of opinions by the measurement of the tangible commitments and the allocation of resources with which people backed them: how large preparations were made specifically for the possibility of war against any other group within the wider community? Consider a case in which the maintenance and indoctrination of troops, and the building and upkeep of fortifications and other strategic facilities, suggested possible military action against some particular smaller political unit, whether a state, a people, or a territory. If such military action was considered a sufficiently practical possibility to war-rant a significant allocation of resources, then there may have existed some other kind of political community, but not a secu-rity-community, between the two political units in question.

We found, as expected, that these tests by opinions and by allocations usually coincided in their results, but that they tended to differ in marginal cases. For example, a war between two states might still be considered possible by some of their leaders, even though no significant preparations for it were being made by either side; and routine preparations for defense of a border might continue even though conflict across it might already appear unthinkable. Even in such rare instances, however, we expected that the achievement of a security-community would involve something like the crossing of a threshold, from a situ-ation where war between the political units concerned appeared possible and was being prepared for, to another situation where it was neither. It was the crossing of this threshold, and with it the establishment of a security-community, that we called inte-gration; and it is in this sense that we are using the term in this book.

Somewhat contrary to our expectations, however, some of our cases taught us that integration may involve a fairly broad zone of transition rather than a narrow threshold; that states might cross and recross this threshold or zone of transition several times in their relations with each other; and that they might spend decades or generations wavering uncertainly within it.

Thus we found that states could maintain armed forces which were potentially available for warfare against each other, but which were not specifically committed to this purpose. The American state militias from 1776 to 1865 and the forces of the Swiss cantons from the thirteenth to the nineteenth centuries, seem to have been available for such purposes if the political temper of their respective communities had warranted such employment, as it did on a few occasions. It would thus be extraordinarily difficult to say just in which year warfare between the Protestant and Catholic cantons ceased to be a practical political possibility after 1712, or when it again became temporarily a practical possibility between 1815 and 1847; or just when integration within the United States was lost in the period between 1820 and 1861, and warfare between North and South became a substantial possibility. Similarly, the lands of the Habsburg monarchy seem to have been politically integrated—though not very deeply—in the period about the middle of the eighteenth century, but it would be extraordinarily difficult to say just when this state of affairs was reached in regard to each of them, and just when it was lost again after the end of the eighteenth century. We know that certain of these lands were permitted at some times to have native troops stationed in them under the command of native officers, drawn from the local aristocracy. At other times, and for certain other lands at most times, the rulers of the Habsburg monarchy tried to avoid stationing native troops in some parts of the monarchy and deliberately attempted to rule its territories by means of troops of different language and culture. These men, recruited from distant territories and under the command of officers culturally alien to their subordinates, were expected to have no loyalty other than to the sovereign residing in Vienna.

The extent to which these conditions prevailed makes it difficult to decide whether the lands of the Habsburg monarchy were integrated at all, or whether they were governed with the possibility of revolution and civil war perpetually envisaged and carefully prepared against. So far as the Habsburg monarchy is concerned, we have found it safest to infer that it reached the threshold of integration in the eighteenth century and persisted somewhere in the transition zone between integration and non-integration during most of the nineteenth century. We assume that integration had already been lost by the beginning of the twentieth century, when secession and warfare among the constituent parts of the monarchy were viewed as possibilities for the moderately distant future; and we conclude that the Habsburg Empire was an amalgamated but no longer an integrated political community when it was destroyed by the strains and stresses of the first World War.[9]

In the case of pluralistic security-communities, we found the transition from non-integration to integration similarly broad and potentially ambiguous. Canada and the United States demilitarized their common border after 1819, but each of them retained other means for retaliatory action in case of military conflict. The United States army could easily have attacked Canadian territory even without the help of American border fortifications, and the Canadian connection with Great Britain insured for Canada the possibility of large-scale British retaliation against American shipping and American ports in case of war with the United States.[10] As the nineteenth century pro-

---

[9] As to general presentations see Franz Krones, *Handbuch der Geschichte Österreichs*, vol. IV, Berlin, 1881; Hugo Hantsch, *Die Geschichte Österreichs*, vol. II, Graz, 1950; on constitutional-administrative development see Alfons Huber, Alfons Dopsch, *Österreichische Reichsgeschichte*, part 3, Vienna, 1901; on military history see A. Wrede, *Geschichte der k. und k. Wehrmacht*, Vienna, 1898, Herman Meynert, *Geschichte der k.k. Armee*, 2 vols., Vienna, 1852-1854; and with regard to the early Maria Theresan period particularly informative, K. und k. Kriegsarchiv, *Österreichischer Erbfolgekrieg 1740-1748*, vols. 1 and 3, Vienna, 1896-1898.

[10] Henry C. Allen, *op. cit.*, 351. "Strictly speaking, this disarmament [under the terms of the Rush-Bagot Treaty of 1817] never extended completely to land fortifications as well, but the Agreement gradually acquired a symbolic value and the so-called 'undefended frontier' between Canada and the United

gressed, these possibilities became increasingly less realistic, and by the middle of the twentieth century they had disappeared for all practical purposes from the calculations of statesmen and the opinions of political elites in both countries.

In Europe, the pluralistic security-community between Norway and Sweden may be dated conveniently from 1906, the year in which the destruction of border fortifications between the two countries was completed. But some Norwegians remained aware of the possibility of foreign aid which was procured by the Treaty of Integrity in 1907 when Norway was guaranteed against aggression by Britain, Germany, Russia, and France. Even so, it seems unlikely that the slogan "we shall mobilize England" (used in the days of the secession crisis) should have been so soon forgotten.[11] It is possible to date at least the beginnings of a pluralistic security-community between Canada and the United States in 1819, and between Norway and Sweden in 1906. It would be far more difficult, however, to specify the exact year in which the United States and Great Britain, or the United States and Mexico, ceased to contemplate the possibility of mutual warfare. It would be equally hard to determine when they ceased to allocate significant resources to its specific preparation, let alone to allocate specific resources to more generalized military organizations and facilities. These would be of the kind that could readily be switched to employment in mutual threats or warfare without being specifically committed to this purpose from the outset.

The threshold of integration thus turned out to be far broader, and far less easy to discern, in our historical cases than we had envisaged at the outset. Not only the approach toward integration, but the very act of crossing the integration threshold, have turned out to be much lengthier and more uncertain processes than had been expected.

States became an object of pride and satisfaction to both peoples."—John Bartlet Brebner, *North Atlantic Triangle*, New Haven, 1945, pp. 88, 103.

[11] Wilhelm Keilhau, in *Det norske folks liv og historie*, x, Oslo, Aschenhoug, 1935, 497-498; also Nils Ørvik, *The Decline of Neutrality 1914-1941*, Oslo, Tanum, 1953.

C. COMMUNICATION AND THE SENSE OF COMMUNITY. Integration has proved to be a more continuous process than our earliest analytical scheme had suggested; but it continues to be characterized by important thresholds. Within this framework of our revised general concept of integration, we have arrived at a somewhat deeper understanding of the meaning of "sense of community." It appears to rest primarily on something other than verbal assent to some or many explicit propositions. The populations of different territories might easily profess verbal attachment to the same set of values without having a sense of community that leads to political integration. The kind of sense of community that is relevant for integration, and therefore for our study, turned out to be rather a matter of mutual sympathy and loyalties; of "we-feeling," trust, and mutual consideration; of partial identification in terms of self-images and interests; of mutually successful predictions of behavior, and of cooperative action in accordance with it—in short, a matter of a perpetual dynamic process of mutual attention, communication, perception of needs, and responsiveness in the process of decision-making. "Peaceful change" could not be assured without this kind of relationship.

If sense of community were a matter of belief in a limited number of common propositions, then political community should be stronger among those people who share such beliefs in a large number of propositions, or who believe in them more fervently than others. But such a concept of sense of community does not fit the evidence of some of our cases. It could hardly explain the deterioration of English–Irish relations between 1880 and 1914: as the Irish became more like the English in matters of education, language, political rights, and even economic attitudes as a result of the rise of an Irish middle class and the effects of English-sponsored land reforms, they became more anti-English. Some of their leaders even sought deliberately to foster additional symbols and values, such as the use of the Gaelic language, that would emphasize the difference. It was not the case that the Irish first preferred Gaelic to English and then revolted against the English connection; rather, many

Irishmen found the link to the unresponsive English community increasingly irksome and then chose the propagation and study of the Gaelic tongue as one way of expressing their desire for a separate group identity. Similarly, if sense of community consisted in an identical attitude toward a set of propositions, it would not explain why, for instance, Texas and Vermont joined the United States while Nova Scotia remained outside it;[12] or why the city of Nice became French in 1860—and remained French thereafter—while most of Piedmont remained Italian after 1859. In all such cases, something can be learned, to be sure, by applying the concept of sense of community as a matter of static agreement; but we found that in all such cases more could be learned by viewing it as a matter of dynamic process.

D. GROWTH AROUND CORE AREAS. As such a process of integrative behavior, sense of community requires some particular habits of political behavior on the part of individuals and some particular traditions and institutions on the part of social groups and of political units, such as provinces or states.

These habits, in turn, are acquired by processes of social learning. People learn them in the face of background conditions which change only slowly, so that they appear at any moment as something given—as political, economic, social, or psychological facts that must be taken for granted for the purposes of short-range politics. The speed and extent of this learning of habits of integrative political behavior are then influenced in each situation by these background conditions, as well as by the dynamics of the particular political process—the particular movement toward integration. Some of our more specific findings deal

12 See Chilton Williamson, *Vermont in Quandary, 1763-1825*, Montpelier, 1949, *passim*; Earle Newton, *The Vermont Story*, Montpelier, 1949, pp. 40-89; W. A. Mackintosh, "Canada and Vermont: A Study in Historical Geography," *Canadian Historical Review*, VIII, March 1927, pp. 9-30; John Bartlet Brebner, *The Neutral Yankees of Nova Scotia*, New York, 1937, *passim*; a more comprehensive study of Texan independence and of the annexation of Texas which includes a survey of the attitudes of Texans comparable to Williamson's and Brebner's studies of Vermont and Nova Scotia unfortunately has not been done. Some useful material can be found in Justin H. Smith, *The Annexation of Texas*, New York, 1911, *passim*; J. W. Schmitz, *Texan Statecraft, 1836-1845*, San Antonio, Texas, 1941, *passim*.

with the importance of certain background conditions in each area studied, while others deal with the successive stages of the integrative political process that occurred.

The outcome, then, of the integrative process among any particular group of countries depends on the interplay of the effects of background conditions with moving political events. One aspect of this interplay deserves to be singled out for particular attention. It is the matter of political, economic, and social capabilities of the participating political units for integrative behavior.

Generally, we found that such integrative capabilities were closely related to the general capabilities of a given political unit for action in the fields of politics, administration, economic life, and social and cultural development. Larger, stronger, more politically, administratively, economically, and educationally advanced political units were found to form the cores of strength around which in most cases the integrative process developed.

Political amalgamation, in particular, usually turned out to be a nuclear process. It often occurred around single cores, as in the case of England, Piedmont, Prussia, and Sweden. Each of these came to form the core of a larger amalgamated political community (even though the Norwegian–Swedish union turned out to be transitory). Sometimes amalgamation occurred around composite cores, as in the cases of the Habsburg monarchy. Its core was formed by the close functional association and later amalgamation of the so-called Alpine-hereditary lands. These lands formed the basis of Habsburg power before 1526; they furnished the base for the later union with Bohemia, Hungary, and other territories and they remained the mainstay of Habsburg power and of loyalties to the monarchy until the dissolution of the latter in 1918. The Swiss political community was created around a double core: on the one hand, the alliance of the three original small cantons of Uri, Schwyz, and Unterwalden, which came to constitute a fairly strong composite core of power and of economic and political attraction, and, on the other hand, the city-state of Bern, which was the largest well-organized political unit in the area.[13] In the case of the United States, Massachusetts formed something of a core of leadership in New England, Virginia fulfilled a similar function in the South, and Pennsylvania did so in the Middle Atlantic region. Together, these three largest states then played a major role in the establishment of the United States; and the federation of the original thirteen colonies later functioned somewhat as a composite core in the integration of the territories and states that were gradually added to the union in the West.

E. THE NEED FOR RISING CAPABILITIES. The extent of integrative capabilities which already existed in the individual political units at the beginning of a major drive toward amalgamation thus turned out to be very important for the future development of the process. But another step was no less important: the further increase of these capabilities in the course of the movement toward amalgamation. The presence or absence of growth in such capabilities played a major role in every integrative process we studied, and particularly in every case of an amalgamation movement.

Generally, amalgamation did not come to pass because the government of the participating units had become weaker or more inefficient; nor did it come to pass because men had been forced to turn away from these increasingly incapable organizations to the building of a larger and less decrepit common government. Rather, amalgamation occurred after a substantial increase in the capabilities of at least some of the participating units, or sometimes of all of them. Examples are the increase in the capabilities of the American colonies before 1789, and in the capabilities of Prussia before 1871. The increase in the capabilities of the political organizations or governments of the in-

[13] Cf. Weilenmann, *op. cit.*, pp. 66-74, 99-104, 166-206, 221-254. *Die vielsprachige Schweiz*, Basel-Leipzig, Rhein-Verlag, 1925, pp. 70-81; *Uri: Land, Volk, Staat, Wirtschaft und Kultur*, Zurich, Rentsch, 1943, pp. 8-22; *Der Zusammenschluss der Eidgenossenschaff*, Zurich, Gutenberg, 1940, *passim*; Anton Castell, *Geschichte des Landes Schwyz*, Zurich, Benziger Verlag Einsiedeln, 1954, pp. 9-28; Leo Weisz, *Die Alten Eidgenossen*, Zurich, Niehans, 1940, pp. 7-76; Wilhelm Oechsli, *History of Switzerland, 1499-1914*, Cambridge University Press, 1922, pp. 1-3. Wolfgang von Wartburg, *op. cit.*, pp. 46-48, 68-72; Nabholz, *op. cit.*, vol. 1, pp. 179-187; etc.

dividual states, cantons, principalities, and the like, formed a
major element in the dynamic political process leading to amalgamation in each instance.

Such capabilities relevant to integration were of two broad
kinds. One was related to the capacity to act of a political unit—
such as its size, power, economic strength, administrative efficiency, and the like. The other kind was related to the ability
of a unit to control its own behavior and to redirect its own
attention. More accurately, this means the ability of its political
decision-makers and relevant political elites to redirect and control their own attention and behavior so as to enable rulers to
receive communications from other political units which were
to be their prospective partners in the integrative process. It
means, further, the ability to give these messages from other
political units adequate weight in the making of their own decisions, to perceive the needs of the populations and elites of
these other units, and to respond to them quickly and adequately
in terms of political or economic action. The first kind of capabilities—those related to the capacity to act and to overcome
external obstacles—are closely linked to what we often call power;
the second kind are linked to what we propose to call responsiveness.

The two kinds of capabilities obviously overlap. Power that
cannot be controlled by the governments or political communities who try to exercise it is likely to dwindle soon by dissipation
or to be checked by growing external resistance; and responsiveness would remain a matter of mere intention, lacking the
measure of power required to put the intended responses into
practical effect. Yet we found that power and responsiveness
were not quite equal in importance. Once a moderate measure
of power had been achieved, the capabilities relating to the
responsiveness of a political unit and its rulers seemed to be of
crucial importance to the success or failure of integration.[14]

This applied particularly to cases of amalgamation, but it

[14] On Prussian responsiveness to Hanoverian needs and desires after that
state's annexation in 1866, see Hans Herzfeld, *Johannes von Miquel*, Detmold,
1938, I, 127-186.

seemed also true to a considerable extent in the political processes leading to the establishment of a pluralistic security-community. Such communities, too, often (though not always)
included substantial increases in the political and administrative
capabilities of the states concerned. This applied particularly
to such matters as mutual communication, consultation, and
decision-making, as well as to the control of their own political
behavior in the direction of increased responsiveness to the major
needs or most urgent messages of their partners.

F. THE RACE BETWEEN CAPABILITIES AND LOADS. Another set of
data we found to be of crucial importance pertained to the
burdens thrown upon the tangible and intangible resources of
political units by the requirements of establishing or maintaining either an amalgamated or a pluralistic security-community.
Such loads or burdens, as we have called them, were of many
kinds. They included military or financial burdens, drains on
manpower or wealth; the burden of risk from political or military commitments; costs of social and economic readjustments,
such as at the establishment of a customs union; and similar
burdens of a material kind. But they also included intangible
burdens upon government, which could be visualized as somewhat similar to traffic loads of vehicles at a road intersection or
of messages at a telephone exchange. In the cases of crossroads
or switchboards, the flow of vehicles or messages requires more
than a certain volume of material facilities for its accommo-
dation; it also requires a certain number of decisions which must
be made in a limited amount of time by the traffic officer who
controls traffic at the intersection, or by the persons or apparatus
that control the flow of calls through the telephone exchange.

It is this burden, imposed by the traffic load of messages and
signals upon the attention-giving and decision-making capabilities of the persons or organizations in control, that has close
parallels in the burden of government upon rulers. It is a burden
upon the attention-giving, information-processing, and decision-
making capabilities of administrators, political elites, legislatures,
or electoral majorities. Thus the failure of the British Parlia-

ment to respond quickly and adequately to the disastrous Irish famine of 1846 was not caused primarily by any lack of material or financial resources to provide relief. Rather, the failure was one of adequate attention, perception, and decision-making to meet the burdens of responsibility which the Parliament had taken upon itself under the terms of Anglo–Irish union. It was none the less a failure that was to have far-reaching effects upon the future of Anglo–Irish relations.

Political amalgamation in general tended to increase the load of demands upon the material resources and the decision-making capabilities of governments, since decisions for larger areas and populations had to be made by fewer central institutions. The success or failure of amalgamation, then, depended in considerable part upon the relationship of two rates of change: the growing rate of claims and burdens upon central governments as against the growing—in some instances, the insufficiently growing—level of capabilities of the governmental institutions of the amalgamated political community. The load of communications, demands, and claims upon the capabilities of government was also growing from independent causes—such as the increasing complexity of economic life, the increasing level of popular expectations in terms of living standards, social opportunities, and political rights, and the increasing political activity of previously passive groups and strata. Hence the outcome of the race between the growth of loads and capabilities sometimes remained precarious for a longer period, or it changed from one period to another.

Thus we find that the political and administrative capabilities of the Habsburg monarchy increased relatively rapidly during the hundred years after 1683, while the burden of claims put upon the central government by the populations and political elites of such territories as Bohemia and Hungary increased at a far slower rate. As far as it ever went, the integration of these territories—as distinct from their mere occupation by military strength—was substantially achieved by the middle of the eighteenth century. In the course of the nineteenth century, on the other hand, political participation and popular claims upon the government began to increase ever more rapidly, and with them grew the load upon the capabilities of the central government at Vienna and Budapest after 1867. The latter also grew, particularly with the aid of such improvements in transportation and communication as the railroad and the telegraph; but the balance between the two rates was shifting so as to make the integration of the monarchy increasingly precarious. By 1914 the Habsburg monarchy could no longer be called integrated, at least not without serious qualifications of the term, and soon even amalgamation ended as a result of the disastrous overcommitment of the monarchy's resources in the first World War.[15]

Perhaps this example will suffice to indicate our notion of political loads or burdens and of governmental capabilities, and of the critical nature of the balance between them. In each case, we studied data bearing on the extent of the prospective burdens of amalgamation, and of the capabilities available for its attainment, as given by the background conditions and as developed further in the course of the political and social processes directed toward the achievement of amalgamation. These data furnished an important set of indications for understanding the eventual outcome. A more detailed discussion of background conditions relating to political capabilities will follow in the appropriate sections of this chapter. These will also discuss the political developments relating to their change in the context of a process aiming at political amalgamation.

B ◈ THE IMPORTANCE OF BACKGROUND CONDITIONS

In general, our cases have left us impressed with the importance of certain background conditions for the success or failure of the integrative process. The influence of background condi-

15 See Huber-Dopsch, op. cit., parts 3-5; Joseph Redlich, Das österreichische Staats-und Reichsproblem, vols. 1/1, 1/2, and 11, Leipzig, 1920-1926; Oscar Jászi, Dissolution of the Habsburg Monarchy, Chicago, 1929, pp. 86-130, 271-429; Henry Marczáli, Hungary in the Eighteenth Century, Cambridge, 1910; Dominic Kosáry, History of Hungary, Cleveland, 1941, pp. 219-396; S. Harrison Thomson, Czechoslovakia in European History, Princeton, 1954, pp. 216-237, 269-325; Louis Eisenmann, Le compromis Austro-Hongrois, Paris, 1904.

tions appears to be larger, and the opportunities for decisive action by political leaders or movements appear to be somewhat more limited, than we had thought at the beginning of our study.[16]

To be sure, we found that the importance of a few background conditions had been somewhat overrated. Certain conditions which had often been considered as essential for the establishment of an amalgamated security-community turned out to be helpful to that end but not essential to it. Such helpful but non-essential conditions included previous administrative and/or dynastic union; ethnic or linguistic assimilation; strong economic ties; and foreign military threats. While all of these turned out to be helpful to integration, none of them appeared to be essential since each of them was absent in the successful establishment of at least one amalgamated security-community. Thus no previous administrative union had linked the Italian states for almost 1500 years. No ethnic or linguistic assimilation had wiped out the differences between the language groups of Switzerland.[17] No strong economic ties existed between England and Scotland,[18] or Norway and Sweden, or among the Italian states, prior to their union in each case.[19] And no unusual foreign military threat played any important role in the adoption of the Swiss

[16] On the perhaps decisive importance of German medieval history, see Hermann Heimpel, *Deutschlands Mittelalter, Deutschlands Schicksal*, Freiburg, 1932, and Fritz Rörig, "Das Mittelalter und die deutsche Geschichte," in Martin Göhring and Alexander Scharff, eds., *Geschichtliche Kräfte und Entscheidungen*, Festschrift for Otto Becker, Wiesbaden, 1954, pp. 1-15.

[17] A possible borderline case was that of the Polish population in Prussia between 1871 and 1918: they remained unassimilated and unintegrated; they constituted no serious threat of violence within the German empire; but they seized the first opportunity to secede at the end of the first World War.

[18] Trade between England and Scotland was curtailed to Scotland's disadvantage, since she imported more from England than she exported during the seventeenth century—by the various restrictions of the English mercantile system. Theodora Keith, *Commercial Relations of England and Scotland, 1603-1707*, Cambridge, 1910, pp. xx-xxi; Ephraim Lipson, *Economic History of England*, London, 1948, 5th edn., III, 126-127; William Law Mathieson, *Scotland and the Union*, Glasgow, 1905, pp. 21-23.

[19] Constantine E. McGuire, *Italy's International Economic Position*, New York, 1926, p. 466, declares that trade between the Italian states actually diminished in this period.

federal constitution in 1848, or in the union between England and Wales.[19a]

Even where foreign threats were present, their effects were transitory.[20] Most often they provided an impetus toward temporary military alliances, while more permanent unions derived their main support from other factors.

To be sure, foreign military threats at times served a useful purpose. Sometimes they induced relatively privileged political units or social groups to become somewhat more generous in sharing their economic, political, or social privileges with individuals or groups from other political units which appeared as potential allies or partners in an amalgamated security-community. Thus in the 1530's, the possibility of an attack by Emperor Charles V, perhaps with support from other Catholic princes, increased English willingness to arrange the union with Wales. Again, after 1701, England's involvement in the War of the Spanish Succession contributed somewhat to the willingness of the English Parliament to concede to the Scots the equal access to all English trading privileges which earlier English parliaments had refused to do.

Sometimes, however, foreign military threats had exactly the opposite effect: they induced a state of fear or at least of intense preoccupation among the political elites of the privileged political unit and rendered them less able or less willing to pay attention to the needs of weaker or less privileged units, or to make concessions to them. Thus the threat of the first World

[19a] The unusual factor in the latter situation consisted rather in the changes introduced by Henry VIII's religious policy.

[20] Thus the threat of the French Revolution and Napoleon failed to produce any political or military revitalization of the Holy Roman Empire. Cf. Heinrich Ritter von Srbik, *Deutsche Einheit, Idee und Wirklichkeit vom Heiligen Reich bis Königgrätz*, Munich, 1935, i, 153ff. Much has been written also on the influence of foreign affairs on the progress of the unity movement during the revolution of 1848. See Alexander Scharff, *Die europäischen Grossmächte und die deutsche Revolution. Deutsche Einheit und europäische Ordnung 1848-1851*, Leipzig, 1942, and Siegfried A. Kaehler, "Die deutsche Revolution von 1848 und die europäischen Mächte" in *Vorurteile und Tatsachen*, Hameln, 1949, pp. 59-89. Whether Russia, for one, however, could or would actually have intervened militarily in Germany in 1848 is most questionable, as is shown in the new evidence in A. S. Nifontow, *Russland im Jahre 1848*, Berlin, 1954, pp. 278-285, 291, 300, 348.

War contributed to the decision of the English Parliament to postpone the enactment of Irish home rule. This contributed indirectly to the secession of Ireland that resulted within the decade that followed. Similarly, the threat of the first World War reduced rather than increased the capabilities and inclinations of the rulers of the Habsburg monarchy to make any timely concessions to the demands of the increasingly disaffected nationalities of the empire.

C ⟡ SOME ESSENTIAL REQUIREMENTS FOR THE ESTABLISHMENT OF AMALGAMATED SECURITY-COMMUNITIES

A number of conditions appear to be essential, so far as our evidence goes, for the success of amalgamated security-communities—that is, for their becoming integrated. None of these conditions, of course, seems to be by itself sufficient for success; and all of them together may not be sufficient either, for it is quite possible that we have overlooked some additional conditions that may also be essential. None the less, it does seem plausible to us that any group of states or territories which fulfilled all the essential conditions for an amalgamated security-community which we have been able to identify, should also be at least on a good part of the way to successful amalgamation.

1. *Values and Expectations.* The first group of essential conditions deals with motivations for political behavior, and in particular with the values and expectations held in the politically relevant strata of the political units concerned. In regard to values, we found in all our cases a compatibility of the main values held by the politically relevant strata of all participating units. Sometimes this was supplemented by a tacit agreement to deprive of political significance any incompatible values that might remain. In this manner the gradual depoliticization of the continuing difference between Protestant and Catholic religious values in the course of the eighteenth century furnished an essential pre-condition for the successful amalgamation of Germany and Switzerland, respectively, in the course of the following

century.[21] Examples of a partial depoliticization of conflicting values include the partial depoliticization of the slavery issue in the United States between 1775 and 1819, and of the race problem after 1876.[22] Similarly, Germany saw a reduction in the political relevance of the liberal-conservative cleavage after 1866 with the emergence of the National Liberal Party. A similar reduction of political relevance occurred in regard to the conflict of Scottish Presbyterianism with the Episcopal Church in England and Scotland after 1690, and in the further abatement of the Protestant–Catholic issue in Switzerland after the mid-eighteenth century, and further after 1848.

Whether values are "main" values can be determined from the internal politics of the participating units independently from the issue of union—although only, to be sure, within broad margins of error. How important is each value in the domestic politics of the participating units? Acceptance of slavery as a "positive good" had become an essential qualification of candidates for public office in many Southern states in the United States before 1861; this value, important in Southern internal politics, was then also important in the relations between South and North. Conversely, the importance of the distinction between Catholics and Protestants was declining in the domestic politics of nineteenth century Prussia and Bavaria, as well as—more slowly—in the relations between them.

Values were most effective politically when they were not held merely in abstract terms, but when they were incorporated in political institutions and in habits of political behavior which permitted these values to be acted on in such a way as to strengthen people's attachment to them. This connection between values, institutions, and habits we call a "way of life," and

[21] For the Swiss solution of the denominational problem, see Weilenmann, *Pax Helvetica*, pp. 300-311; Kohn, *op. cit.*, pp. 77-78, 88-94; Bonjour, Offler and Potter, *op. cit.*, pp. 272-273, 296-299, etc.

[22] Any survey of American history of the period up to about 1819 reveals how small a part the slavery issue played in politics in the early years of the republic. For the temporary depoliticization of the race problem after 1876 see Paul H. Buck, *The Road to Reunion*, Boston, 1947, pp. 283, 296-297; C. Vann Woodward, *Origins of the New South, 1877-1913*, Baton Rouge, 1951, p. 216.

it turned out to be crucial. In all our cases of successful amalgamation we found such a distinctive way of life—that is, a set
of socially accepted values and of institutional means for their
pursuit and attainment, and a set of established or emerging
habits of behavior corresponding to them. To be distinctive,
such a way of life has to include at least some major social or
political values and institutions which are different from those
which existed in the area during the recent past, or from those
prevailing among important neighbors. In either case, such a
way of life usually involved a significant measure of social innovation as against the recent past.

Putting the matter somewhat differently, we noted in our
cases that the partial shift of political habits required in trans-
ferring political loyalties from the old, smaller political units,
at least in part, to a new and larger political community has
only occurred under conditions when also a great number of
other political and social habits were in a state of change. Thus
we find that the perception of an American people and an American political community, as distinct from the individual thirteen
colonies, emerged between 1750 and 1790. This occurred at the
same time as the emergence of a distinct American way of life
clearly different from that of most of the people of Great Britain
or French Canada. This way of life had been developing since
the beginnings of colonial settlement in the seventeenth century,
but had undergone accelerated change and development in the
course of the American Revolution and its aftermath. Another
example of this process is the emergence of a distinct way of life
of the Swiss people, in contrast to the way of life of the peasants
and to a lesser extent of the town dwellers in most of the rest of
Europe; here, too, the emergence of this distinctive way of life
furnished the social and political background for the gradual
emergence of Swiss political community.[23] Similarly, the unifications of Germany and of Italy occurred in the context of a
much broader change in political values, institutions, and habits

[23] Cf. Weisz, *op. cit.*, pp. 7-156. Oechsli, *op. cit.*, pp. 1-7, 17-21; Castell,
op. cit., pp. 26-33. Wolfgang von Wartburg, *op. cit.*, pp. 31-56. Weilenmann,
Die vielsprachige Schweiz, pp. 20-42, 50-51, 54-57, 60-63, 68; *Pax Helvetica*,
pp. 221-284.

of behavior. These new values were implicit in the modern, liberal nineteenth-century way of life in contrast to the values and institutions of the "old regime" still represented by the policies of the Metternich era.

In regard to expectations, we found that in all our cases amalgamation was preceded by widespread expectations of joint rewards for the participating units, through strong economic ties or gains envisaged for the future. By economic ties, we mean primarily close relations of trade permitting large-scale division of labor and almost always giving rise to vested interests. It was not necessary, however, for such strong economic ties to exist prior to amalgamation. Expectations of rewards were conspicuous in the Anglo–Scottish union of 1707;[24] in the unification of Italy, where the South found itself to some extent disappointed; and in the unification of Germany, where such economic expectations were brilliantly fulfilled.

Only a part of such expectation had to be fulfilled. A "down payment" of tangible gains for a substantial part of the supporters of amalgamation soon after the event, if not earlier, seems almost necessary. This was accomplished by the land policies of Jefferson and the fiscal policies of Hamilton in the case of the United States, by Bismarck's "National Liberal" policies in the 1870's,[25] and by Cavour for at least Northern Italy. Somewhat different economic gains may result from the joint or parallel exploitation of some third resource, rather than from trade between one unit and another. Thus, exploitation of Western lands offered joint rewards to members of the American union, apart from the benefits of mutual trade; many Scotsmen, too, in 1707 were more impressed with the prospect of a Scottish share in English overseas markets than in direct trade with England.

24 One of the more important rewards from the Scottish point of view was participation in trade with England and England's colonies. P. Hume Brown, *History of Scotland*, Cambridge, Eng., 1911, III, 57-58; George S. Pryde, *The Treaty of Union of Scotland and England 1707*, Edinburgh, 1950, 13ff.

25 Cf. Adalbert Wahl, *Deutsche Geschichte von der Reichsgründung bis zum Ausbruch des Weltkriegs (1871 bis 1914)*, Stuttgart, 1926, I, 61-107; and Johannes Ziekursch, *Politische Geschichte des neuen deutschen Kaiserreiches*, Frankfurt, 1927, II, 279-308.

Some noneconomic expectations also turned out to be essential. In all our cases of successful amalgamation we found widespread expectations of greater social or political equality, or of greater social or political rights or liberties, among important groups of the politically relevant strata—and often among parts of the underlying populations—in the political units concerned.[26]

2. *Capabilities and Communication Processes.* Values and expectations not only motivate people to performance, but the results of this performance will in turn make the original values and expectations weaker or stronger. Accordingly, we found a number of essential conditions for amalgamation which were related to the capabilities of the participating units or to the processes of communication occurring among them. The most important of these conditions was an increase in the political and administrative capabilities of the main political units to be amalgamated. Thus the amalgamation of Germany was preceded by a marked increase in the political and administrative capabilities of Prussia from 1806 onward, and by a lesser but still significant increase in the corresponding capabilities of Bavaria and of other German states. Similarly, there were important increases in the capabilities of Piedmont in the course of the last decades preceding Italian unification.[27] In the case of the American colonies, considerable increases in the capabilities of American state governments after 1776, and particularly the adoption of important and effective state constitutions by Pennsylvania, Virginia, Massachusetts, and other states, paved the way for the Articles of Confederation and later for federal union.[28]

[26] Hermann Oncken, *Lassalle, Eine politische Biographie,* 4th edn., Stuttgart and Berlin, 1923, pp. 236-237; Erich Eyck, *Der Vereinstag Deutscher Arbeitervereine 1863-1868,* Berlin, 1904; Gustav Mayer, *Johann Baptist von Schweitzer und die Sozialdemokratie,* Jena, 1909; and Eugene N. Anderson, *The Social and Political Conflict in Prussia 1858-1864,* Lincoln, Neb., 1954, pp. 119-175.

[27] The development of Piedmont is discussed in great detail by Giuseppe Prato in *Fatti e dottrine economiche alla vigilia del 1848: l'Associazione agraria subalpina e Camillo Cavour,* published in *Biblioteca di Storia Italiana recente (1800-1870),* IX, Turin, 1921, pp. 133-484.

[28] Allan Nevins, *The American States During and After the Revolution, 1775-1789,* New York, 1924, 117ff., 621ff.

Another essential condition for amalgamation, closely related to the increase in capabilities, is the presence of markedly superior economic growth, either as measured against the recent past of the territories to be amalgamated, or against neighboring areas. Such superior economic growth did not have to be present in all participating units prior to amalgamation, but it had to be present at least in the main partner or partners vis-à-vis the rest of the units to be included in the amalgamated security-community. The higher economic growth rates of England, Prussia, and Piedmont, both immediately before and during amalgamation, are conspicuous examples.

Another essential requirement for successful amalgamation was the presence of unbroken links of social communication between the political units concerned, and between the politically relevant strata within them. By such unbroken links we mean social groups and institutions which provide effective channels of communication, both horizontally among the main units of the amalgamated security-community and vertically among the politically relevant strata within them. Such links thus involve always persons and organizations.

Some of the links are horizontal or geographic between different participating units; others involve vertical communications, cutting across classes. An example of geographic links occurred during the course of the Industrial Revolution. The rapid growth of settlement and economic activity in Northern England and Southwestern Scotland deepened the integration of England and Scotland during the century after 1707.[29] Another example would be the rapid growth in population and economic activity in the Middle Atlantic states and in Kentucky, Tennessee, and Ohio which tended to strengthen the links between North and South in the United States during the first decades after 1776.

[29] This, strictly speaking, cannot be documented, since the two areas are not fused industrially even today. They are, however, very close to one another, and there has been an extensive migration back and forth. The term "Geordie" as used to describe a Tyneside Scottish migrant is one indication, however, of the extent of population flow over the border. For evidence of the continuing distinctiveness of the two areas even so late as the early nineteenth century, see John Clapham, *Economic History of Modern Britain*, Cambridge, Eng., 1950, 2nd edn., I, pp. 50-51.

A third example is the role of commerce and transport over the St. Gotthard Pass, and of the institutions and organizations related to it, in the consolidation of Switzerland.[30]

An example of a vertical link within Scotland was that between the aristocracy and the middle classes and the people at large, made possible by the ministers and elders of the Scottish Presbyterian Church. In the course of the seventeenth century, the horizontal links of the Scottish Presbyterians to English Protestant sects facilitated Scottish participation in English theological disputes, and this in turn contributed to the acceptance of English (rather than lowland Scots) as the standard language of Scotland.[31] Another example would be the German financial and industrial community that came to link major interests in the Rhineland, Berlin, Darmstadt, Leipzig, and other German centers and states during the 1850's and 1860's.[32]

Another essential condition, related to the preceding one, is the broadening of the political, social, or economic elite, both in regard to its recruitment from broader social strata and to its continuing connections with them.[33] An example of such a

[30] See, e.g., Nabholz, *op. cit.*, vol. 1, pp. 105-106, 126, 150-152, 203, etc., Wolfgang von Wartburg, *op. cit.*, pp. 32-33, 43, 58, 82, etc., Weilenmann, *Pax Helvetica*, pp. 99-127, 177-181, 197-200, 205-207.

[31] For evidence of the growth of an Anglicized Scottish language during the early seventeenth century see Marjorie A. Bald, "The Anglicisation of Scottish Printing," *Scottish History Review*, xxiii, 1925-1926, pp. 107-115, and "The Pioneers of Anglicised Speech in Scotland," *Scottish History Review*, xxiv, 1926-1927, pp. 179-193.

[32] Cf. the great work of Pierre Benaerts, *Les Origines de la Grand Industrie Allemande*, Paris, 1933, which also indicates the extent to which Austria was increasingly excluded from German economic life. For basic statistical data on this subject see A. Bienengräber, *Statistik des Verkehrs und Verbrauchs im Zollverein für die Jahre 1842-1864*, Berlin, 1868.

[33] An exception must be made here for Germany. In Prussia, in particular, both before and after 1871 there was little, if any, broadening of the political "decision-making" elite; the top offices in the government, the foreign services, the bureaucracy, and the army, continued to be filled with aristocrats; and political considerations continued to govern individual appointments: no Social Democrat or Linksliberaler could hope for a government career, and members of the Catholic Center Party could only if their politics were known to be reliably conservative. Only in some of the South German states, notably Baden and Württemberg, was a somewhat greater political toleration to be found. Cf. Theodor Eschenburg, "Die improvisierte Demokratie

broadening of the elite was the emergence of a new type of political leader among the landowners of Virginia, such as George Washington, who retained the respect of his peers and at the same time also knew, well before the American Revolution,[34] how to gain the votes of poorer farmers and frontiersmen at the county elections in Virginia. Another example might be the shift in leadership in the Prussian elite, during the two decades before 1871, from a noble such as Edwin von Manteuffel, who was unwilling to work with the middle classes, to Bismarck, who retained the respect of his fellow aristocrats but knew how to attract and retain middle-class support.[35]

3. *Mobility of Persons.* Another condition present in all our cases of successful amalgamation was the mobility of persons among the main units, at least in the politically relevant strata. It is quite possible that this condition, too, may be essential for the success of amalgamation. In any event, our cases have persuaded us that the mobility of persons among the main political units of a prospective amalgamated security-community should be given far more serious consideration than has often been the case. Full-scale mobility of persons has followed every successful amalgamated security-community in modern times immediately upon its establishment. Examples of the inter-regional mobility of persons preceding amalgamation are the cases of the American colonies,[36] the German states, and the Anglo–Scottish union. Examples of personal mobility accompanying amalgamation are the unification of Italy, and the union of England and Wales. Taken together with our finding that the free mobility of com-

---

der Weimarer Republik von 1919," in *Schweizer Beiträge zur Allgemeinen Geschichte*, IX, 1951, pp. 164-165.

For an important new comparative analysis of the Prussian and Austrian political and military elite in the nineteenth century, see Nikolaus von Preradovich, *Die Führungsschichten in Österreich und Preussen (1804-1918) mit einem Ausblick bis zum Jahre 1945*, Wiesbaden, 1955.

34 Cf. Charles S. Sydnor, *Gentlemen Freeholders: Political Practices in Washington's Virginia*, Chapel Hill, 1952.

35 Cf. Gordon A. Craig, *The Politics of the Prussian Army, 1640-1945*, Oxford, 1955, pp. 148-179.

36 See Michael Kraus, *Intercolonial Aspects of American Culture on the Eve of the American Revolution*, New York, 1928, pp. 42ff., 51, 53, 55, 75-89, 91-102, 146, 160-161, 208.

modities and money, like other economic ties, was not essential for political amalgamation, our finding of the importance of the mobility of persons suggests that in this field of politics persons may be more important than either goods or money.

4. *Multiplicity and Balance of Transactions.* We also found that it was not enough for a high level of communications and transactions to exist only on one or two topics, or in one or two respects, among two or more political units if their amalgamation was to be successful. Rather it appeared that successfully amalgamated security-communities require a fairly wide range of different common functions and services, together with different institutions and organizations to carry them out. Further, they apparently require a multiplicity of ranges of common communications and transactions and their institutional counterparts. Thus the unification of Germany on the political level in 1871 had been prepared by the setting up of common institutions in regard to customs policies, to postal matters, and to the standardization of commercial laws; and beyond the sphere of politics, amalgamation had been prepared by a multiplicity of common institutions in cultural, educational, literary, scientific, and professional affairs.[37] Similarly we find in the American colonies, in the period prior to the Articles of Confederation, a wide range of mutual communications and transactions, as well as of common institutions. The latter included intercolonial church organizations, universities training ministers and physicians, and a postal service, together with ties of travel, migration, friendship, and intermarriage among important elements of the colonial elites.

Two other conditions may well turn out to be essential for

[37] On the German postal union see Josef Karl Mayr, "Der deutschösterreichische Postverein," in *Gesamtdeutsche Vergangenheit. Festgabe für Heinrich Ritter von Srbik,* Munich, 1938, pp. 287-295; on the German commercial code, Rudolph von Delbrück, *Lebenserinnerungen,* Leipzig, 1905, ii, 90ff. and 161ff.; and Enno E. Kraehe, "Practical Politics in the German Confederation, Bismarck and the Commercial Code," *Journal of Modern History,* xxv, March 1953, pp. 13-24; on the national significance of the new academic societies see R. Hinton Thomas, *Liberalism, Nationalism, and the German Intellectuals (1822-1847): An analysis of the academic and scientific conferences of the period,* Cambridge, Eng., 1951.

the success of amalgamation, but these will have to be investigated further. The first of them is concerned with the balance in the flow of communications and transactions between the political units that are to be amalgamated, and particularly with the balance of rewards between the different participating territories. It is also concerned with the balance of initiatives that originate in these territories or groups of population, and finally with the balance of respect—or of symbols standing for respect—between these partners. In the course of studying cases of successful amalgamation, we found that it was apparently important for each of the participating territories or populations to gain some valued services or opportunities. It also seemed important that each at least sometimes take the initiative in the process, or initiate some particular phase or contribution; and that some major symbol or representative of each territory or population should be accorded explicit respect by the others. Thus it seemed significant to us that in the unification of Wales and England, and of Scotland and England, it was a family of Welsh descent (the Tudors) and the Scottish Stuart dynasty who were elevated to the English throne during important stages of the process; and that in the reunion between North and South in the United States, the name of General Robert E. Lee became a symbol of respect even in the North,[38] and that of Abraham Lincoln even in the South. In the case of the Swiss Confederation the very name of the emerging political community was taken from the small rural canton of Schwyz rather than from the more populous and powerful cantons of Bern or Zurich. Likewise, in the unifications of Germany and Italy it was the strongest participating units, Prussia and Piedmont respectively, that had to accept some of the symbols of the larger unit with which they merged, rather than insist on first place for symbols of their own prestige.

The second condition follows from the preceding one. It was not essential that the flow of rewards, of initiatives, or of respect should balance at any one moment, but it seems essential that

---

[38] Buck, *op. cit.*, pp. 251, 255. However, Lincoln never became as much a national hero to the South as Lee did in the North.

they should balance over some period of time. Sometimes this was accomplished by alternating flows or by an interchange of group roles. Territories which received particular prestige, or material benefits, at one time might become sources of benefits for their partners at another; or initiatives might pass from one region to another; or territories whose political elites found themselves ranged with a majority on one political issue might find themselves in a minority on another, without any one particular division between majorities and minorities becoming permanent. Where this was not the case, as in the instance of the permanent minority of Irish Catholics in Protestant Great Britain under the terms of the Anglo–Irish Union, amalgamation eventually failed.[39] In contrast, most political divisions in Switzerland since amalgamation in 1848 have showed every canton, Protestant as well as Catholic, alternating between majority and minority status in accordance with political divisions in terms of agricultural versus industrial cantons, liberal versus conservative, Alpine versus lowland, and the like. This frequent interchange of group roles seems to have aided in the consolidation of the Swiss political community, but further study would be required to say to what extent, if any, this condition was essential in all the other cases of successful amalgamation.

5. *Mutual Predictability of Behavior.* A final condition that may be essential for the success of amalgamation may be some minimum amount of mutual predictability of behavior. Members of an amalgamated security-community—and, to a lesser extent, of a pluralistic security-community—must be able to expect from one another some dependable interlocking, interchanging, or at least compatible behavior; and they must therefore be able, at least to that extent, to predict one another's actions. Such predictions may be based on mere familiarity. In this way, the Vermonters or English-speaking Canadians may know what to expect of their French-Canadian neighbors and

[39] Similarly, the Norwegian fears of a permanent minority status in an amalgamated Norwegian-Swedish union did much to prevent full amalgamation and to destroy eventually even the partial amalgamation that had existed.

to what extent to rely on them, even though they do not share their folkways and culture and do not know what it feels like to be a French-Canadian. Even so, familiarity may be sufficiently effective to permit the development of an attitude of confidence and trust. (The opposite of such successful predictions of behavior are the characteristic fears of the alleged treacherousness, secretiveness, or unpredictability of "foreigners." Such fear of unpredictable "treachery" seems to be more destructive, as far as the experiences from our cases go, than do any clearcut and realistic expectations of future disagreements. Thus Norwegians and Swedes in the nineteenth century often could predict fairly well the unfavorable response which a given political suggestion from one country would find in the other; but these two peoples, while they failed to maintain even limited amalgamation, did retain sufficient mutual confidence to establish later a successful pluralistic security-community.) While familiarity appears to have contributed successfully to the growth of mutual trust in some of our cases, such as that between Scottish Highlanders and Lowlanders, and later between Scots and Englishmen, or between German, French, and Italian Swiss during much of the eighteenth century, we found in a number of our cases that mutual predictability of behavior was eventually established upon a firmer basis.

This firmer basis was the acquisition of a certain amount of common culture or of common group character or "national character." In this manner, an increasing number of Germans in the German states, of Italians in the Italian principalities, and of Americans in the American colonies, came to feel that they could understand their countrymen in the neighboring political units by expecting them, by and large, to behave much as they themselves would behave in similar situations; that is to say, they came to predict the behavior of their countrymen in neighboring political units on the basis of introspection: by looking into their own minds they could make a fairly good guess as to what their neighbors would do, so they could trust them or at least understand them, to some extent much as they would trust or understand themselves. The extent of mutual predictability of behavior, however, seems to have varied from case to case, and it also seems to have varied with the particular political elites or relevant strata concerned. That some mutual predictability of political behavior is an essential condition for an amalgamated security-community seems clear from our cases; but the extent of such predictability must remain a matter for further research.

6. *Summary.* Altogether we have found nine essential conditions for an amalgamated security-community: (*1*) mutual compatibility of main values; (*2*) a distinctive way of life; (*3*) expectations of stronger economic ties or gains; (*4*) a marked increase in political and administrative capabilities of at least some participating units; (*5*) superior economic growth on the part of at least some participating units; (*6*) unbroken links of social communication, both geographically between territories and sociologically between different social strata; (*7*) a broadening of the political elite; (*8*) mobility of persons, at least among the politically relevant strata; and, (*9*) a multiplicity of ranges of communication and transaction. And we have found indications that three other conditions may be essential: (*10*) a compensation of flows of communications and transactions; (*11*) a not too infrequent interchange of group roles; and, (*12*) considerable mutual predictability of behavior.

Among a given number of territories eligible for amalgamation, all these essential conditions may already be present among the background conditions that prevail before "take off"—that is, before any major political amalgamation movement gets under way.[40] In our successful cases of amalgamation, most of these background conditions were indeed present, at least in good part, by the time of take-off. While this part of our findings emphasizes the importance of background conditions for the success or failure of amalgamation, we also found that much could be accomplished toward fulfilling many or all of these conditions for amalgamation in the course of the political proc-

---

[40] For a fuller discussion of the concept of "take-off," see Chapter III, Section C.

ess that followed after take-off. We shall have to say a little more on this point in our discussion of the amalgamative political process later in this chapter.

D ◈ BACKGROUND CONDITIONS CONDUCIVE TO DISINTEGRATION

Several conditions were found present in all cases of disintegration of amalgamated political communities which we studied, and they appear likely to promote disintegration wherever they occur. This does not mean, however, that they are sufficient by themselves to produce disintegration. We have found these conditions also present in some cases where disintegration did not follow but where other factors favoring integration were present in particular strength. The establishment and preservation of amalgamated security-communities thus turned out to depend upon a balance of favorable and adverse conditions. Amalgamation does not seem likely to be established, or to persist, except in the presence of the nine essential conditions for amalgamation which we listed earlier in this chapter; but even in their presence, the disintegrative conditions which we shall discuss below could prevent, destroy, or at least endanger an amalgamated security-community.

In our earlier general discussion, we have described integration as a process depending upon a balance between political loads upon a government, and its capabilities for maintaining amalgamation, or its capabilities for maintaining integration within a pluralistic security-community. In accordance with this general view, we may group the disintegrative conditions in our cases under two headings: conditions that increased the burdens upon amalgamated governments, and conditions that reduced the capability of such governments to cope with the burdens put upon them.

One of the outstanding conditions that tended to destroy amalgamated security-communities by placing excessive burdens upon them was the effect of excessive military commitments. Common armies with light burdens and conspicuous gains in prestige or privileges, or short wars of similar character, were helpful, though not essential, to the deeper integration of a political community; but heavy military burdens with few conspicuous gains over the status quo tended to have the opposite effect. Thus the British attempt to impose a larger defense burden upon the American colonies after 1763 contributed to the movement which ended in the American Revolution. The Napoleonic kingdom of Italy made the idea of Italian unification unpopular for a considerable time afterward as a result of its conscription policies and other military and financial burdens resulting from its commitments in the Napoleonic wars.[41] In more recent times, the strain of war played an essential part in the destruction of Austria–Hungary in 1918; and the same year saw the beginning of the secession of Ireland from the United Kingdom after a period of common war burdens and sacrifices; and it appears that the British attempt to introduce conscription in Ireland in April 1918 accelerated the trend toward secession.[42] In the case of the Norwegian–Swedish union, military burdens of both countries were relatively light, but in the 1890's influential Swedish leaders felt that more should be done to strengthen the joint defense of the two countries against Russia, while most Norwegians remained conspicuously cool to the suggestion. This difference of opinion contributed to the dissolution of the limited political amalgamation between the two countries, but it did not prevent their subsequent integration in a pluralistic security-community.[43]

On the other hand, in several instances deliberate efforts to

[41] R. John Rath, *The Fall of the Napoleonic Kingdom of Italy*, N.Y., 1941, and Eugene Tarlé's *Le blocus continental et le royaume d'Italie*, Paris, 1928, especially Tarlé's brilliant summary of the economic situation, pp. 366-372.

[42] Though the act was never enforced there, the very threat to do so gave a great impetus to the extremists' demands for separation. By the time the law was passed in April 1918, even the strongest Unionists, among whom were Sir James Campbell and Sir Edward Carson, were counselling against any attempt to enforce it in Ireland. See David Lloyd George, *War Memoirs*, London, 1938, new edn., ii, pp. 1597-1601.

[43] On the 1890's cf. Keilhau, *op. cit.*, 392-394, 424-429. On defense and security considerations see the discussion in Leroy Karlstrom, *The "Scandinavian" Approach to Political Integration*, Mss. doctoral thesis, University of Chicago, 1952. By permission of the author.

avoid placing any heavy military burdens on weaker or smaller states or regions, or upon populations psychologically and socially unready or unwilling to bear them, were followed by the successful preservation of the wider political community. Thus no burdens in manpower or money were imposed by Britain upon French Canada between 1776 and 1783; and as late as the second World War, French Canadians were not drafted for overseas service. As in French Canada, Britain during the second World War relied in Northern Ireland on volunteers rather than on conscripts for overseas service. In the case of the American union, effective conscription for the Federal Army was introduced only in 1917. Throughout the formative years of the union, including the wars of 1776-1783 and 1812-1815, the military strength of the union continued to be based on state militias and on voluntary enlistments for limited terms, with no effective Federal coercion of unwilling states or populations. Even as late as the Civil War of 1861-1865—which was fought, after all, for the preservation of the union—volunteer enlistments, and not conscription, were the mainstay of the Union forces.

Another condition which tended to increase greatly the load upon governments, and thus tended to disintegrate amalgamated security-communities, was a substantial increase in political participation on the part of populations, regions, or social strata which previously had been politically passive. Such a substantial increase in political participation meant in each case that the needs, wishes, and pressures of additional social strata or regions had to be accommodated within an old system of political decision-making that might be—and often was—ill-suited to respond to them adequately and in time. Thus the rise of political participation and of a new peasant party in Norway during the second half of the nineteenth century, together with the lack of any corresponding increase in responsiveness on the part of the Swedish governments of the time, greatly increased the difficulties of the Norwegian–Swedish union. Similarly, the Anglo–Irish union became increasingly strained with the rise of Irish mass participation in politics. In the United States between

1830 and 1860, increased political participation tended to magnify sectional tension as politicians facing a mass electorate found it expedient to appeal to emotional issues.[44] Similarly, the destruction of Austria–Hungary, too, was greatly advanced by the rise of mass interest, and often active participation, in politics among her politically and economically underprivileged people (the Rumanians, Ruthenians, Slovaks, Slovenes, and Serbs), as well as among her privileged nationalities (the Germans and Magyars), and among those critical national groups whose intermediate position left them underprivileged in some respects and relatively privileged in others (the Croats, Czechs, Poles, and possibly the Italians). In all these groups, the coming of mass participation in politics was followed by serious disappointments and frustrations of many of the new hopes, claims, and expectations that had been advanced by the newcomers to politics. These experiences of disappointment with the old political institutions and processes of the monarchy were followed by the rise of more extremely nationalistic leaders, platforms, or parties within each ethnic group, and by a more exclusive stress on ethnic in-group values and interests, together with a growing disregard for the claims and feelings of other groups and regions.[45]

A further disintegrative condition related to this rise in political participation is the increase in ethnic or linguistic differentiation. Another aspect of the same condition is a rise in the political awareness of such differentiation as already may exist. Both of these are likely to be a consequence of the rise in political participation among groups that are already thus differentiated, in language and culture, from the predominant nationality or regional-cultural group within the political community in question. Thus, in the mid-nineteenth century, the

---

[44] Roy Franklin Nichols, *The Disruption of American Democracy*, New York, 1948, pp. 514-516; Nichols, "Political Processes and Civil War," in Edward N. Saveth, ed., *Understanding the American Past*, Boston, 1954, pp. 303-314; Avery Craven, "The 1840's and the Democratic Process," *Journal of Southern History*, XVI, April 1950, pp. 161-176.

[45] See Oscar Jászi, *op. cit.*, pp. 271-429; Robert A. Kann, *The Multinational Empire*, New York, 1950, vol. 1 and vol. 2, conclusions.

social and political rise of the Norwegian peasants—whose speech differed considerably from the Dano-Norwegian of the small educated classes in the towns—was accompanied by the rise of the *landsmaal* movement, led by Ivar Aasen, which aimed at the national emancipation of Norway from both Danish and Swedish influence.[46] The rise of the Slavic populations of Austria–Hungary certainly made the preservation of its unity more difficult. Sometimes the differentiation was social and cultural rather than linguistic. The growing differentiation of the German-speaking Swiss from the Germans during the fifteenth, sixteenth, and seventeenth centuries,[47] and the rapid differentiation of American colonists from Englishmen after the middle of the eighteenth century, may serve as examples of this process. The acute awareness of Belgian–Dutch differences which helped to end the Belgian–Dutch union of 1815-1830 might be explored from this point of view; and so might the trend toward the rise of new states based on language differences within the federal system of India.

Another group of disintegrative conditions tends to weaken or destroy amalgamated security-communities by reducing the capabilities of their governments and political elites for adequate and timely action or response. One such condition in our cases appeared to be any prolonged economic decline or stagnation, leading to economic conditions comparing unfavorably with those in neighboring areas.

Another disintegrative condition of this kind was the relative closure of the established political elite. This tended to promote the rise of frustrated counter-elites, somewhat in Pareto's sense, among ethnic or cultural out-groups, or in outlying regions.

Another disintegrative condition, related to the foregoing, was the excessive delay in social, economic, or political reforms which had come to be expected by the population—reforms which sometimes had already been adopted in neighboring areas.

[46] Oscar J. Falnes, *National Romanticism in Norway*, New York, Columbia University Press, 1933; Karen Larsen, *History of Norway*, Princeton University Press for the American-Scandinavian Foundation, 1948, pp. 441-443.

[47] For details, see Weilenmann, *Die vielsprachige Schweiz*, pp. 49-57; cf. also Oechsli, *op. cit.*, pp. 1-14.

Another aspect of the same complex of factors was the disintegrative result of any major failure on the part of a formerly strong or privileged state, group, or region to adjust psychologically and politically to its loss of dominance as a result of changed conditions. The cases of the North Irish Protestants in Ulster before 1918, and of the Bohemian Germans during the same period, are relevant in this connection;[48] and so are the attitudes of most of the Austro–German and Magyar political leaders during the last years of the Habsburg monarchy, as well as the attitudes of many British conservatives toward Southern Ireland in 1918-1921, and, to a lesser extent, the attitudes of some Swedish conservative leaders toward Norwegian claims between 1895 and 1905.

On the other hand, instances of successful adjustment to a loss of dominance tended to contribute to the preservation of a greater measure of political community than otherwise would have been likely. Such cases of successful adjustment to the loss of dominance often led to the preservation or establishment of a pluralistic security-community among areas or peoples where an amalgamated security-community had become impracticable. Examples include British adjustment to American independence and equality after 1819, together with American adjustment to the continued separate existence of Canada; this permitted the demilitarization of the American–Canadian frontier and the gradual consolidation of a pluralistic security-community between the two countries, which became substantially complete after the Treaty of Washington of 1871. Other examples of successful adjustment include the Swedish acceptance of Norwegian independence after 1905, and of Finnish cultural and social equality or near-equality with Swedes after 1918. The first of these adjustments permitted the establishment of a plural-

---

[48] Though in fairness it must be pointed out that most Ulstermen did not and do not think of themselves as striving to maintain a "privileged" or "dominant" position. What they were and are afraid of is that their own folkways and religious beliefs would be swallowed up by the overwhelmingly Catholic south if they were forced to enter into political union with the rest of Ireland. In any case, theirs was never a "dominant" position in the same way that that of the Anglo-Irish aristocracy was.

istic security-community between Norway and Sweden, as well as Denmark, after 1907. The second may have contributed to bringing Finland ever more closely into this Scandinavian community. Still another example might be seen in the successful British adjustment in 1947 to their loss of dominance in India which permitted the continuing membership of India in the Commonwealth.

E ◈ SPECIAL FEATURES OF PLURALISTIC SECURITY-COMMUNITIES

In regard to the problem of a pluralistic security-community, we found that its attainment would be favored by any conditions favorable to the success of an amalgamated security-community, and that it was sometimes hindered by conditions or processes harmful to the latter. Pluralistic security-communities sometimes succeeded, however, under far less favorable conditions than the success of an amalgamated government would have required; and they sometimes survived unfavorable or disintegrative processes which would have destroyed an amalgamated political community. The survival of the Swiss Confederation under the relatively unfavorable conditions of the seventeenth and eighteenth centuries is a case in point. Another is the survival of the Scandinavian pluralistic security-community under the strains and stresses of two world wars.

The argument can be put more strongly. We have noted a considerable number of pluralistic security-communities in the North Atlantic area: United States–Canada since somewhere between 1819 and 1871; United States–Britain since perhaps 1871 or perhaps the end of the century; United States–Mexico since the 1930's; Norway–Sweden since 1907; Sweden–Denmark and Denmark–Norway since some time in the late nineteenth or early twentieth century; Austria–Germany between 1876 and 1932; Britain–Netherlands; Britain–Belgium and Belgium–Netherlands since 1928, if not earlier; and Britain–Norway, Britain–Denmark, and eventually Britain–Sweden since 1910 or earlier. Several of these pluralistic security-communities comprised states of markedly unequal power, but their existence always implied acceptance by both parties of a political situation between them which neither side expected to change by force. Small states in pluralistic security-communities did not have to expect an attack by the larger ones, nor did large states have to fear that their smaller neighbors were merely biding their time while preparing to join their enemies in some future military crisis.

Of these thirteen communities, only one seems to have deteriorated again to a point where war between the participating countries seemed a serious possibility, and where some tangible preparations were made for it. This one case was Austria–Germany in 1933; and in this case the tension was brought about by the threat of forcible amalgamation of Austria into Nazi Germany which was consummated in 1938. With this one exception, all other cases of pluralistic security-communities have persisted to this day and thus, in our terms, have been successful.[49] Pluralistic security-communities between different peoples and countries thus appear to have had a much higher rate of survival than their amalgamated counterparts.

Of the twelve conditions that appeared to be essential for the success of an amalgamated security-community, or at least potentially so,[50] only two or possibly three were found to be very important for a pluralistic security-community as well. The first of these was the compatibility of major values relevant to political decision-making. The second was the capacity of the participating political units or governments to respond to each other's needs, messages, and actions quickly, adequately, and without resort to violence. In the case of a pluralistic security-community, such capabilities for political responsiveness required in each participating state a great many established political habits, and of functioning political institutions, favoring mutual communication and consultation. To be effective, such habits and institutions had to insure that messages from other member govern-

[49] The earlier conflict between Austria and Prussia in 1866 has been referred to above, Section A, 2, A.

[50] These conditions are listed in Section C, 6, above.

ments or units would not merely be received, but would be understood, and that they would be given real weight in the process of decision-making. A third essential condition for a pluralistic security-community may be mutual predictability of behavior; this appears closely related to the foregoing. But the member states of a pluralistic security-community have to make joint decisions only about a more limited range of subject matters, and retain each a far wider range of problems for autonomous decision-making within their own borders. Consequently the range and extent of the mutual predictability of behavior required from members of a pluralistic security-community is considerably less than would be essential for the successful operation of an amalgamated one.

Compared with these three major conditions for a pluralistic security-community, the remaining nine conditions seem to be less important. A distinctive way of life was helpful, as in the case of the Scandinavian political community, but it was not essential, as exemplified by the very considerable differences in the ways of life of Mexico and the United States, which nevertheless have come to form a pluralistic security-community. The requirement of superior economic growth might seem more important; it certainly played a role in the attraction of the United States for Mexico, but this condition could play at most only a very minor part in the successful initiation of a pluralistic security-community between the United States and Canada in 1819, or between Norway and Sweden in 1907. Similarly, the expectation of strong economic ties or gains was not essential; few such ties were expected by either Norwegians or Swedes in 1907.[51] Likewise the broadening of elites and the development of unbroken links of social communication are not essential for a pluralistic security-community; neither of these conditions was present to any marked degree between the United States and Canada in 1819. The same was true for the multiplicity of ranges of communication and transactions, for the interchange of group roles, and for the balance or compensation of flows of such

[51] Note the debate on the concessions law in 1908-1909 in Keilhau, *op. cit.*, 486-489.

communications or transactions between the participating states. None of these conditions seems to have played a major role in the Norwegian–Swedish, the United States–Canadian, and the United States–Mexican cases.

The last of our twelve conditions—the free mobility of persons—surprisingly enough existed, at least to a considerable degree, in all cases of a pluralistic security-community that we have looked into. The movement of persons was substantially free between the United States and Canada during the nineteenth century. It was also free to a considerable extent between Sweden and Norway after 1907,[52] and it was even free to a considerable degree between the United States and Mexico during the most recent decades. But relatively few Norwegians or Swedes actually moved between their countries after 1907; mobility between these two countries was affected but little by the change from amalgamation to pluralism and the growth of Norwegian–Swedish economic, cultural, and social cooperation in later years. On the North American continent, while there has been considerable movement of Canadians to the United States, and there was a somewhat lesser migration of Americans to Canada at certain periods during the nineteenth century, the movement of Mexicans to the United States has been increasingly curtailed. This has been done by United States legislation and by the stricter enforcement of legislation already on the books, without any fatal effects upon the continuing existence of the pluralistic security-community between the two countries.

Of the twelve conditions we found essential for an amalgamated security-community, or possibly so, at most three seem essential for its pluralistic counterpart. The additional four conditions found helpful but not necessary, even for an amalgamated security-community, appear to be completely unessential

52 By 1956, the movement of persons had become nearly unlimited; no passports, no job problems (common labor market for Norway, Denmark, and Sweden), no social security problems, etc. Even professors may apply and be accepted for posts in another country, e.g., a philosophy professor at the University of Bergen is a Swede, a sociology professor at the University of Copenhagen is a Swede, Danish professors teach in Sweden, Norwegian professors teach in Sweden, etc.

for a pluralistic one. At the same time, pluralistic security-communities have shown themselves capable of persistence over long periods, as in the case of the United States and Canada, and perhaps in the case of the Swiss cantons at various periods in their history.

Pluralistic security-communities have also shown themselves capable of further gains in depth, as in the Norwegian–Swedish case that led to the still-developing security-community of the Scandinavian states, and again in the case of the Swiss cantons before they formed an amalgamated national state under a federal constitution.

Altogether, our findings in the field of background conditions tend to bring out the great and potentially restrictive importance of these conditions for the establishment and preservation of amalgamated security-communities. Further, our findings tend to bring out the very considerable potentialities of pluralistic security-communities for overcoming even partially unfavorable background situations.

◇◇

CHAPTER III

Main Findings: Integration as a Process

◇◇

A ◈ POLITICAL INTEGRATION AS A DYNAMIC PROCESS

The transition from background to process is fluid. The essential background conditions do not come into existence all at once; they are not established in any particular fixed sequence; nor do they all grow together like one organism from a seed. Rather, it appears to us from our cases that they may be assembled in almost any sequence, so long only as all of them come into being and take effect. Toward this end, almost any pathway will suffice. As each essential condition is fulfilled, it is added, one by one or a few at a time, as strands are added to a web, or as parts are put together on an assembly line.

So long as this assembling of conditions occurs very slowly, we may treat the status of each condition and the status of all of them together at any one time as a matter of stable, seemingly unchanging background. Indeed, in our historical cases they were so considered, as practically unchanged or slow-changing situations, by most of their contemporaries. But as the last of the conditions in each sequence are added to those whose attainment was assembled previously, the tempo of the process quickens. Background and process now become one. A multiplicity of ranges of social communication and transaction was a background condition for amalgamation, but the rapid adding of new ranges of such communications and transactions is a process. Moreover, it is a process that may become accelerated as a by-product of other processes of political and social change. A balance of flows of transactions between the different units eligible for amalgamation is another of the necessary background conditions for amalgamation. This is particularly true in regard to a balance of initiatives, of rewards, and of respect. But substantial progress toward the establishment of some such balance may be a matter of political process, or else a political process directed toward the attainment of amalgamation may produce a better balance of transaction flows as one of its by-products.

In this assembly-line process of history, and particularly in the transition between background and process, timing is important. Generally speaking, we found that substantial rewards for cooperation or progress toward amalgamation had to be timed so as to come before the imposition of burdens resulting from such progress toward amalgamation (union).[1] We found that, as with rewards before burdens, consent has to come before compliance if the amalgamation is to have lasting success. Thus in the growth of the American federation, the citizens of Vermont, and later of Texas, were each in effect given for a time the privileges of American citizenship without any of its attendant burdens in terms of any liability as to tariffs, taxes, or military service. As their populations became more accustomed and attached to the union, each of these territories eventually joined the United States; and their populations accepted willingly and loyally all duties and burdens which this membership entailed.[2] In the English–Scottish case, the English parliament appropriated a large sum for the compensation of the stockholders of the Darien Company—which comprised a very large part of Scottish society—as part of the settlement connected with

[1] In the case of German unification Bismarck found it expedient to concede certain special rights (*Reservatrechte*) to Bavaria, Württemberg, and a number of other states, even before the Empire was formally agreed to. On Bavaria he conferred the chairmanship of a new Committee on Foreign Affairs to be established in the Bundesrat (the upper house of the imperial legislature), as well as certain other concessions connected with the operation of the Bavarian Army, internal administration and foreign representation (cf. Michael Doeberl, *Bayern und die Bismarcksche Reichsgründung*, Munich, 1925, pp. 132-135). Not to be forgotten either is the annual life pension-subsidy Bismarck conferred on King Ludwig II, in November 1870, to help him out of some of his acute financial difficulties, the result of his expansive building projects. See Wilhelm Schüssler, "Das Geheimnis des Kaiserbriefes Ludwig II," in Martin Göhring and Alexander Scharff, eds., *Geschichtliche Kräfte und Entscheidungen*. Festschrift for Otto Becker, Wiesbaden, 1954, pp. 206-209.

[2] See Chapter II, Section A, 2, c, n. 12.

the union of 1707.[3] In the United States, federal aid to public creditors was associated with the adoption of the federal Constitution, just as federal control of western lands had aided in the acceptance of the Articles of Confederation.

The emergence of strong core areas of amalgamation—either in the form of some one particularly large or strong political unit, or of an increasingly closely-knit composite of smaller units —provides another occasion at which background merges into process. If the other essential background conditions for amalgamation were absent, the emergence of so strong a political unit or coalition tended to arouse fear and to provoke counter-coalitions on the principle of the balance of power. Where the other conditions for amalgamation were present, however, this was not the case. While the emerging core power or federation might be viewed with some misgivings or suspicions, its growth was on the whole tolerated or even welcomed; and in time the other units joined it in some form of wider political amalgamation. An example is the amalgamation first of England, then of England and Wales, prior to that of England–Wales with Scotland. Another is the case of Switzerland, where the confederation of the original three Forest Cantons was joined only two generations later by Zurich and Bern. A third example is the amalgamation of the original thirteen United States, which were later joined by Vermont and Texas, and all the territories which eventually became Western states. A fourth case would be the North German Confederation, which soon afterward grew into the German Empire.

This growth of acceptance of the emergence of core areas or coalitions was somewhat related to the decline in the expectations of war, and to the increasing reluctance to wage war, between the political units that were eventually to join in amalgamation. But there was a condition even more important than the decline in actual expectations and preparations for such

[3] A great part of the sum was used for this purpose. The rest went to pay the current national debt of Scotland, to promote Scottish fishing and other industries, and to recompense individuals who might suffer loss as a consequence of the change-over in coinage. Brown, *History of Scotland*, III, p. 86.

wars among the units eventually to be amalgamated; this was the decline in the willingness to institutionalize preparations for such warfare and to consider war legitimate. In all the cases of lastingly successful amalgamation we studied, warfare among the units concerned became somewhat less than respectable for one or more generations before these units amalgamated.

The devices by which this was accomplished varied, but they all had the effect of making war fratricidal or treasonable, in any event no longer a normal and expectable part of politics. War between England and Wales prior to 1536 had long ceased to be respectable by reason of the common crown, and the two countries had been united under a Welsh dynasty since 1485. Between England and Scotland war began to lose some of its respectability, though it was still waged, after the Stuart–Tudor Marriage of 1503; and it lost almost all respectability with the union of the crowns in 1603 which preceded by more than a century the union of the two countries—even though they were involved in military conflict during this period and threats of war were mentioned as late as the eve of their union in 1707. A decisive step in this decline of expectations of English–Scottish warfare, the coming of the Scottish Reformation, led to dissolution of the Scottish alliance with France against England in the 1560's, and to its eventual replacement by an alliance with England.[4] Thus the military actions between English and Scottish forces between 1638 and 1660 were perceived as aspects of the disordered state of the two kingdoms in a period of civil war, and uprisings of a Scottish Jacobite minority in 1715 and 1745 were viewed as acts of either treason or legitimate revolt. But none of these actions or uprisings generally appeared either in Scotland or in England as a normal aspect of international politics between the two kingdoms.[5]

[4] The Protestant sentiment common to both kingdoms was well expressed by the Scottish divine, Samuel Rutherford, in 1644: ". . . England sent an armie to free both our soules and bodies from the bondage of Popery [in 1560] . . . for which we take Gods name in prayer, seeking grace never to forget that kindness." Samuel Rutherford, *Lex Rex: The Law and the Prince,* 1644, p. 383.

[5] The above statement is made in full awareness of the fact that Covenanting Scotland rose against its king in 1637-1640 (though it remained loyal to

In the case of the American colonies, war between them had never been considered legitimate.[6] Nor had it been systematically prepared for between the beginnings of colonization and independence, since all the colonies had been members of the same British Empire; and from the Declaration of Independence to the adoption of the Constitution, public opinion in the colonies would overwhelmingly have considered warfare between the colonies as fratricidal. Among the Italian principalities, wars undertaken on Italian initiative ceased in the middle of the seventeenth century. By the time of Italian unification in 1859-1860, Italians had not initiated any major war against each other for two centuries. Even though they had on occasion fought each other as allies or vassals of foreign powers, they had long come to consider any such warfare essentially as a cause for regret, while the Italian patriots continued to consider warfare against France or Austria as a possible cause for legitimate glory. Between the Protestant and Catholic cantons of Switzerland, warfare flared up in the course of the religious controversies of the sixteenth century, but already in the course of the Thirty Years' War, Switzerland as a whole remained neutral. Her cantons, with the exception of Graubünden, remained at peace, or rather in a state of cold war, that was only broken by relatively minor incidents, and this cold war finally evaporated in the eighteenth century. By the time of final amalgamation, in 1848, the unity of all Swiss cantons had long become accepted by public opinion throughout the country, and the attempt of a minority of cantons to secede in 1847 led only to a very short "war" with minor casualties.

The war between the German principalities in 1866, in which

---

him and to the monarchical principle) also because Scotsmen felt that English influences in the administration of Scottish ecclesiastical affairs had become far too strong. In this sense—and in some others as well—Scottish national sensibilities were outraged. Englishmen later revolted against the king but, in most instances, for very different reasons from those of the Scots.

[6] A marginal exception to this was the conflict of the original Dutch colonies with the New England colonies which led to minor skirmishes in 1634 and 1635. These, of course, had no significant effects on eighteenth century politics. See Curtis P. Nettels, *The Roots of American Civilization*, New York, 1947, p. 213.

a number of them, including Bavaria, Hanover, and Saxony, fought as allies of Austria against Prussia, would seem to constitute an exception to this pattern. On closer examination, however, Germany too appears to confirm our rule. The German states had initiated no war against each other for more than a hundred years, from 1763 to 1866; and their actual military action against Prussia in 1866 was perfunctory in the extreme, in striking contrast to the serious military effort of the Austrian monarchy. Where Austrian casualties against Prussia were counted in the thousands and tens of thousands, Bavarian and Hanoverian casualties had to be counted in the hundreds. In 1866, the Bavarian army engaged in a good deal of marching and counter-marching that kept it effectively out of any important engagement with the Prussians.[7] Yet only four years later, Bavarian and Hanoverian soldiers—the latter serving in the Prussian army, and the former serving as Prussian allies—fought most vigorously in the bloody war against France (1870-1871). The inference seems inescapable that the Germans by the 1860's had already come to regard warfare among the states that were to become united in the German Empire of 1871 as something far less legitimate or desirable than war against non-German powers. The most that many German liberals would admit was the possibility of a short war against Austria in order to cut the Gordian knot of Austrian opposition to German amalgamation.[7a] In the Norwegian–Swedish case, Norwegian opinion by 1905 had been willing to accept the possibility of a short war against Sweden in order to cut the last ties of Norwegian dependence on that country, but there were no other serious quarrels between the two countries once their partial amalgamation was liquidated. Many Norwegians hoped to achieve separation without actually having to go to war; and the preponderance of Swedish opinion at the very end in 1905 found war against

---

[7] See Generalquartiermeisterstab, *Antheil der Königlich Bayerischen Armee am Kriege des Jahre 1866,* Munich, 1868.

[7a] In Austria, on the other hand, in 1866 there was tremendous public clamor for war with Prussia. Cf. Chester Wells Clark, *Franz Josef and Bismarck: The Diplomacy of Austria Before the War of 1866,* Harvard University Press, 1954, pp. 511-512.

Norway unacceptable as a policy, so that the transition to pluralism occurred without bloodshed.

We found another indication of a quickening of the integrative process in the decline of party divisions which reinforced
the boundaries between political units eligible for amalgamation,
and in the rise in their stead of party divisions cutting across
them. Thus the issue of the reformation cut across the boundaries
of England and Wales in the period of English–Welsh union;
the division between Whigs and Tories cut across the boundaries
between England and Scotland during the generation before
1707.[8] In the case of the American colonies, the division between
conservatives and radicals, and later between Federalists and
Democratic Republicans, cut across colonial or state boundaries.
In the case of the Federalists this was a matter of deliberate de-
sign, as well as a result of the partial merging of colonial elites
between Virginia and New York, and between New York and
Massachusetts. On the side of the radicals, the cry of states'
rights was taken up, but it seems characteristic that the outstanding leader of the radicals, Thomas Jefferson, had not remained content with a role in Virginia politics; he eventually
came to base his political fortunes upon the success of a political Virginia–New York alliance among the anti-federalist elements in both states and eventually throughout the union. This
alliance, to be sure, took shape only in the 1790's, but it had
its forerunners in the parallel attitudes of American radicals
on many issues during the 1770's and 1780's, exemplified perhaps in Jefferson's well-known expression of sympathy for Shays's
Rebellion in Massachusetts (1786).

In the unifications of Italy and Germany, the division between
liberals and conservatives, or between liberals and reactionaries,
cut across state boundaries, and so in Italy did the division
between pro-clericals and anti-clericals. In Germany, moreover, the territorial changes which had resulted from the Napole-

---

[8] Though not in any clearcut or simple way. Scottish party alignments before the Union were rather more complicated than the simple division into
Whigs and Tories. In Scotland a man who attempted to stand upon Tory
principles found himself outside the law and often drifted into Jacobitism.

onic Wars had greatly increased the extent to which the division between Protestants and Catholics crossed the state boundaries that emerged in 1815.[9] In Switzerland, the division between liberals and conservatives also cut across many cantonal boundaries in the period between 1815 and 1858, though a few predominantly Catholic and conservative cantons took part in the abortive attempt at secession in 1847. Even in the lands of the Habsburg Monarchy, the division between the Catholic Counter-Reformation and its Protestant opponents cut across the boundaries of the kingdoms and principalities concerned. In all these territories (except for the major part of Hungary, then under Turkish rule) the Counter-Reformation tended to strengthen the centralization of the Habsburg government throughout the sixteenth and seventeenth centuries.[10] As we have seen, not only amalgamation but integration of the Habsburg lands was achieved, though not in great depth, in the course of the eighteenth century; but it is important to remember that the loss of this integration in the nineteenth century and the eventual dissolution of the monarchy in the twentieth were accompanied by the further rise of political movements which continued to cut across territorial and national boundaries—such movements as liberalism in the middle of the nineteenth century and, toward its end, that of organized labor.[11]

Here again we find that the effect of party divisions cutting

[9] On the role of the Catholics in the German unity movement, see the illuminating new study of George G. Windell, *The Catholics and German Unity, 1866-1871*, Minneapolis, 1954; also Franz Schnabel, *Der Zusammenschluss des politischen Katholizismus in Deutschland im Jahre 1848*, Heidelberg, 1910, and Else Mülker, *Der konfessionelle Gegensatz und das deutsche Einheitsproblem 1848-1849*, Marburg, 1935.

[10] Hantsch, *op. cit.*, vol. 1, pp. 240-371; Krones, *op. cit.*, vol. 3; Huber-Dopsch, *op. cit.* part 2; Thomas Fellner and Heinrich Kretschmayr, *Die österreichische Zentralverwaltung*, 1. Abt. *Von Maximilian I bis zur Vereinigung der österreichischen und böhmischen Hofkanzlei (1749)*, Vienna, 1907; see also Dominic Kosáry, *op. cit.*, and S. Harrison Thomson, *op. cit.*, pp. 130-153.

[11] Redlich, *op. cit.*, vol. 1/1, 59-220, vol. 1/2, 25-63; Kann, *op. cit.*, vol. I, 90-108, 137-149, 180-181, vol. II, 138-178; Jászi, *op. cit.*, 177-185, 318-320; as to the administrative amalgamation in the Maria Theresan period see particularly Friedrich Walter, *Von der Vereinigung der österreichischen und böhmischen Hofkanzlei bis zur Einrichtung der Ministerialverfassung (1749-1848)* in *Die österreichische Zentralverwaltung*, ed. by Heinrich Kretschmayr, Vienna, 1938.

across the units depends largely on the presence or absence of other essential conditions for integration. Where some of these are present, party divisions cutting across units may hasten integration. Where these other conditions are absent, parties standing within each unit for apparently the same abstract ideology—such as liberals, conservatives, clericals and the like—may in fact come to express within these seemingly similar ideologies the actually clashing perspectives and interests of the separate political elite of each unit. They may thus merely add a somewhat deceptive common vocabulary to the actual conflicts that continue to divide such units from each other.

Our last geographic area, that of the Norwegian–Swedish union, offers an interesting variation to this problem. During most of the nineteenth century, party divisions tended to reinforce Norwegian–Swedish cleavages rather than to cut across them. Peasants and liberals had far greater weight in Norwegian politics than they had in Sweden, while throughout the nineteenth century conservatives and aristocrats continued to wield great political influence in the latter country. Swedish liberalism did not become sufficiently powerful to form a Swedish government until 1905, the year of Norway's secession; and the emergence of liberal and later of strong labor parties in both countries, with a greater share of political divisions now cutting across the boundary between them, did not follow until the decades after secession. Then, however, this development contributed there, too, to the integration of the two countries; but this time it did so within the looser framework of a pluralistic security-community.

On the matter of party divisions, one observation should be added. In all the cases we studied, the victorious party—and sometimes even both parties—stood for something new in the way of social institutions and individual opportunities, and not for mere defense of a status quo. This was true of the Reformation and the Tudors in the case of England and Wales; of the Whigs, and to some extent even of the Tories, in the case of England and Scotland; of the liberals in the cases of Switzerland,

Italy,[12] and Germany; and in the latter two countries it was true even to some extent of those conservatives such as Cavour and Bismarck who knew how to incorporate part of the liberal program into their own policies. In the case of the United States, finally, both the Federalists and the radicals (and later Jeffersonians) stood for many and substantial new positive institutions and achievements. The cases where this element of positive social and political reform was least pronounced were those of England–Ireland in 1801, of the Habsburg Monarchy, and of the Swedish attitude toward the Norwegian–Swedish union of 1814; and all these cases ended in an eventual dissolution.

B ◆ THE ISSUE OF FUNCTIONALISM AS A PATHWAY TO AMALGAMATION

Our finding that the bringing together of the necessary background conditions for amalgamation in our cases resembled an assembly-line process, suggests indirectly an answer to an old question: does merging of one or more governmental functions among two or more political units promote progress toward later over-all amalgamation of their governments? Or, on the contrary, does what we shall call functional amalgamation impede such over-all amalgamation by inadequate performance of the few already amalgamated functions? Does it take the wind from the sails of the movement for full-scale amalgamation by making the few already amalgamated functions serve adequately the main needs which had supplied most of the driving power for the over-all amalgamation movement?

Before we answer this question, we must say exactly what we mean by functionalism. As we are using the term here, it includes all cases of partial amalgamation, where some governmental functions are delegated by the participating units on a low or a high level of decision-making. Whether a particular function or institution is so important that its pooling with another

---

[12] A splendid study of the role played by liberals and by liberal ideas in the Risorgimento is Kent Roberts Greenfield, *Economics and Liberalism in the Risorgimento*, Baltimore, 1934.

government would have the effect of over-all amalgamation rather than partial—and thus take it out of the field of functionalism—depends on the importance of this particular function or institution in the domestic politics of the participating units. Thus the union of the crowns between Britain and Canada today, with effective power in each country vested mainly in its legislature, is a case of functional amalgamation. In 1770, joint monarchial rule did constitute over-all amalgamation. In the case of the Habsburg Monarchy, the power of the monarch in Bohemia and Hungary after 1526 vis-à-vis the estates of these countries was not great enough to insure that the dynastic union of these countries with Austria would constitute over-all amalgamation; but by the early eighteenth century the power of the monarchy in all these countries was so great that they were without doubt amalgamated.[13]

We have also found historically a number of quasi-functional arrangements in which participating units delegated some of their governmental functions, not to a joint authority, but to one or more other units. Arrangements of this type were, notably, the arrangements for joint citizenship between Geneva and Bern early in the sixteenth century; the arrangements for joint citizenship of persons born after 1603 between England and Scotland in the seventeenth century; and the full faith and credit clause in the Articles of Confederation. These, too, we have included under the heading of functionalism.

How helpful, then, has functionalism been? We have found, first of all, that over-all amalgamation can be approached functionally and by steps, with successful over-all amalgamation at the end. This occurred in the cases of Germany with the Zollverein (of which, significantly, Austria was not a member); the United States with the common administration of Western lands under the Articles of Confederation; the Swiss cantons since the fourteenth century, and the common citizenship between Geneva, Bern, and Fribourg, and later other Swiss cantons from

---

[13] Fellner-Kretschmayr, *op. cit.*, Walter, *op. cit.*; see also J. Beidtel, *Geschichte der österreichischen Zentralverwaltung* (1740-1848) 2 vols., Innsbruck, 1896-1897.

the sixteenth century onward; finally, between England and Wales and England and Scotland before the union of crowns preceding full amalgamation. In all these cases amalgamation eventually was successful. But functional amalgamation was also proposed and rejected among the Italian states in the 1840's, and eventually amalgamation was achieved without its aid. Moreover, functional amalgamation took place in at least three of our cases that were eventually unsuccessful: there was the union of crowns between Austria, Bohemia, and Hungary from 1526 onward;[14] there was the union of crowns between Norway and Sweden in 1814; and there were various forms of partial amalgamation between England and Ireland before 1801.

These examples are taken from a sample collection of historical cases and situations in which instances of successful amalgamation outnumber the unsuccessful ones by more than two to one.[15] From this it should be clear that the historical evidence in favor of functionalism is quite inconclusive.

It seems safest to conclude that the issue of functionalism has been greatly overrated. Functionalism, it appears, is a device that has been widely used both in successful and in unsuccessful movements toward amalgamation, somewhat as functional devolution and decentralization have been used in successful and in unsuccessful attempts at secession. The outcome in all such situations seems mostly to have been the result of other conditions and other processes—depending largely on whether functionalism mainly was associated with experiences of joint rewards or of joint deprivations—with functionalism in itself doing little to help or to harm. Among our cases there is none in which functional amalgamation prevented later attempts at over-all amalgamation; in England–Ireland and the Habsburg Monarchy, some form of over-all amalgamation was indeed accomplished, but this eventually proved to be brittle.

[14] See Huber-Dopsch, *op. cit.* parts 1, 2; Arnold Luschin-Ebengreuth, *Grundriss der Österreichischen Reichsgeschichte*, Bamberg, 1899; H. J. Bidermann, *Geschichte der österreichischen Gesamtstaatsidee*, Innsbruck, 1867, 1889.

[15] For a discussion of the limitations of such partly quantitative statements, see Section E, 1, below.

Our evidence seems to show that carefully limited functional amalgamation among a few countries might well be used as an approach toward eventual more far-reaching amalgamation or integration among them. But there seems to be no evidence in our cases that functionalism, in general and as such, would make any major contribution to success.

Perhaps the most that can be said for functionalism as an approach to integration is that it seems less hazardous than any sudden attempt at over-all amalgamation. Successful over-all amalgamation from the outset occurred in only two of our situations. One was the amalgamation of England in 1066 by the strong personal rule of a foreign conqueror; the other was the accomplishment of a deeper, broader kind of English amalgamation as a result of the growth of native and more impersonal legal and political institutions after 1215. In all other situations, over-all amalgamation came only after a prolonged period of functional and pluralistic associations, or else it was unsuccessful for both. As in England in 1066, over-all amalgamation was imposed by force between Austria and Bohemia after 1620, and to a degree between Austria and Hungary in the 1680's.[16] It was imposed by substantial political and military pressure, as well as by bribery, between England and Ireland in 1801; and its forcible imposition was attempted unsuccessfully by Sweden in her relationship to Norway in 1814. With the exception of England in 1066—and perhaps with the exception of England and Northern Ireland—all the cases just listed ended in eventual failure. Of course, the goal of an amalgamated security-community was attained at a late stage of the amalgamation movement in a number of well-known cases, such as Italy, Germany, England and Scotland, England and Wales, the American colonies, and Switzerland, but these instances of its eventual success as a goal do not make it appear any less unsuccessful as a method. Where an amalgamated over-all govern-

---

16 D. Kosáry, op. cit., pp. 132-134; S. H. Thomson, op. cit., pp. 130-153; Anton Gindely, Geschichte der Gegenreformation in Böhmen, Leipzig, 1894; Th. Mayer, Verwaltungsreform in Ungarn nach der Türkenzeit, Vienna, 1911; Fellner-Kretschmayr, op. cit.

ment was imposed by military conquest, or by related forms of pressure, the chances were more than even that the enterprise would eventually end in failure; and if we recall once again that in our collection of situations the instances of failure form less than one-third of the total, our doubts as to the wisdom of early over-all amalgamation as an approach to political integration under modern conditions become even stronger.

If early over-all amalgamation was likely to end in eventual failure, and if the functional approach proved practicable but unlikely to contribute much to eventual success, what are the early approaches to amalgamation that promise to be more successful under present-day conditions? For answers to this question we must look at the early stages of the political amalgamation movement. The first of these questions is: when can a political amalgamation movement be said to begin?

C ◈ *THE CONCEPT OF TAKE-OFF FOR INTEGRATION*

The image of take-off is borrowed from some recent students of economic development.[17] As an airplane speeds along the runway, its wheels gradually lose touch with the ground; rolling becomes flight, a change in the amount of speed turns into a change in kind of motion. For the economist, take-off means the period in the history of an underdeveloped country during which efforts at economic development undergo a change in magnitude or in coordination that brings about a change in kind for the development process of the country concerned. Prior to take-off, efforts at economic development were slow, small-scale, scattered; after take-off they are large and coordinated, making for new successes or new difficulties on a larger scale.

In studying political movements directed toward integration, we may similarly speak of take-off as a period in which small, scattered, and powerless movements of this kind change into larger and more coordinated ones with some significant power behind them. Before take-off, political integration may be a matter for theorists, for writers, for a few statesmen, or a few small

---

[17] See Walt W. Rostow, "The Take-Off into Self-sustained Growth," in *The Economic Journal*, vol. LXVI, March 1956, pp. 24-48.

pressure groups. After take-off, integration is a matter of broad political movements, of governments, or of major interest groups, often an affair of more or less organized mass persuasion and mass response, or else of the organized persuasion of large parts of the political elites or the politically relevant strata of the time. Before take-off, the proposal for integration is a matter of theory; after take-off, it is a political force.

While the concept of take-off is applicable both to drives for political integration and to drives for mere amalgamation, the distinction between the two is important. Integration, as we have defined it, requires expectations of security based on a large measure of sense of community among the politically active groups. Amalgamation was sometimes accomplished by mere conquest, and was maintained by force and fear. Sometimes the two drives coincided: among the American colonies a unified government was established during the same period that consent developed among the groups who counted in politics in the course of the years between 1765 and 1791. In some other cases, however, amalgamation was enforced by conquest, and the drive for political integration based on consent came only much later. Thus, England completed the conquest of Wales in 1282, but the drive for a political union based on consent among the political elites of the two countries began at the earliest in 1485. It should be noted, however, that this conquest did not lead to any major amalgamation of the legal, administrative, and social institutions of the two countries; in many ways the conquest of 1282 thus enforced merely a functional union; full amalgamation did not come until after 1536. Finally, the drive for integration based on consent may begin long before the drive for amalgamation, as it did in the cases of Italy, Germany, and Switzerland.

In this study, we are interested in the establishment and consolidation of a security-community (whether amalgamated or pluralistic) as a goal, and in amalgamation only as a possible instrument for its attainment. Where the take-off periods for the drives toward integration or amalgamation should happen to differ, therefore, we shall use the take-off toward integration as the starting point for our analysis in this section. It should be made clear, furthermore, that the concept of take-off does not necessarily imply a sudden, new beginning or an abrupt break with the past, but rather a marked quickening or strengthening of the political process moving toward integration.

We may consider take-off to have occurred as soon as at least one major social or political group, or political institution, has become committed to the cause of integration. In most of our cases, the period of take-off was followed, within a period of one to two generations (or between twenty and sixty years), either by the attainment of integration or by the abandonment of the attempt; but in some cases the decision took longer, up to five generations, or about one hundred and fifty years. It is to this period of between one and two generations after take-off that the following discussion will largely apply.

D ◈ EARLY ISSUES AND LEADERS IN THE INTEGRATION MOVEMENT

In all our cases, the basic issue of integration became acute in the course of a double process of habit-breaking.

The most important element in this process was the emergence of a distinctive way of life, as discussed in Chapter II among the essential background conditions for an amalgamated security-community. Such an emerging way of life involved necessarily a change in many habits of behavior. It created a climate within which the political habits of loyalty to a particular political unit could be more easily shifted to a political unit of another size, either larger or smaller, if this seemed to offer a more promising framework within which this attractive way of life could be developed.[18]

A secondary element in the same process of habit-breaking was constituted by the presence of some external challenge to the emerging new way of life. This would make men aware of the

---

[18] See the interesting new study of Wolfgang Von Groote, *Die Entstehung des Nationalbewusstseins in Nordwest-Deutschland 1790-1830*, Göttingen, 1955, esp. pp. 122-129.

extent to which the new way of life had already developed, and of the extent to which they had already become attached to it.

This coincidence of a new way of life and of an external challenge to it could, in principle, make for secession as easily as for amalgamation. If the new way of life was common to several political units otherwise eligible for amalgamation, an external challenge to this way of life might be perceived as a challenge to all these units and might drive them closer together. If, on the other hand, the way of life was prevalent or strongly established only in some of the units but not in others, an external challenge to it might separate the political units from each other in proportion to their attachment or lack of it to the new way of life that was being challenged. The distribution of the institutions, habits, values, and social groups characteristic of the new way of life among the different political units would thus tend to determine the direction of the process either toward secession or amalgamation. The impact of an external challenge would then speed up the timing of the process and precipitate the decision in which direction it would go, whatever that direction might turn out to be. The common way of life thus constituted the major premise for the outcome, and the external challenge provided the minor one.

A still more minor aspect of this process of habit-breaking was the arrival of a new generation in politics; the younger men were usually more committed to new ways of doing things and more willing to accept the new size of political units than their predecessors had been. Of these three elements in the process of habit-breaking, we have called the emergence of a new way of life the most important because it was the least probable. After all, new ways of life do not emerge very often in either history or in politics. Compared with this basic factor, external challenges are fairly probable; they occur very frequently—indeed, almost all the time—in history and in politics. Finally, the coming into politics of a new generation of leaders is so highly probable as to become virtually certain with the passage of time. Nevertheless, it seems that it was characteristically the coincidence of an improbable event (the emergence of a new way of life) with a far more probable event (the impact of some external challenge) and a highly probable event (the appearance of a new generation of leaders in politics) which in their interplay tended to make integration an acute issue in politics.

At the same time it is important to remember that in the early stages of integration movements, local political issues—that is, issues related to the politics of the participating units—were always dominant. The details of these issues were too varied to permit enumeration here, but on the whole they had one characteristic in common: they all dealt in some way with the capabilities of governments, and in particular with their responsiveness to the needs of the population within each participating political unit. The issue of political integration thus arose primarily when people demanded greater capabilities, greater performance, greater responsiveness, and more adequate services of some kind from the governments of the political units by which they had been governed before. Integration or amalgamation[19] were first considered as possible means to further these ends, rather than as ends in themselves.

Consistent with this, we found that functional and pluralistic approaches were dominant in the early stages of the integration movement in all cases we studied. In most of our cases the goal of setting up an amalgamated security-community played only a minor role at the outset of the movement. This was particularly true of the cases of Italy, Germany, Switzerland, the American colonies, and England and Scotland. Even in the cases of England and Wales, and of England and Ireland, administrative amalgamation came rather late. Even in the case of the Habsburg monarchy after 1526, the early emphasis was on functional union, limited to the crowns, while leaving the estates of Bohemia and Hungary for a considerable time in possession of

[19] Integration, and amalgamation *without* integration (amalgamation forcibly imposed, for example), were sometimes alternative goals which were found intermingled in some unification movements. See Chapter I, A. Thus at the end of the American Civil War the adherents of the Union included some who wanted to reconcile the South and others who wanted to rule it by coercion.

much of their power.[20] Finally, the union between Norway and Sweden, after the failure of the early Swedish attempts to force amalgamation, remained essentially functional in character. The functional approach was thus used both in successful and in eventually unsuccessful cases, presumably because it appeared at each time as the most promising approach to take. Attempts at immediate integration, as well as immediate amalgamation without integration, usually proved to be far more unpromising.

Leadership in the early stages of an integration or amalgamation movement was furnished typically not by any single social class, but rather by a cross-class coalition. Such a coalition characteristically united some of the "most outside of the insiders"— that is, some of the less secure members of the established ruling class who were least closely connected with its other members— in a political alliance with the "most inside of the outsiders." These were some of the members of those social groups or classes outside the seats of power who had already become, or were in the process of becoming, the most serious contenders for a share of political power from among those strata hitherto excluded from it. It seems noteworthy that cross-class coalitions of essentially the same kind seemed also characteristics of the leadership of movements aiming at secession. In other words, many of the movements that aimed at changing the scale of the political unit, either by dividing a large political community into several smaller ones, or by uniting several small political units into a larger one—the leadership of such movements, we say, seemed to unite characteristically some of the least secure among the powerful with some of the most powerful among those who were just ceasing to be powerless.

Leaders of amalgamation movements were thus usually drawn from previously established elites. But we often found in their backgrounds some evidence of partial alienation from their own elite or from the political community within which they were functioning.[21] The perception by these leaders of their own

---

[20] Huber-Dopsch, *op. cit.*, pp. 146-227; Fellner-Kretschmayr, *op. cit.*; H. J. Bidermann, *op. cit.*

[21] Cf. George W. F. Hallgarten, "Heinrich von Treitschke: The Role of the

political communities with which they identified themselves was thus often problematical; they could not take them naïvely for granted. At the critical time, such leaders perceived their own community of political allegiance, and their own membership role within it, as more problematical and as more open for re-interpretation and redefinition than did their more securely affiliated peers.

Integration or amalgamation was promoted in its early stages not only by cross-class coalitions, but also by political coalitions—and occasionally even by involuntary cooperation—between conservatives and liberals or radicals. In the United States it was the radicals who first pressed for a break with England and emphasized the unity of the colonies in the common struggle; but it was mostly the conservatives, who had opposed this break, who afterward turned nationalist and shaped much of the character of the Constitution. In Germany, early German nationalism had been a liberal movement in the eighteenth century. The reform sentiment that stood behind the national idea in 1813-1814 was liberal in domestic politics; and to the extent that German na-tionalism made progress between 1815 and the 1830's, including the achievement of the Zollverein, it was primarily a product of liberal thought and policy. In 1848, the liberals sought German unity, though without success; and after their failure it was the Prussian conservative von Radowitz who attempted to salvage something through the Northern Union movement. Again, it was the revival of liberalism in Prussia at the end of the 1850's that led to the revival of the unity issue, but it was Bismarck who then took over direction of the unity movement after 1862 and carried it through to a successful—conservative—conclusion in 1871. In Italy, the liberalism of the Carbonari and of Maz-zini, and the conservatism of Piedmont, both contributed to the development of the sentiment for Italian unity. Then the union movement culminated in the dramatic contribution of the radical Garibaldi, with his One Thousand, to the final unification of

---

'Outsider' in German Political Thought," in *History*, xxxvi, October 1951, pp. 227-243.

the country. But at the same time it was far more conservative statesmen, Cavour and men like him, who did most to shape the character of the new state.

As these examples suggest, integration or amalgamation movements in their early stages did not require any high degree of like-mindedness from their early leaders and promoters. Rather, these men could and did differ widely from each other in their values and their political philosophies, provided only that they could somehow work together, or at least add their contributions together. The basis of such cooperation was not necessarily similarity of values or outlook, but rather complementarity—that is, an interlocking relationship of mutual resources and needs. A crucial condition for the success of the early leaders or promoters of integration movements was thus their skill in making compromises, or the lack of it.[22] Frequently, such compromises were not mere halfway houses between opposed positions on one and the same issue, but rather these compromises themselves followed something like a dovetail pattern. That is to say, a far-reaching acceptance of demands of one side or group was not frustrated by compromise, but rather was compensated for by a similarly far-reaching acceptance of some other demand by another group or faction on some other issue. Thus, characteristically, the Articles of Confederation already combined far-reaching concessions to the radical and states' rights position with far-reaching federal powers over Western lands.[23] In a more general way, far-reaching concessions to radical desires in the state constitutions came to be balanced by the greater conservatism of the federal Constitution; and this conservatism of the federal Constitution in turn came to be compensated for in part by the far more radical principles of the first ten amendments

---

[22] In Germany, particularly, the unity movement was seriously retarded by an inability to come to speedy and effective compromises on basic political questions. Cf. Karl Wolff, *Die deutsche Publizistik in der Zeit der Freiheitskämpfe und des Wiener Kongresses*, Plauen, 1934, and Wilhelm Mommsen, *Grösse und Versagen des deutschen Bürgertums; Ein Beitrag zur Geschichte der Jahre 1848-1849*, Stuttgart, 1949.

[23] Merrill Jensen, *The Articles of Confederation*, Madison, Wis., 1948, pp. 150ff., 161ff.

to that Constitution known as the Bill of Rights, which were adopted almost immediately after its ratification.

In the absence of such dovetailing of mutual needs and mutual concessions, even a high degree of similarity in institutions and of like-mindedness in outlook would not produce any particular progress toward either integration or amalgamation. Thus, during the first two-thirds of the nineteenth century, many of the German princes were remarkably similar in background and political outlook, and there was a great deal of similarity between many of the aristocratic (and in part absolutistic) political institutions from which many of them drew their power. Yet most of these princes did nothing to promote either amalgamation or integration. Rather, most of them showed their like-mindedness in opposing and in retarding these movements.

Thus far we have mainly spoken of the politically active elite. Perhaps a few words should be added in particular about the role of the intelligentsia. The intellectual and professional classes were usually marginal members of the elites of the countries in which they lived. They were the peers of aristocrats and great merchants in the matter of education, but not at all in the matter of power or wealth. They were thus likely recruits for some of the cross-class coalitions which we mentioned earlier. Beyond this, these strata were the carriers of the traditions of independent state existence on the part of political units, on the one hand, as well as carriers of the traditions of the unity of the larger political community, on the other. Bureaucrats and intellectuals were the major carriers of the memories of Scottish independence, as well as of the image of a possible greater British unity. Intellectuals wrote and retransmitted the ancient history of Bavaria or of Venice, and intellectuals preserved and developed the competing traditions of the larger political units, such as Germany or Italy. The intellectual classes, and the leading intellectual figures within them, were thus of considerable importance for the success of movements aiming either at union or at separation.

An interesting aspect of some of the successful integration movements was the relative massiveness of their intellectual sup-

port: most prominent German historians after the middle of the
nineteenth century were nationalists of one sort or another and
thus generally in favor of German unity. The intellectual classes
in Italy and in the United States similarly tended on the whole
to favor national union, and scattered indications suggest that
the same was true of Switzerland. In the cases of Ireland, Bohemia,[24] Hungary[25] and Norway, the intellectual classes gradually shifted from lukewarm endorsement of the larger political
communities to which these countries for a considerable length
of time belonged, to an increasing stress first on their distinct-
ness and eventually on their likely separation.

In movements aiming at either union or separation, the importance of intellectuals tended to increase when they were
united. So long as most intellectuals disagreed among themselves,
their opinions tended to cancel out. Thus in 1815, the German
intellectuals were still to a considerable extent divided as to
whether greater unity was at all desirable for Germany. By
1848 this division had almost disappeared, but it had been replaced by strong difference of opinion as to what sort of union
was desirable. In 1815 the medieval imperial idea of German
unity still cast a strong spell over many intellectuals; by 1848
its influence had greatly declined; by the 1860's it had virtually
disappeared. But in 1815 there was no marked intellectual trend
toward any acceptance of Prussian leadership in a German unity
movement; by 1848 there was definitely such a trend; and by the
1860's it had become strongly predominant.

In addition to the extent of their unity, the political influence
of intellectuals depended, of course, on the number of non-
intellectuals whom they could lead in politics, and on the
strength of their hold upon them. As mass participation in politics increased, and as larger numbers of persons acquired literacy,
the potential public of the intellectuals increased and, with it,
their potential power. At an earlier level of social development,

[24] Herman Münch, *Böhmische Tragödie*, Braunschweig, 1949, pp. 167-296;
Elizabeth Wiskemann, *Czechs and Germans*, London, 1938, pp. 19-44; Ernest
Denis, *La Bohème depuis la Montagne Blanche*, vol. 2, Paris, 1903.
[25] L. Spohr, *Die geistigen Grundlagen der Nationalismus in Ungarn*, Berlin, 1936; Jules Szekfü, *État et Nation*, Paris, 1945, pp. 202-224.

many of the political non-elite followed their traditional authorities, such as the landlord and the priest. At a much later stage, they would have become thoroughly accustomed to being literate and to forming their own interests, organizations, or pressure groups, such as agricultural organizations, labor unions, and the rest. It was during the transition period between the first and the last of these stages, when large numbers of people began to know enough to enter into some sort of political activity, but did not yet know enough to act politically without the guidance of the intellectuals, that the potential influence of intellectuals on politics was at its height.

Despite these circumstances, active direct popular support played only a minor role in the early stages of integration and amalgamation movements. Popular attitudes, to be sure, set limits to what was politically practical from an early stage, both in regard to movements aiming at amalgamation or at secession; and the importance of these popular attitudes tended to increase with growing mass participation in politics. Active popular support, however, tended to come only at a later stage; but it is important to note that the enlisting of popular participation was one of the most successful methods used to promote successfully a movement for amalgamation.

In their early stages, drives toward integration or amalgamation frequently met with temporary failures. The main causes of such failures seem to have been, first of all, lack of essential background conditions, and lack of motivation among both the elites and the broader strata of the population to support the movement. Other causes included lack of skill in the making of compromises; and lack of agreement on accepted policies. The amalgamation or integration issue had failed, in such cases, to emerge as the paramount political issue at this place and time, nor had there been any agreement on the main method of strategy by which its aims were to be pursued. There was division between federalists and centralists in Italy in the 1840's, and between those who wanted to include the Pope in a proposed Italian federation and those who wanted to keep the Papal political power out of the new Italian state; and there were others who wanted to abolish the temporal power of the Papacy. All these divisions contributed to the failure of the Italian attempts at unification in 1848.[26] Similarly the division between the "Great Germans," who wanted to include Austria in the future German Empire, and the "Little Germans," who wanted to keep her out of a German Empire that was to be organized under Prussian leadership, contributed very materially to the failure of German unification in 1848.

These causes of failure were somewhat related to the overburdening of the attention of contemporaries by a multiplicity of urgent but apparently unrelated problems, all competing with the amalgamation or integration issue for attention. Thus in Germany the problems of major administrative and political reforms in 1813-1814, and of political and social reform in 1848, were not clearly related to the issue of union; they detracted from its urgency. On the other hand, after these issues had at least in part been dealt with, integration did emerge as the paramount issue. Where the inability to relate these different issues to the problem of amalgamation or integration contributed to its temporary defeat, the ability to relate such social, administrative, or local issues to the problem of over-all integration contributed, on the contrary, to its victory. In the case of the American Revolution, relating of local to federal issues was accomplished sooner; but even there, many problems had to be solved first on the state level by the adoption of state constitutions before the issue of federal union could gain the center of attention.

Among the cases we studied, we found that a striking number of the early failures left behind them a legacy of improved background conditions for the next drive toward amalgamation or integration. On the face of it, this evidence would seem to suggest that early defeats were, if anything, beneficial to the cause of eventual integration. This impression, however, may be somewhat spurious, for we had deliberately selected a set

[26] The point is made in all the discussions of the causes of the failure of 1848 in Italy. See, for example, Bolton King, *A History of Italian Unity*, London, 1899, i, pp. 347-350.

of cases of successful integration, or of cases where integration was unsuccessful only after complete or partial amalgamation had at first succeeded. In other words, we do not have, in our sample, any cases where a major attempt at integration was made without ever meeting with success. We do not know, therefore, to what extent, if any, the early defeats of an amalgamation or integration drive might contribute not only to its early, but also to its eventual, failure. The most likely example for this possibility is the effort for fuller amalgamation of Norway and Sweden in the period 1855-1871, at a time when the two countries had gone far toward integration, although the extent of amalgamation between them had remained limited. Most of the drive came from the Swedish side. It failed for lack of Norwegian support. It strengthened the Norwegian peasant movement which opposed amalgamation; and the failure of the drive helped to shift Swedish conservative opinion toward a policy of greater firmness and potential coercion vis-à-vis Norway, thus contributing to the eventual failure of the union.

Pending further study, we should perhaps say that if most of the essential background conditions for an amalgamated security-community are present, even an early defeat of a drive toward amalgamation may end with a further gain in some of the background conditions required. Early defeats of amalgamation drives would then be neither helpful nor unhelpful in themselves to the eventual success of amalgamation, but their helpfulness or lack of it could be judged more accurately in terms of their positive or negative contribution to the assembly of the background conditions essential for eventual success.

E ◈ SOME WAYS IN WHICH MOVEMENTS SPREAD

After the first leaders and promoters had begun their activities, and after the amalgamation or integration movement had received the first setbacks, the movement could ordinarily spread only by involving formerly disinterested or passive persons in their appeals. So far as we could find, the motives of formerly passive persons or groups or strata that came to support the movement were primarily *local* in character. That is to say, these people were motivated by economic, political, or social concerns within their own political units, and they came to support the amalgamation or integration movement in so far as they expected to reap from its success some gains in the local matters that concerned them. In addition to this, we found that formerly passive individuals or groups were frequently motivated to activity by seemingly accidental or adventitious pressures, such as famine, economic depression, and the like, with which their existing political institutions somehow had failed to cope. On the face of it, these pressures, such as the economic distress in Germany in 1847-1848, would seem quite unrelated to the problem of amalgamation; and we find indeed that similar apparently accidental pressures, such as the Irish potato famine of 1846, also accelerated the drift toward eventual secession.

On second thought, however, the effect of these adventitious pressures does not seem to be quite so accidental. Stable and well-organized governments with ample resources—political, economic, and psychological—ordinarily can cope quite successfully with temporary loads or burdens put upon them by natural catastrophes, wars, or economic difficulties. The fact that a particular government of a small or large political unit has no such reserves and is thrown into a crisis by such a transient load is in itself an indication of latent trouble. A well-integrated political community, such as that of Italy or Germany in the twentieth century, survived extreme stresses of war, revolution, and all kinds of economic distress without any major movements aiming at secession. On the other hand, a poorly integrated community, such as the Habsburg Monarchy, could have been thrown into a serious crisis by a wide variety of pressures after 1900. If the first World War had never occurred, the economic depression of 1933 might still have put an extremely serious strain upon Habsburg institutions—as it did strain conspicuously the relations between Czechs and Germans in one of Austria's successor states, the Czechoslovak Republic, after 1933. Transient pressures thus had the effect of testing the capabilities of the governments of small or large political units, and of motivating previously passive groups of their populations to reappraise their governments more critically and eventually to take some political action about them.

1. *Political Appeals.* The main appeals employed usually did little to clarify these underlying relationships. Frequently we found that the appeals were couched in general and ambiguous terms. They asserted values such as "liberty" or "justice" which lent themselves to an extremely wide variety of interpretations. In the actual situation, of course, these appeals naturally took their content from the experience of contemporaries, and in particular from the local and personal experiences of the groups and individuals concerned. Here again we found that the broader amalgamation or integration movements were usually extensions of domestic politics and pressures within the participating units.

We evaluated these appeals in three ways. We tried to group similar instances of political propaganda so as to be able to identify more general appeals—or, strictly speaking, types of appeal—which might recur more or less frequently in amalgamation or integration movements. Then we tried to gauge the frequency of these types of appeal. And we tried to assess the apparent decisiveness of each type of appeal—that is, the frequency with which each of these appeals occurred in situations in which amalgamation was ultimately successful, as against its occurrence in situations in which amalgamation eventually failed. Later, we used the same three-step attack on political methods used to promote amalgamation.

The advantages of this approach seemed to us twofold. It permitted a more systematic and careful comparison of the occurrence of each appeal with others, as well as a comparison of the association of each of these appeals with situations ending in failure or success. It thus helped us to make judgments about each of these appeals—and later about each of the main political methods of fostering amalgamation—which we could not have made otherwise with nearly as much ordered information at our disposal.

Our judgments of these appeals and methods thus are informed judgments arrived at with the help of some "quantitative" comparisons, but they are not a mechanical product of statistical calculations. Our sample of sixteen situations would have been in any case too small, and the inevitable element of judgment in identifying and grouping appeals would have been too large, to permit any confidence in the use of statistical methods alone. Yet this sample, and the ways in which we tried to bring out some of its quantitative as well as qualitative implications, played a significant part in the process by which each judgment was eventually made.

In order to keep our readers alert to this double process by which we made these judgments, we shall present this part of our findings together with the number of situations from which they were derived. The list of relevant situations which we compared has already been given.[27] In the pages that follow here, we shall refer frequently, as far as our brief space permits, to the numbers of situations which we found relevant in evaluating a particular political method or appeal. Taken together, these data will remind readers of the smallness of our sample, and perhaps of the complexity of the problem of combining quantitative and qualitative considerations in this kind of study.

By means of this approach, we can discern some more specific appeals. Among these, five groups of appeals stood out. Beginning with the most frequent and ending with the least, they were as follows: First, appeals to the strengthening or defense of an already existing or emerging sense of social or cultural community, usually based on a common and distinctive way of life. Second, appeals promising greater social or political equality. In third place, in terms of frequency, there were appeals promising more power as a result of political amalgamation. They thus treated power to some extent as a value in itself, or they elevated it to a position of relatively greater prominence than the purposes it was supposed to serve (in contrast to the appeal of power as a mere instrument for the attainment or safeguarding

[27] See Chapter I, Section D.

of other values). Fourth, there were appeals promising additional specific rights or liberties to individuals or groups.

Last in frequency among the important appeals, we found the appeal made to the defense of some existing privilege or privileged status for certain peoples, regions, or cultural or social groups. Such promises, explicit or implied, of defending some privileged status were largely absent in the early stages of the case of the American colonies, but became increasingly important after 1781, and they played a major role in promoting unity among the Norman conquerors of England after 1066, and again in promoting unity among the different denominations of Protestants in Northern Ireland after 1795.[28] Efforts at defending a somewhat privileged geographic, social, and economic position played also at least a secondary role in the efforts of the Swiss cantons to strengthen their unity from the thirteenth through the sixteenth centuries. This was specifically true in the union of the original three forest cantons in 1291, in the accession of the cities of Luzerne, Zurich, and Bern between 1332 and 1353, and in the developing alliance between Geneva and some of the main members of the Swiss Confederation from 1526 onward. Finally, the defense of some legal and economic standards believed to be higher played a part in promoting the increasing movement toward unity among Austria, Bohemia, and Hungary about 1526 in the face of the Turkish challenge.[29] Moreover, considerations of defending or extending a dominant status played a part in motivating Austria in pressing for amalgamation with Bohemia in and after 1620 and in Hungary in the 1680's, as well as in the English pressure in favor of Anglo-Irish union in 1801, and in motivating Swedish pressure in favor of Norwegian–Swedish union in 1814.

The other four major kinds of appeal were more frequent than the last named; yet an appraisal of the importance of all

[28] "Privileged status" they indeed had as Protestants, but they were genuinely concerned with something more than that, as we have seen (Chapter II, n. 48). They were also interested in their own survival as a religious group.

[29] H. J. Bidermann, *op. cit.*, Fellner-Kretschmayr, *op. cit.*

these appeals in terms of their frequency alone would be almost entirely misleading.

The fact that an appeal was used frequently in different instances of amalgamation or integration movements says nothing about its *decisiveness*—that is, it says nothing about the effectiveness of its contribution to the success or failure of the undertaking. A very rough indication of the decisiveness of an appeal used can be found in the relative frequency of its application in successful cases as against its frequency in unsuccessful ones. Since our universe of cases, and of the several amalgamation and integration situations which some of them contain, includes more than twice as many successful instances than unsuccessful ones, crude probability suggests that a widely used appeal might be expected to be found about twice as often in successful as in unsuccessful movements. This is not the place to discuss the details of our method of computation; suffice to say that two different indices of decisiveness gave an extremely close agreement on the rank-order of the appeals. These indicated in almost every case large and well-marked differences in decisiveness between each appeal and its neighbors in the rank-list. Decisiveness, so defined, was thus an indicator of the probability that an amalgamation or integration movement in which a particular appeal was employed would turn out to be a successful rather than an unsuccessful one.

In these terms, the appeal for more individual rights and liberties, or more additional rights and liberties for groups, turned out to be the most decisive; and it was closely followed by the appeal for more equality. Both of these appeals were found about three times more often in successful movements than one would have expected on a basis of blind probability. At a small distance they were followed, in terms of decisiveness, by appeals involving the development, strengthening, or defense of a distinctive way of life. Such appeals occurred in successful movements about twice as often as blind probability would have led us to expect. The remaining two major appeals, that for more privileges and that of greater power, turned out to be not decisive at all. These two appeals occurred about as often in unsuccessful movements as in successful ones; and since the unsuccessful movements formed only somewhat less than one-third of the total number of movements examined, it turned out that the appeals for more privileges and for more power were about twice as frequently correlated with movements that ended in failure as mere probability would have suggested.

2. *Methods of Promoting Amalgamation.* A similar type of analysis can be applied to the evaluation of the methods used to promote the spread of the amalgamation or integration movements and to bring them closer to success. Among the many different methods used to promote such movements, fifteen stood out sufficiently to claim our particular attention, and nine of these were used in more than one half of all situations studied.

Ranking the political methods used in order of their frequency seems mainly to document the obvious. It shows that the promoters of most amalgamation movements did what promoters of political movements do in general: they set up organizations and political institutions, they used symbols, they resorted to legislation, they promised to oppose institutions that were unpopular, and they employed propaganda. These five methods were the first in order of frequency, in the sequence listed. The stress on over-all amalgamation as a presumably attractive political goal comes only in sixth place; and this method is almost exactly paralleled in frequency by the seventh-ranking method—the stress on functional amalgamation, which leaves intact the over-all separateness of the governments of the political units concerned. This in turn is closely related to the eighth most frequent political method used—the emphasis on the pluralistic approach, usually coupled with specific promises to respect the independence and sovereignty of the units concerned. The ninth most frequent method again is a standard procedure in politics: it is the appointment of individuals favorable to the aims of the movement to positions of political influence or power.

The remaining six political methods were identified in only a minority of the situations studied. In declining order of frequency, they were: direct popular participation in the amalgamation movement or in the operation of amalgamated institutions; promises of political or administrative autonomy; and outright military conquest. A still less frequently used method was that of concluding military alliances as instruments of amalgamation policy (although they were used effectively for this purpose by Prussia and some other German states after 1866); and an even less frequent method used in the movements we surveyed was the method of creating a "monopoly of the legitimate use of physical force"[30] for a certain area.

This last-named method has played a considerable role in recent writings proposing various programs for federal union among states. It consists in essence in effectively disarming, or promising to disarm effectively, every power-holder in the area with the exception of a central government. Promises of such a monopoly of the legitimate use of physical force are frequently associated in theoretical writings with promises of a rule of law; both are taken in large part from the experiences of the consolidation of the English monarchy during the Middle Ages and to a lesser extent from the consolidation of royal power in Western European states in the late Middle Ages and the early modern period. In the situations we studied, an effective monopoly of legitimate physical force was established in the early stages of an amalgamation movement in only four situations: England in 1066, England–Wales after 1485, Austria–Bohemia in and after 1620, and perhaps England–Scotland in 1603. The latter case, however, is doubtful. The capabilities of Scotland for warfare by no means disappeared during the reign of James I after 1603, and under his successor Charles I (1625-1649) the royal claim to any such monopoly of force was effectively contested in both Scotland and England by a Scottish army. While the English, Welsh, and Scottish cases ended in successful amalgamation, the Austrian–Bohemian case eventually ended in separation. Two other cases in which establishment of a monopoly of the legiti-

---

[30] This is Max Weber's phrase; see *The Theory of Social and Economic Organization*, translated by A. M. Henderson and Talcott Parsons, New York, 1947, p. 154.

mate use of physical force was attempted, likewise did not end in long-run success: Austria–Hungary in 1687, and England–Ireland in 1801.

The least frequent political method, finally, among those we identified was that of opposing unpopular legislation and promising its abolition as a result of political amalgamation. This tactic obviously required a very special situation within which to be effective. It played a considerable role in the movement of the American colonies against British rule, particularly in the agitation against the Stamp Act, and it contributed eventually to their unity. Later, during the Confederation period, the promise of abolishing legal-tender laws and other state legislation favoring debtors played a part in the appeal to creditor groups to support a stronger federal constitution. Promises to repeal unpopular legislation also played a role in promoting the amalgamation between England and Wales; English–Irish union likewise was made palatable in 1801 by the promise of Catholic emancipation even though this was not fulfilled until 1829; the modification of the legal disabilities imposed upon Protestant Dissenters helped to make union with England popular among North Irish Protestants from the 1790's onward; and in the case of Italy, adherents of Italian unification promised the abolition of sundry distasteful laws and administrative practices—particularly those relating to privileges of the clergy or powers of the police—if the amalgamation movement should be victorious.[31]

Here again it is far more illuminating to rank the political methods used in order of their apparent decisiveness. Again, we should assume that any political method used should turn up about twice as often in cases of successful amalgamation or integration movements as in instances of unsuccessful ones, since we studied twice as many cases of successful amalgamation as unsuccessful ones. As before, we shall consider that the more decisive a method is, the more the number of successful amalgamation movements in which it is employed exceeds the number of such successes that could be expected from blind probability.

[31] Arturo C. Jemolo, *Chiesa e stato in Italia negli ultimi cento anni,* Turin, 1948, stresses the importance of anticlericalism in the unity movement.

With this perspective in mind, we found that the two most frequently used methods, the setting up of political institutions and the use of symbols, have no apparent decisiveness at all. They were used in all successful and in all unsuccessful cases, and the proportion of successes and failures in which they played a part is thus exactly the same proportion as that in our sample as a whole. Two other methods, on the other hand, move up to the top of the rank-list of decisiveness. These are popular participation in the amalgamation movement and in the operation of amalgamated institutions, and political pluralism.

Popular participation did not occur in a single unsuccessful case; and it occurred in more than half a dozen situations where the amalgamation movement was successful. Even if we invented an instance of an unsuccessful amalgamation movement in which popular participation played a significant role—and we repeat that no such instance was found in our cases—popular participation would still have approximately three times more successes to its credit than could be expected from probability alone.

The second most highly decisive method, pluralism, played only a partial role in two cases that were eventually unsuccessful: the Habsburg Monarchy in 1526, and the Norwegian attitude toward Norwegian–Swedish union in 1814.[32] Its successes included, on the other hand, England–Scotland in 1608, after the failure of James I's efforts at promoting over-all amalgamation; England and Wales after 1485; the American colonies after 1765; the Swiss cantons in 1291, in 1351-1353, and the accession of Geneva to the Swiss political community after 1526; the German movement toward the Zollverein from 1825 onward; and, to a lesser degree, the early stages of the debate about Italian unification in the 1830's and 1840's.[33] Pluralism was thus likewise asso-

[32] For discussion of this point see Sverre Steen, *1814* in *Det frie Norge*, Oslo, Cappelen, 1951, and Arne Bergsgård, *Året 1814*, 2 vols., Oslo, Aschehoug, 1943-1945.

[33] For Gioberti, the great advocate of the pluralistic solution in Italy, see Antonio Anzilotti, *Gioberti*, Florence, 1922. There is an interesting and highly critical essay on Gioberti by Adolfo Omodèo in his *Figure e Passioni del Risorgimento Italiano*, Palermo, 1932.

ciated over three times more often with successful amalgamation movements than could have been expected on a random basis.

Measured by the same yardstick, the next two high-ranking methods, the use of propaganda and the promise to abolish specific items of unpopular legislation, are found in about twice as many successful amalgamation movements as would be expected. In rank-order of decisiveness, the fifth method was the promotion of political or administrative autonomy; this occurred in one-and-a-half times more successful cases than would have corresponded to the mere composition of our sample. Three other methods were still associated slightly more often with successful movements than were found in our sample as a whole: the opposition to specific political institutions, the use of military alliances, and the promotion of specific legislation.

The ninth and tenth methods on our rank-list of decisiveness were the promotion of specific political institutions, and the use of symbols. As mentioned above, these methods were used in all successful and in all unsuccessful cases and thus appeared to have no decisiveness at all one way or the other. The same was true of the appointment of individuals; these methods were used in about three-fifths of all the situations we studied, but the proportion of successful to unsuccessful movements in which they occurred was almost exactly the same as in the sample as a whole.

The remaining three political methods—over-all amalgamation, monopoly of violence, and military conquest—rank at the bottom of the list of decisiveness. They occurred in about twice as many movements that ultimately failed, or in only half as many movements that succeeded, as could be expected on the basis of probability. If anything, they seem to have been somewhat more of a burden than a help.

F ◆ OPPOSITION TO AMALGAMATION MOVEMENTS IN THEIR EARLY STAGES

In the cases we studied, the main sources of opposition to early amalgamation movements were first of all peasants, farmers, or similar groups in the rural population; and in the second place, privileged groups, classes, or regions whose members feared some loss or dilution of their privileges as a result of integration or amalgamation.

In seven out of the sixteen situations[34] we surveyed, peasants were of relatively small importance in politics: England in 1066 and 1315, England–Wales, England–Scotland, the Habsburg Monarchy in 1526, Austria–Bohemia after 1620, and Austria and Hungary in 1686. In six out of the remaining nine situations, in which peasants or farm groups did play a political role, they were sources of some opposition to amalgamation or integration: American farmers—with the exception of some frontier districts—supplied the bulk of the anti-federalist vote in opposition to the ratification of the United States Constitution between 1787 and 1789, while the pro-ratification vote was strongest in the cities, on the seaboard, and along the main communication lines;[35] and peasants were conspicuous among the supporters of Bavarian separatist opposition to German unification in the 1860's and thereafter.[36] Italian unification was effectively hampered by the apathy or outright hostility of peasants in many Italian states.[37] In Switzerland, the Catholic mountain cantons, which were overwhelmingly rural in character, opposed the admission of the city of Geneva to the Swiss Confederation after 1526, so that Geneva had to be content with being linked to the Swiss Confederation only indirectly through a perpetual alliance with Zurich and Bern until the end of the eighteenth century. In Ireland during the late eighteenth and nineteenth centuries, Catholic peasants were on the whole apathetic or hostile toward

[34] See Chapter I, Section D, for the list of these.

[35] See map in Orrin Grant Libby, *The Geographic Distribution of the Vote of the Thirteen States on the Federal Constitution, 1787-1788*, Madison, Wis., 1894.

[36] Kläre Kraus, *Der Kampf in der bayrischen Abgeordnetenkammer um die Versailles Verträge 11-21, Januar 1871*, Cologne, 1935, p. 18. See also Hans Zitzelsberger, *Die Presse des Bayrischen Partikularismus von 1848-1900*, Munich, 1937.

[37] This point is made by virtually all the historians of the Risorgimento. See, for example, Alberto Maria Ghisalberti, "Ancora sulla participazione populare al Risorgimento," *Rassegna storica del Risorgimento* xxxi-xxxiii, combined volume, 1946, pp. 5-13.

the English connection; and the rise of their influence in politics led to the rise of a succession of nationalist movements tending increasingly toward separation. In the case of the Norwegian–Swedish union, similarly, Norwegian farmers were on the whole cool or unfriendly toward closer union with Sweden; and the rise of a strong Norwegian peasant party from the 1870's onward was followed by an increasing strain on Norwegian–Swedish relations.

Several other situations from the same geographic areas tend to reinforce this impression. Peasant apathy or unfriendliness toward closer amalgamation or integration in the larger political unit played a part in the attempted secession of the Swiss Catholic cantons in 1847, and the amalgamation of Switzerland under a federal government in 1848 followed only after their defeat. The dissolution of the Habsburg Monarchy in 1918 occurred again against a background not only of mounting dissatisfaction among labor and professional groups, but also in certain areas of increasing peasant apathy or hostility toward the Monarchy under the strains and burdens of the first World War.[38]

On the eve of the Civil War in the United States, anti-slavery sentiment in the North was strongest in rural areas such as rural New England, upstate New York—from where John Brown had come—and in rural Michigan, Wisconsin, and Northern Ohio, while the main cities (such as New York and even Boston) long retained trade and other ties to the South and favored moderation of the conflict and preservation of the Union.[39] In the South, likewise, some of the most extreme advocates of secession came from rural areas or states which were characterized by concentrations of plantations and Negro slaves, such as Mississippi, rather than from Richmond, Charleston, or New Orleans. Among the poor white farmers of the Southern hill country, Unionist sentiment in some counties was high when compared to the rest of the South, though it was less than in much of the North. In much of the pro-Confederate area, rural sentiment

[38] See O. Jászi, *op. cit.*
[39] See Philip Foner, *Business and Slavery*, Chapel Hill, North Carolina, 1941, *passim.*

was cool toward the idea of tighter amalgamation of the Confederate states, and the hill country was rich in deserters from
the Confederate Army.[40] In only three situations did we find
clearcut rural or peasant support for an amalgamation or integration movement: Switzerland in 1291 and in 1351, and England–Northern Ireland after 1795, in so far as the Ulster population was concerned.

While peasant opposition was thus frequent, however, it was
not at all decisive. Amalgamation or integration movements opposed by peasants succeeded or failed in just about the same
proportion as all such movements in our cases. On the other
hand, active support of an amalgamation or integration movement by the rural population, though rare, was invariably associated with success: every single amalgamation or integration
movement so supported was successful. Finally, in the cases where
peasants were irrelevant in politics, successes were relatively
somewhat more rare, and failures relatively somewhat more frequent, than was the case in our sample as a whole.

Concessions were frequently made by the proponents of amalgamation or integration movements to the wishes of peasants or
farmers. In almost three-quarters of all those situations in which
peasants or farmers counted for something in politics they received concessions; but no specific concessions were made to the
rural population where its political importance was small or non-
existent. In only one case, Italy, amalgamation was successful
without any major concessions to the peasantry, and in this
case peasant influence in politics had been small and the peasants, particularly of Southern Italy and Sicily, had been promised
considerable gains from amalgamation, even though these promises were not fulfilled for many decades, if indeed they are fulfilled even today.[41] In one other case, England–Ireland, no sub-

[40] Robert Royal Russel, "Economic Aspects of Southern Sectionalism,
1840-1861" in *University of Illinois Studies in the Social Sciences*, XI, March,
June, 1923, pp. 232-239-243, 278, 284-288; Georgia Lee Tatum, *Disloyalty in
the Confederacy*, Chapel Hill, 1934, *passim*; Ella Lonn, *Desertion during the
Civil War*, New York, 1928, pp. 3-126, 225-230.

[41] On this point see the article of Costanzo Maraldi, "La Revoluzione
Siciliana del 1860 e l'opera politico-amministrativa di Agostino Depretis,"
Rassegna storica del Risorgimento, XIX, 1932, pp. 434-574.

stantial concessions were made to the peasant population at the time of the union of 1801 or for several decades thereafter. Here, too, peasant influence in politics was very small at the time of amalgamation, but here amalgamation eventually ended in failure.

Taking together all cases where no specific concessions were made by the amalgamation or integration movement to rural needs or viewpoints, we find that the ratio of failures to successes was about twice as high as it was in all our situations taken together; refusal to make concessions to farmers or peasants was thus associated with distinctly unfavorable long-run prospects for eventual integration or amalgamation. This was true both of the situations where peasants had some political influence and of those where they had none at the time of amalgamation. By contrast, in those cases where concessions were made to the farmers or peasants, eventual successes were three times more frequent, relative to failures, than could have been expected on the basis of probability alone. Such concessions to rural viewpoints occurred, of course, in all those cases where the amalgamation movement had peasant support from the outset, as in Switzerland in 1291 and 1351, and in Northern Ireland from the 1790's onward. But this also occurred in the concession to the opposition of the mountain cantons against the admission of Geneva to the Swiss Confederation in the sixteenth century, as well as in the concessions to Bavarian sentiment in the eventual form of federal government adopted for the German Empire in 1871 (which preserved the exclusively Bavarian administration in most fields touching directly the lives of the country population), and most notably in the concessions to anti-federalist sentiment adopted at the time of the ratification of the United States Constitution in the form of the first ten amendments to that document.

In only one situation among all those we studied, that of the Norwegian–Swedish union, we found that concessions to peasant needs and views were apparently followed by eventual failure of amalgamation. In this case, however, concessions were made in the name of the Norwegian State, but not in the name of the union; and concessions often tended to lag consistently behind the rising needs and expectations of the Norwegian rural population, so that association with Sweden did not cease to be felt as unrewarding or even frustrating by many Norwegian farmers.[42] It is also worth noting, on the other hand, that while the attempted amalgamation between Norway and Sweden failed, integration between the two countries was eventually achieved after 1907 in the form of a pluralistic security-community. Since then, while peasant influence diminished in all countries of the Norwegian–Swedish pluralistic security-community with the growth of urban majorities in both countries, governmental policies in both kingdoms continue to aim at a certain amount of protection and subsidization for agricultural producers.

In contrast to the peasants, the privileged classes, of course, were never neutral or irrelevant in politics. Some opposition from privileged classes, groups, or regions to amalgamation or integration movements was found in ten out of the sixteen situations we surveyed. In seven of these ten instances, amalgamation was successful despite this opposition: England–Wales, England–Scotland, England–Northern Ireland, Germany, Italy, and Switzerland in 1291; another instance of success, despite upper-class opposition, occurred in 1526 when some of the important privileged groups in Geneva opposed the Genevan connection with Switzerland and preferred to retain the Genevan association with Savoy. In three cases, where there had been some opposition on the part of groups fearful of losing their privileges, amalgamation eventually failed: England–Ireland, Austria–Bohemia in and after 1620, and Austria and Hungary after 1686. Of the six situations in which the main privileged groups supported amalgamation or integration, four ended in success: England in 1066 and in 1215; the United States; and Switzerland in 1351. Two cases in which the weight of support among the privileged classes was in favor of union ended nevertheless in failure: the Habsburg Monarchy in 1526 and the Norwegian–Swedish union in 1814.

---

[42] Note the opposition to king and to Sweden which developed within the Norwegian farmer's party, *Venstre*, in Jacob S. Worm-Müller, Arne Bergsgård and Bernt A. Nissen, *Venstre i Norge*, Oslo, 1933, pp. 34-73.

In the latter case, Norwegian conservatives were divided in their views, with only a part of them supporting the idea of more far-reaching amalgamation. The Swedish aristocracy, on the other hand, at all times favored complete amalgamation; and Norwegian conservatives after 1884 had to favor Norwegian independence or be branded as "traitors" by many of their countrymen. In both the Norwegian–Swedish and Austro–Hungarian cases, the partial association of union with conservatism and aristocracy eventually became a liability in politics.

Somewhat surprisingly, the mere fact of support or opposition on the part of privileged groups or regions did not appear to have any decisive effect upon the long-run success or failure of the amalgamation or integration movements concerned. Like all successful movements for political changes, amalgamation eventually came to be supported by a sufficient number of the politically influential. But among the movements which found preponderant upper-class support and support in the relatively privileged regions or units, instances of success and failure occurred in just about the same proportion as in our sample of situations as a whole. In regard to movements which encountered some serious opposition on the part of at least some privileged groups or regions, successes and failures occurred in almost the same proportion, with a very slightly higher proportion of eventual successes despite such initial opposition.

While the support or opposition of privileged groups or regions did not in itself decisively influence the long-run outcome of amalgamation or integration movements, these groups or regions did succeed almost invariably in winning significant concessions to their interests and views. The concessions made to the Prussian nobility in the course of German unification are particularly well known. We found in only two of our sixteen situations that the resistance of a privileged group was completely overridden: the bishop and the influential pro-Savoyard faction were driven from Geneva in 1526; and the Bohemian nobility which had resisted closer amalgamation in the Habsburg Monarchy was in large part wiped out by 1621 and replaced by other nobles more favorable to the Habsburg cause. It appears from our cases that the making of such concessions to the views of privileged classes was something in the nature of a standard operating procedure in amalgamation movements; in the fourteen situations where such movements were either supported by privileged groups and regions from the outset, or else where concessions were made to them, the proportion of successes and failures was almost the same as in our sample as a whole. But if we exclude those movements which found support from privileged groups and regions from the start, and concentrate on those which were originally opposed by such regions or groups but where concessions were later made, we find that successes were about one-and-a-half times more numerous in proportion to failures than in our sample as a whole. The making of such concessions to privileged opponents thus seemed to have a low but distinct effect in favor of success. Similarly, the proportion of failures to successes in the extremely small sample of movements where no such concessions were made, shows a somewhat higher ratio of failures to successes than could be expected from probability.

Taken together, our findings concerning retarders of amalgamation or integration movements tend to confirm our earlier findings concerning the cross-class character of successful movements of this kind. They also tend to confirm our findings concerning the importance of the skill of their leaders in bringing about compromises which would satisfy at least some of the major needs and aspirations of each major group concerned.

In order to reach a successful conclusion, amalgamation or integration movements had not only to acquire broad support among the politically relevant strata—and this often included mass support in periods of growing mass participation in politics— but they had to overcome the resistance of apathetic or opposed groups by means of concessions or pressure or combinations of the two. In addition to all this, the amalgamation or integration movements had to bring about a closure in the attitudes of the politically relevant strata in regard to the "union" issue. They had to get people finally to make up their minds. That is to say, they had to bring about a state of affairs in which the multiplicity of urgent political, economic, and social issues would appear to be reduced, at least temporarily, to the single issue of union. This could be brought about by solving some of the competing issues by means of reforms, or by the workings of time and history. Or these competing issues might be relegated temporarily to the background, or become less urgent for other reasons; or finally, the proponents of the amalgamation or integration movement might succeed in presenting a "more perfect union" as a convincing prospective solution to all the main political and social problems pressing upon the political units concerned.

In either case, the proponents of union had to make the union issue paramount in politics. They had to link the remaining urgent local pressures and issues to it; and they had to present eventually the practical approach to union in terms of a single political plan. Eliminating rival plans was crucial. Important and useful as the Articles of Confederation had been in strengthening the bonds of union among the American states at a certain stage of their development, they had to be discredited in order to provide a favorable political climate for the adoption of the Constitution. In the unification of Germany, the "great German" idea and the leadership of Austria had to be discredited before a smaller Germany could be united under Prussian leadership. In the unification of Italy, plans for a confederation of Italian states under the leadership of the Pope had to be discredited—as had also plans for a unitary Italian Republic as envisaged by Mazzini—before Italian opinion became ready to accept a unitary Italian monarchy under the House of Savoy. The growing unanimity among outstanding intellectual figures, and eventually the growing consensus among the intellectual classes as a whole, as these two processes can be observed, for example, in Germany between 1815 and 1870, are indicative of this process of closure in terms of intellectual opinion.

G ◈ THE FORMING OF POLITICAL INSTITUTIONS: A CHALLENGE TO ORIGINALITY AND INNOVATION

As we have seen, the attainment of closure of opinion on the issue of union implies the attainment of a considerable degree of consensus within the political elite, and the absence or elimination of any major opposition or cross-pressures from within the elite, or from broader strata of the population just entering political life. We found that a significant role in bringing about this end was played in several of our cases by the originality and resourcefulness of proponents of amalgamation or integration in formulating practical plans for approaching union and for organizing specific political institutions to make it work.

In this connection our studies of the more promising strategies of integration have left us strongly impressed with the importance of political innovation and invention. Many of the decisive advances in bringing about political integration involved the making of political decisions in a manner such that improbable or original measures were adopted rather than their more obvious or probable alternatives. Many of the central institutions of amalgamated security-communities thus were original and highly improbable at the time they were adopted. The American Articles of Confederation, the Federal Constitution, and the land and settlement policy of the Northwest Ordinance with its automatic admission of territories as new states—none of these has any close counterpart in eighteenth century politics or law. The Anglo–Scottish union of 1707, the German Zollverein, and the rights of peasants in the Swiss forest cantons all are similarly unusual for their time and place.

It seems worth adding that a number of amalgamated political communities were wrecked precisely as a consequence of decisions which were highly probable at the time and place at which they were made. Statesmen did the obvious thing when they tried to subject the American colonies to routine British administration according to the usual standards of the eighteenth century. A century later, routine ideas and convictions of Swedish and Norwegian statesmen, which were entirely normal for their times and social classes, prevented integration and helped destroy the union of the two countries. The rulers of Austria–Hungary did nothing unusual in the decades before 1914 when they decided to take their monarchy into a system of alliances which seemed routine and almost inevitable to contemporaries, even though it led eventually into the first World War and the dissolution of the Empire.

From the study of successful as well as of unsuccessful cases, we have gained the impression that there are few areas of politics in which originality and creativeness appear to be as important as in the building of amalgamated security-communities.

H ◇ THE POLITICAL PROCESS OF ESTABLISHING A PLURALISTIC SECURITY-COMMUNITY

The broad principles of our findings concerning the processes of establishing amalgamated security-communities apply also to the establishment of their pluralistic counterparts, so long as we make allowances for much looser organization of pluralistic security-communities and the less stringent requirements for their establishment and preservation.

The outstanding issue leading to the emergence of a pluralistic security-community in the cases we studied seems to have been the increasing unattractiveness and improbability of war among the political units concerned. War became unattractive because it promised to be both devastating and indecisive, as in the case of the United States and Canada after 1815: American land power could easily devastate much or all of Canada, while British sea power could easily inflict great harm upon American shipping and American seaports. But American armies could not have destroyed Britain's ability to make war, nor could British seapower have destroyed the military capabilities of the United States on the North American continent. Since war became unpalatable to both Canada and the United States after 1815, the basic conditions were created for the demilitarization of their common border and the emergence of a pluralistic security-community between the two countries.

In other cases, war became unattractive because of the danger of international complications that might engulf the contestants: the possibility of German, Russian, or British intervention, or of a war involving eventually several of the great powers, acted as a deterrent against the possibility of a Norwegian–Swedish war at the time of Norway's secession from the union of the two countries in 1905 and thereafter; here again, a pluralistic security-community between Norway and Sweden emerged as a far preferable alternative. Another factor in the increasing unattractiveness of war was sometimes its unpopularity in the domestic politics of all, or at least of the strongest, of the countries concerned. Thus the idea of war against Norway remained extremely unpopular in Sweden from 1905 on, until it grew unthinkable; and the rise of liberal and labor influence in Swedish politics enhanced this trend.[43] Similarly, the idea of a war against Mexico was clearly unpopular in the United States in the late 1920's and early 1930's, while such a war would clearly have been military folly from the point of view of Mexico; despite the tense dispute over American oil properties in Mexico, the period saw the emergence of a pluralistic security-community between the two countries.

Pluralistic security-communities, like their amalgamated counterparts, benefited from intellectual movements and traditions preparing the ground for them. The rapprochement between Britain and the United States after the peace of 1815 and the parallelism in the attitude of the two countries at the time of the Monroe Doctrine facilitated the establishment of a pluralistic security-community, and the increase in self-government in Canada during the nineteenth century contributed to its preservation. The pluralistic security-community among the Scandinavian countries was prepared for and strengthened by the cultural and political movement of Scandinavianism and the network of actual inter-Scandinavian communications, transactions, and institutions in social, cultural, and scientific fields which developed during the nineteenth century and became even stronger thereafter. In the case of the United States and Mexico, the developing tradition of Pan-Americanism and later of Inter-American cooperation gradually found increasing embodiment in specific legislation and institutions. This contributed to a favorable background for the pluralistic security-community between the two countries.

---

[43] Raymond E. Lindgren's forthcoming study, tentatively titled, *Union, Disunion, Reunion: A Study of the Dissolution of the Union of Norway and Sweden and Scandinavian Integration* (in preparation), Princeton, *passim*.

CHAPTER IV

◇◇

Current State of Integration in the North Atlantic Area

◇◇

What have we learned from our study of history that might apply to the contemporary problem of integration?

There are two ways in which we could go about answering this question. One would be to examine some of the current suggestions for integrating particular parts of the globe. These suggestions or plans run all the way from a tiny Benelux (Belgium, the Netherlands, and Luxembourg) to Little Europe (sometimes referred to as The Six—Belgium, the Netherlands, Luxembourg, France, West Germany, and Italy) to Big Europe (the 15 Council of Europe countries—Belgium, Denmark, France, West Germany, Greece, Iceland, Ireland, Italy, Luxembourg, the Netherlands, Norway, the Saar, Sweden, Turkey, and the United Kingdom), to Atlantic Union (at least the democracies in the North Atlantic area), to federation of democracies anywhere, and even to world federation. The other way toward finding an answer would be to examine the main living issues in the field of international organization in the light of our findings. Some of these are the functional vs. the federal or constitutional approach, the political vs. the economic-social approach, gradual vs. abrupt timing, and the regional or partial vs. the universal approach.

In this brief volume, we shall use a portion of each of these ways. For the sake of coherence, we shall examine with some care the idea of integration for a single geographic area—the North Atlantic.[1] While focusing on that area, we shall bring in once in a while at the edges of that focus some of the main issues in the study of international organization.

Our first need is a rough estimate of the current situation in the North Atlantic area with respect to integration, but mainly

[1] This area has been defined, and its 19 countries listed, in Chapter I, Section B.

in terms of our historical findings. After we have presented that picture, we can move in the next chapter to the implications of those findings for a policy with regard to further integration.

A ◈ SOME GENERAL CONDITIONS

1. It is hardly necessary to point out that the North Atlantic area is not already integrated. It is not a security-community, although it does contain several security-communities within it— United States–Canada, United States–United Kingdom, Norway–Sweden, and others. But it also contains at least one country that is not entirely trusted by some of the others—Germany. Also, who can say with certainty that Spain and France will never go to war against each other? Ten years after a world war is too soon for a conviction that permanent peace has arrived. The North Atlantic area is, however, a political community[2] and 13 of the 19 countries in the area belong to a primarily military alliance—the North Atlantic Treaty Organization. The entire area is also sometimes considered to form a distinct civilization.[3]

2. The North Atlantic area probably cannot count on a tide of internationalism to carry it toward integration. One of our findings has cast serious doubts on the idea that modern life tends to be more "international" than life in the past,[4] and hence more conducive to the growth of international or supranational institutions. It cast special doubt upon the probability of amalgamation as a route to integration. Although this does not mean that the need for international or supranational institutions is any the less great today than it was earlier, it does indicate that to set them up may be harder than many well-informed people realize. Can a historical trend be discerned from

[2] As defined in Chapter I, Section A.

[3] After reviewing the main literature on this question, an American and a French historian recently have concluded that the Western European and North American civilizations do come together to form a vague North Atlantic civilization. See Jacques Godechot and Robert R. Palmer, "Le Problème de l'Atlantique du xviiième au xxème siècle," especially pp. 216-218, in *Relazioni del X Congresso Internazionale di Scienze Storiche*, vol. v, Florence, 1955.

[4] See Chapter II, Section A, 1, first three paragraphs.

this? If so, the trend would certainly not show that "all the streams of modern history are surging toward the unification of our world."[5]

3. The same general conclusion is implied by our finding that states do not seem to grow by a "snowballing process."[6] We found that successful amalgamation of smaller units into larger ones tended to increase both the resources and the skills necessary for integration on the part of the larger unit. But we found that this also might increase the preoccupation of these units with domestic affairs, reducing their ability to respond promptly and effectively to the needs and interests of people outside the national borders. This ability of governments to respond to the interests of "outsiders" has always been important, but it has become even more important in our own time. To the extent that very large states may tend to imprison the minds of their rulers in a web of domestic complexities, pressures, and preoccupations, the growth of states might turn out to be a self-limiting process. The larger a state, the less attention and understanding might its political leaders be able to give to any additional small territory or population that might be tempted to join it, or whose loyalties after amalgamation might have to be secured and maintained. At the end of such a development, very large states, empires, or federations might find it impossible to absorb any more people or territory, or even to retain the loyalties of all the smaller groups and political units that had become joined to them in the past. This means that greater political responsiveness—which, we shall see later, is of great importance to integration—cannot be expected to emerge automatically as a by-product of historical evolution. Instead, governments and leaders who

[5] Milton Eisenhower, "Education for International Understanding," *Educational Record*, vol. 35, October 1954, p. 243. A more cautious statement along the same lines came in 1887 from Woodrow Wilson: "There is a tendency . . . clearly destined to prevail, towards, first the confederation of parts of empires like the British, and finally of great states themselves."— "The Study of Administration," reprinted in Ray Stannard Baker and William E. Dodd (eds.), *The Public Papers of Woodrow Wilson, College and State*, New York, Harpers, 1925, i, pp. 157-158.

[6] See Chapter II, Section A, 1.

wish to promote integration may have to strive for greater responsiveness as a distinct aim.

Using figures of foreign trade and foreign mail as compared with domestic trade and domestic mail for several countries in the North Atlantic area, we have found that the ratio between foreign and domestic transactions has been increasingly favoring the domestic during the past quarter-century—and even longer in the case of mail. Indices like these give some evidence that the greater the population, area, wealth, and literacy of a community, the greater is its self-preoccupation.[7]

This gives a warning that size may bring less responsiveness to the needs of "outsiders." But we have no idea at what size and under what conditions this self-limiting process sets in. The United States, with a population of 165,000,000 and an area of over 3,000,000 square miles, is certainly integrated. But for purposes of assessing the situation in the North Atlantic area this figure would not mean as much as the size of the United States at the time when it became integrated, somewhere between 1790 and 1820. In 1790 the United States had less than 4 million people and 900,000 square miles. At the time of its reintegration after the Civil War (about 1877) it had nearly 50 million people and 3,000,000 square miles. Germany, when it was amalgamated in 1871, comprised 41 million people and 212,000 square miles. "The Six" of Western Europe today total about 160 million people living on 453,000 square miles of land area, while the North Atlantic area, as we have defined it, totals some 440 million and over 9,000,000 square miles of land area. This area is increased greatly in one sense, of course, by the ocean between the two parts so that the distance from one part of the area to another can be as great as 7,000 miles (from Southern California to Southern Italy). If size were the determining factor, obviously the amalgamation of the North Atlantic area would be much

[7] See Karl W. Deutsch, "Symbols of Political Community," in Lyman Bryson, Louis Finkelstein, Hudson Hoagland, and Robert M. MacIver, *Symbols and Society*, Harpers, 1955, p. 31 and p. 32. For more detail on the studies of this point, made at the Center for Research on World Political Institutions, see Karl W. Deutsch, "Shifts in the Balance of Communication Flows: A Problem of Measurement in International Relations," in *Public Opinion Quarterly*, xx, 1, Spring 1956, pp. 143-160.

more difficult than that of Germany or the United States. But in view of the differences in modern transportation and communication discussed earlier,[8] and in view of the fact that no firm upper limit of size has been established by our historical studies, we do not conclude that amalgamation of a larger area—such as the North Atlantic—is impossible.

4. We found that the actual process of state-building was quite different from the "snowballing" process that turned out to be an illusion. The essential background conditions for integration could be assembled in almost any sequence, so long as all of them eventually took place. There was a wide variety of pathways.[9] This finding has a double-edged application. It shows that steps can be taken toward any or all the essential conditions at any time, without jeopardizing over-all progress by failure to take steps in the proper order. For that very reason, it warns us of the difficulty of gauging progress even roughly at any point, because that progress depends so largely upon the extent to which all *other* essential conditions are assembled that it cannot be gauged by the presence of any one or two conditions. Achieving several of the essential conditions does mean some sort of progress, but it does not guarantee success, because one condition does not necessarily lead to another. It is well to keep this in mind when we try to look at the current state of integration in the North Atlantic area. It may be unnecessary to add that integration has by now reached different levels in different parts of the area, and that we cannot in this study explore the situation in these subregions at all thoroughly.

5. One of our findings should be discussed at this point because it draws the framework in which we have to present our judgments about the North Atlantic area. We found that the attainment of a pluralistic security-community was favored by any of the conditions or processes that were favorable to the success of an amalgamated security-community, and also that sometimes factors that hindered the one also hindered the other.[10]

---

[8] See Chapter I, Section C.
[9] See Chapter III, Section A.   [10] See Chapter II, Section E.

We found, further, that pluralistic security-communities succeeded under somewhat less favorable conditions than would have been required for the success of an amalgamated one, and that they survived unfavorable or disintegrative processes which would probably have destroyed an amalgamated security-community.[11] Thus the pluralistic type was easier to achieve and also, because of its stability, seemed just about as effective as the amalgamated type in performing the main function of a security-community—keeping the peace. This indicates that the path toward closer community went in generally the same direction for both amalgamation (union or federation) and pluralism (functionalism or tight cooperation), instead of diverging at an early stage into two paths. And in this respect we do not see that the contemporary world is decisively different from the earlier periods from which we took our cases.

In this connection, we found that integration was not an all-or-none process, but required the crossing of a rather wide threshold.[12] The fact that the threshold of integration can be crossed, stood upon, and recrossed does not injure the concept of integration that we have adopted for this study. In fact, it brings out the usefulness of the concept in evaluating the *direction* in which the relations of two or more countries are developing at any particular time. Since integration seems not to be won or lost in all-or-nothing terms, partial steps toward it may be more promising, and their partial character less disheartening, than if integration were conceived in absolute and final terms.

The existence of a broad threshold also means that if integration *seems* to be achieved at some future time, we should be careful not to assume that it is permanent. Disintegration has, of course, taken place in the past after a long period of apparent integration, and this could also happen to an ostensibly integrated North Atlantic area.

For these reasons, we are inclined to emphasize, to a greater extent than we foresaw when the study began, the pluralistic approach in presenting our findings. And we must stress that

[11] See Chapter II, Section A, 2, A, and Section E.
[12] See Chapter II, Section A, 2, B.

in assessing roughly the state of integration in the North Atlantic area (and even more roughly some of the subregions within it), we are considering mainly those conditions that arose from comparing the findings of our historical studies. These we have grouped into conditions (*a*) that turned out to be essential for achieving either a pluralistic or an amalgamated security-community, (*b*) those that were helpful for pluralism though not essential, and yet were essential to amalgamation, and (*c*) those that were helpful to both but were not essential to either.

B ❖ SOME CONDITIONS ESSENTIAL FOR BOTH PLURALISTIC AND AMALGAMATED SECURITY-COMMUNITIES

When we use the term "essential," great caution is in order. Judging from our historical cases, both of the essentials that we are about to discuss had to be present if integration was to be achieved. Yet neither of them separately, nor both of them added together, made a sufficient condition for integration. They had to be present, but their presence was not enough.

1. *Compatibility of Major Values.* For integration of either of the two types, we found that there had to be a compatibility of the main values held by the relevant strata of all the political units involved; and with this condition there sometimes had to be also a tacit agreement to deprive any remaining incompatible values of their political significance.[13]

What this finding means today depends largely upon what we decide to call "main" values. Yet there is no systematic and practical way of deciding, any more than there was in the historical inquiry. To avoid circular reasoning, we have called "main" values those which seem to be of major importance in the domestic politics of the units concerned. This means that no value will be considered important in the relations between political units unless it is important within each of them, and is also considered important in their common relations. Thus we

---

[13] See Chapter II, Section C, 1.

can verify in part the importance of these values in a context different from the issue of amalgamation itself.

One of these values, clearly, is basic political ideology. In the North Atlantic area—with the notable exceptions of Spain and Portugal—this is covered for the most part by the terms "constitutionalism" and "democracy." By democracy we mean, in brief, government by broad representation and by discussion, with the right to organize lawfully in opposition to the government. Democracy thus includes a practicing devotion to the "rule of law." The law is thus linked to democratic control, so that we can consider these two values—constitutionalism and democracy—as one, which may be expressed within a written or an unwritten framework.

It may be that a third value is economic—not just communism contrasted with capitalism, but socialism contrasted with modified free enterprise. In this day of widespread government controls over the individual and government services to the individual, some economists almost take it for granted that a nationalized economy and a comparatively free economy cannot be merged, although of course they can deal with one another. It seems to us that devotion to government ownership or controls, or, on the contrary, free enterprise patterns could hamper integration only on two conditions: first, that these economic institutions should come to be regarded as values in themselves instead of merely as instruments for promoting other values; and second, that at least one of the states concerned should develop a militant missionary attitude toward them. In the absence of the second condition, a pluralistic security-community should be attainable, even without major change in the economic institutions of any participating country. If both conditions are absent, amalgamation should be possible, at least in principle, through peaceful adjustment. Under present conditions, pluralism thus seems somewhat more easily attainable, since it is less hampered by the variety of systems.

Some of the main values that were taken out of politics in successful cases of integration in the past have, on the whole, remained outside of politics up into the present. Religion is one that, however, still causes misgivings in some places. While the North Atlantic area is entirely Christian except for Algeria, the Catholic–Protestant split might still hamper integration. Northrop may be correct in concluding that the living basis of European religions is not common enough to make what he calls a community.[14] In our judgment, religion is not so lacking in controversy that amalgamation could be achieved without having religion largely removed from politics; but we are not sure that this removal would be needed for pluralistic integration. Religion was depoliticized in the Swiss and German cases before amalgamation. The Dutch, the Canadians, and the Americans are others who have accepted a common political union embracing large numbers of Catholics and Protestants.

The liberal–conservative contrast does not seem to be an issue of such great moment as the three we have already mentioned. As long as conservatives and liberals both genuinely support the democratic-constitutional framework and operate within it, the discrepancy between their ideologies would probably not be a solid bar to integration. Neither would the question of monarchy, since all those remaining in the North Atlantic area are constitutional monarchs. In the case of amalgamation, however, it is hard to see how the monarchs could be fitted into an amalgamated North Atlantic area unless it were a confederation or a loose federation. The British Commonwealth is not a suitable illustration, since it is not amalgamated.

This finding also calls attention to the need for making a distinction in diplomacy between those values that can be depoliticized and those that cannot. But how can one tell them apart? We feel that a distinction should be made between those values that have an important bearing on the power position of a country and those values that do not. Values of one country that are incompatible with values of another are not dangerous in themselves. So far as the question of a security-community is concerned, such forms of national power as moral influence or propaganda become dangerous only when linked to the control

---

[14] See Filmer S. C. Northrop, *European Union and U.S. Foreign Policy: A Study in Sociological Jurisprudence*, Macmillan, 1954, p. 76.

of military force. For example, if a strong country—such as West Germany may become—developed an undemocratic form of government, this would not necessarily by itself be a cause for dangerous friction. If, on the other hand, expansionism or ideological crusading or militarism were built into the value system so firmly that they would have an important effect upon national power, then such values could hardly be depoliticized.

There is a tendency in popular thinking to consider too many values as incompatible with each other. The public is apt to become upset about a seemingly incompatible value that may actually be irrelevant to the formation of a security-community. A widespread American attitude toward Socialism in Great Britain is an example. Socialist countries and capitalist countries need not attempt to change one another's domestic economic systems; indeed, they would probably have to accept the difference in advance of amalgamation. Communism is another matter, not so much because of incompatible economic systems as because of more fundamental differences in such matters as civil liberties and democratic procedure.

What is the situation in the North Atlantic area today? Looking back to the two "main values" we selected as being crucial—democracy (including constitutionalism or the rule of law) and non-communist economics—we conclude that compatibility is high except for Spain and Portugal. Those two countries are as clearly undemocratic[15] as the others in the area are clearly democratic, at least in their current practices. Of course it is too early to know whether Western Germany has become a reliable member of the democratic camp. A few years ago, the status of France and Italy might have been questionable also, with their threatening number of extremist voters of the Left and Right, but today their basic democratic alignment seems somewhat more assured.

[15] In Spain, at least, the official rejection of democratic values is quite explicit. The latest evidence of this is a statement of Generalissimo Franco: " 'Nobody should wonder why we should not want for Moroccans that which is repugnant to us,' he explained in referring to the democratic system of government."—Camille M. Cianfarra, in the *N. Y. Times*, 16 December 1955, p. 12.

The situation is not quite so clear with regard to economics. While all the countries are non-Communist, the contrast between those with largely nationalized economies and those with largely "free" economies might seriously hinder amalgamation, even though it did not hinder pluralism. For example, the Netherlands, with its strict governmental controls, and Belgium, with its very loose controls, have not been able to achieve even an economic amalgamation over a land area of such modest proportions as Benelux. The controls that are thought necessary in Scandinavia would not be easy to reconcile with those in the United States. These discrepancies would not, however, seem to be a bar to pluralistic integration.

It is illuminating to see what the official statements of NATO say about its main objectives in ideological terms. NATO includes 13 of the 19 countries in the North Atlantic area as we have defined it; only Austria, Ireland, Sweden, Switzerland, Finland, and Spain are not members. The preamble to the North Atlantic Treaty refers to the "common heritage and civilization of their peoples, founded on the principles of democracy, individual liberty, and the rule of law"; it also refers to "stability and well-being" and "the preservation of peace and security." The first excerpt records values that are dominant in the whole area except Spain and Portugal. The last two excerpts cover such universal values that they are obviously compatible; but at the same time they are too broad to have useful meaning for our purposes. The preamble to the Statute of Europe expresses "devotion to the spiritual and moral values which are the common heritage of their peoples and the true source of individual freedom, political liberty and the rule of law, principles which form the basis of all genuine democracy." It also speaks of "economic and social progress." These professions do represent important values held in theory, whether or not they are realized in practice.

One piece of evidence concerning the compatibility of major values within the North Atlantic area is worth summarizing here. Probably no act of government is closer to the core of democracy (and especially the rule of law) than the act of criminal arrest and trial. A "fair trial" is the culmination of centuries of constitutional struggle in many Western countries. One test of the compatibility of judicial systems would be the answer to this question: What happens when large numbers of citizens of one country are stationed for long periods on the soil of other countries? All members of NATO operate under an executive agreement[16] specifying the rights and duties of the foreign military and of the domestic authorities. This includes the handling of crimes by foreign troops when off duty. Each country believed that its system of justice was fair, so none was willing to grant an extralegal status to foreign troops stationed on its own soil. The guarantees that the United States required in order to insure justice to its personnel were so nearly the same as those obtainable in the courts of the other NATO members that the agreement has caused virtually no trouble. A United States representative has been allowed to follow the proceedings in each trial, and the Department of State has testified that there "was not a single case in which there was a basis for the United States to protest that the safeguards assured by the Status of Forces Agreement for a fair trial were not met, or that there was any other unfairness."[17] Except for occasional leniency of sentences, there has apparently been no serious objection by Europeans that United States troops were overprivileged. Of the 6,000 United States cases falling within the primary jurisdiction of the local courts, 70% were waived by local authorities in favor of trial by United States military authorities.[18] Where the trials were held in local courts, "In not one of these cases do we believe that an innocent man has gone to jail,"[19] although many have been punished by jail sentences.

Most of our troops are stationed in the United Kingdom, France, and West Germany. These countries, one with its Anglo–Saxon law and the other two with their Roman law traditions, represent the judicial systems of all the North Atlantic countries.

---

[16] Status of Forces Agreement of 1951.—U.S. Department of State, *Treaties and Other International Acts* Series, 2846.

[17] Deputy Under-Secretary of State Robert Murphy, testifying before the Committee on Foreign Affairs of the United States House of Representatives on 19 July 1955, as reported in the *State Department Bulletin*, 1 August 1955, p. 183.

[18] *Ibid.*, p. 183.   [19] *Ibid.*, p. 178.

It could be argued that the need for any special agreement at all was an indication of our unwillingness to risk the system of justice practiced by our allies. Yet the utility of clearcut agreements even among trusted friends needs no defense, especially where large numbers of foreigners live on the soil of each other's countries in peacetime. There was a great deal of opposition in the United States Congress to this executive agreement on the status of forces, on the ground that the protection which American soldiers had under United States military law was being waived. Led by Senator John W. Bricker of Ohio, a considerable segment of opinion felt strongly that the agreement "fails to protect the American soldier and his basic rights."[20] The fact that in spite of full debate and wide publicity the agreement was ratified (in July 1953) with Administration backing is a real indication that one of our major values in this touchy field of social and political relationships is quite compatible with that of our NATO allies.

In sum, we conclude that as far as this condition is concerned —compatibility of major values and the possibility of taking other significant values out of politics—the North Atlantic area rates high.

2. *Mutual Responsiveness.* We found that "sense of community" was much more than simply verbal attachment to any number of similar or identical values. Rather, it was a matter of mutual sympathy and loyalties; of "we-feeling," trust, and consideration; of at least partial identification in terms of self-images and interests; of ability to predict each other's behavior and ability to act in accordance with that prediction. In short, it was a matter of perpetual attention, communication, perception of needs, and responsiveness. It was not a condition of static agreement, but a dynamic process—a process of social learning. It resulted in mutual responsiveness to the needs of the units involved in prospective integration, leading to appropriate political and economic action. The need for this was

20 Frank E. Holman, *Story of the "Bricker" Amendment,* Committee for Constitutional Government, Inc., New York, 1954, p. 56.

even more evident for amalgamated than for pluralistic integration.[21]

This finding brings out the need for constant communication, which is the requirement basic to all the others in this cluster which adds up to "responsiveness." "Peaceful change" does not seem assured without a continuous learning process, together with a continuous process of keeping in touch to prevent unlearning. This means the transmission of messages, personal contact through travel and foreign residence, and the exchange of ideas, goods, and services. Naturally, this kind of communication is greater among certain countries in the North Atlantic area than among others, but it appears to be rather lower for the area as a whole than it should be for even pluralistic integration. To compare the North Atlantic area with an already amalgamated security-community is too harsh a test, but it may indicate roughly how far from amalgamation some parts of the area now stand. As one measure, within a well-integrated area the volume of domestic mail is vastly greater than the volume of mail exchanged with other countries. For example, in the Netherlands in 1949 more than 10 letters were transmitted at home for every letter sent to or received from abroad, and during 1946-1951 the average ratio of domestic to foreign letters in the United States was 65 to 1. A pluralistic security-community (Scandinavia) shows the same order of magnitude for foreign mail: Sweden, for example, exchanged only about 5 out of 100 letters with any other member of the Scandinavian area and about 7 more with countries outside that area.[22] It would be illuminating to have figures for the entire North Atlantic area vis-à-vis countries outside it, but we do not believe the result would approach the ratio for an integrated area. Other data about communication within the area are woefully lacking and need to be gathered in order to help assess the state of integration in the area.

A special aspect of responsiveness was found to lie in the disintegrative effect when a once strong or privileged country or

[21] See Chapter II, Sections A, 2, c and e.

[22] These figures are among those compiled at the Center from the *UN Statistical Yearbook*, 1950-1952, and various reports of the Universal Postal Union.

group failed to adjust psychologically and politically to its loss of dominance that came from changed conditions.[23] In the North Atlantic area there is little to worry about from this standpoint except in France, where the fear of being left out of major-power consultations has haunted that country ever since the end of the War, and where that fear seems to be increasing with the recovery of West Germany. The Saar is returning to Germany; Indochina, Morocco, and Tunis have been lost; and the challenge in Algeria is another threat. It remains to be seen whether the French can adjust as well as the British, who demonstrated realistic responsiveness in two ways: in gradual and graceful adjustment to the growing influence of the United States, and in their consent to the emancipation of India, Pakistan, Burma, and Ceylon. By such adjustments, Britain has retained an appreciable amount of influence which might have been lost.

Another specific aspect of responsiveness we found was the disintegrative effect of reacting with excessive delay to the social, economic, or political reforms that came to be expected by people in the area.[24] Mainly, this is the responsibility of national governments within their own borders. But those governments sometimes needed help from outside, and other countries had a chance to demonstrate international responsiveness. The United States and Canada, as the predominant security-community of the area, have risen to the occasion. The United Nations Relief and Rehabilitation Administration (UNRRA), early American assistance to Greece, the Marshall Plan, and NATO are the outstanding instances. Canada's unsolicited loan of a billion and a quarter Canadian dollars to the United Kingdom in 1946 (plus cancellation of about $300,000,000 of debt) is another example. Counter-response has come in such forms as the financing of scholarships and teacher exchanges with the U.S. by European governments. Within Europe, the Coal and Steel Community and the proposed atomic energy pool and common market plan seem to be further evidence of responsiveness. Even more recently, the President of the United States has proposed to Congress the liberalization of the present restrictive immigration law.

[23] See Chapter II, Section D.   [24] See Chapter II, Section D.

One more special aspect of responsiveness appeared from our historical cases. This was the disintegrative effect of a substantial increase in political participation on the part of populations, regions, or social strata that had previously been politically passive.[25] A closely related finding concerns an increase in ethnic or linguistic differentiation, and also a rise in the political awareness of such differentiation as may already exist. Both of these had a disintegrative effect. Where these conditions existed, they called for special responsiveness on the part of the governments concerned.[26]

This finding indicates that only countries with a high degree of political participation and awareness among their people should try to amalgamate, though pluralistic integration without that requisite would not be so difficult. The North Atlantic area today seems to fulfill these qualifications, again with the exception of Portugal and Spain. Political participation is already very high in almost all the countries, and there are no substantial new groups remaining to be plunged into politics. It is not significant that in Portugal very few women are allowed to vote, and in Switzerland none. Nor is it significant in this connection that many Negroes are barred from the polls in the United States. If experience in the United States and France is any guide, the sudden enfranchisement of women makes little difference in political life. The same is true of Negroes voting in those parts of the United States where they do participate fully. And substantially all other persons in the North Atlantic area are already enfranchised.

Neither is there apt to be new ethnic or linguistic differentiation. The danger to watch, in this connection, might be any sharp rise in the awareness of such differentiation as already exists. After all, long-established and highly differentiated languages and national traditions are characteristic of most of the peoples and countries of the North Atlantic areas.

On balance, we conclude that as far as mutual responsiveness is concerned, the North Atlantic area rates rather low at present as compared with what is probably needed for integration, even

---

[25] See Chapter II, Section D.   [26] See Chapter II, Section D.

of the pluralistic type. We believe, however, that since the second World War there is evidence of a trend toward greater responsiveness, at least on the part of the major countries in the area.

C ◈ SOME CONDITIONS THAT WERE HELPFUL FOR PLURALISTIC, BUT ESSENTIAL FOR AMALGAMATED, SECURITY-COMMUNITIES

Beside the two conditions we just discussed that were essential to both pluralistic and amalgamated security-communities, we identified eight others that were also essential to amalgamation, but were not essential—though they were helpful—to pluralism.

3. *Distinctive Way of Life*. Somewhat different from the need for a set of compatible major values is another, but closely related, condition. It was necessary, we found, that quite a network of major and minor values be accepted over the area in question, and that institutional means for the pursuit and fulfillment of those values be also established and accepted. Furthermore, there had to be a set of established or emerging habits of behavior corresponding to these values and institutions. This is as close to defining a distinctive "way of life" as we can come. To be distinctive, however, it had to include at least some major social or political values and institutions that were *different* from those which existed in the area during the recent past or from those currently prevailing among important neighbors. It seemed to us that the successful transfer of loyalties from one political unit to a new and larger political community has occurred only where a wide range of other political and social habits was also in a state of change.[27]

One possible indication of a way of life is economic. Most of the North Atlantic countries are characterized by a remarkably high level of per capita income, as compared with the rest of the world. Taking annual per capita incomes for the three-year period 1952-1954 as a measure, the median level for the countries of the North Atlantic area was $685, as compared with $273 for

[27] See Chapter II, Section C, 1.

the U.S.S.R. and the seven Soviet-dominated countries of Europe. The median level for the 20 Latin American countries was $172 for the same period. Not one country in those two areas came close to the median for the North Atlantic area.[28]

But in addition, these high income levels of the North Atlantic area in general are supplemented by high levels of social welfare services, individual liberties, and civil rights. It is this combination of incomes, welfare services, and individual liberties that makes up much of that "Western" way of life which is so often felt and referred to but which seems so hard to define. The long Western tradition of rational and scientific thought is closely related to this complex. Western levels of income, welfare, and material equipment have provided more widely diffused opportunities for rational and scientific effort. Western traditions of divided authority and of widespread individual freedom have offered more opportunities for the questioning attitude of mind and for the assertion of both individual faith and reason against mere power.

In all these respects, the past traditions and present practices of the following countries have so much in common that they enjoy to a great extent a common way of life: the United States, Canada, the United Kingdom, Sweden, Denmark, Norway, Iceland, the Netherlands, Belgium, Luxembourg, and Switzerland. National income is both an effect and a cause where a social, political, and economic way of life is concerned, and for this reason a few income data may be illuminating. All of these countries except the Netherlands (which was in the $350-$550 group) had per capita real incomes of over $600 in the years 1952-1954 (averaged), and the similarity of many of their values and institutions is such that the term "a common way of life" can be used about them with very little strain.

Several other countries in the North Atlantic area are a little less close, but still have many similarities to the countries in the

---

[28] Those and the figures in the next few paragraphs were computed from two sources. National income figures are found in UN Document no. ST/STAT/SER.H/8, Sept. 1955, *Statistics of National Income and Expenditure*, table 1, part A. Exchange rates for conversion into dollars are found in *UN Monthly Bulletin of Statistics*, vol. IX, no. 12, Dec. 1955, table 52.

preceding group. They have somewhat more checkered political traditions, and their per capita incomes were between $350 and $550 in 1952-1954 (averaged): West Germany, Austria, Ireland, and Finland. France and the Saar also belong in this group, though their income was higher (in the over-$600 group).

In a third category we find those countries with predominantly Mediterranean culture, and with 1952-1954 (averaged) per capita incomes well below $350: Italy,[29] Portugal, and Spain. These countries are to some extent on the economic and political periphery of the North Atlantic world. Their democratic traditions are rather weak, to say the least; by this test, they are the countries that seem to be linked the least closely to the common way of life that we speak of in the North Atlantic area.

We must emphasize again that in speaking of high-, middle-, and low-income countries, we are only using a kind of shorthand: the differences between these groups of countries are neither caused by income alone nor limited to it. Rather, their income levels are relatively easily measurable indications of more basic differences between these groups of countries.

Turning from our first test of distinctiveness—a related way of life in contrast with *other* areas—and looking at the present way of life as compared with that of the recent past in the *same* area, we find that two major differences stand out. The first is a political attitude which may mean a decisive break with the past: the new realization that wars are almost certain to be totally destructive for all parties to a conflict. This leads to the widespread realization that physical defense is impossible for the small states alone, and may be impossible for even the larger states. This realization may make such a difference in popular feeling about national sovereignty that it would affect political behavior seriously and constitute a distinct "way of life" that could be compared to that which seemed essential in our historical cases.

The other break with the past is the acceptance by the govern-

---

[29] Italy is a borderline case. Its northern and central regions would belong in the same category as France; the south, in economic and social terms, begins with the regions below Rome, and includes both Sardinia and Sicily; and it is still characterized by an "Iberian" level of poverty.

ment of each country of substantial responsibility for high and stable levels of employment, for rising standards of living, and for security for most individuals against one or more hazards like old age, workmen's accidents, illness, unemployment, high rents and costs of housing, and excessive fluctuations in the prices of agricultural products. In the United States, these trends have been associated with such legislation as the Social Security Act of 1935 and its subsequent extensions; the Employment Act of 1946; the various items of housing legislation; and the succession of farm price support bills. Broadly similar legislation, with similar social effects, has been enacted in all countries belonging to the first and second of our income groups in the North Atlantic area. The particular items covered have varied, of course, from country to country, and so has the manner in which each particular problem was dealt with in each case. In their cumulative impact, however, these changes have been astonishingly similar—not the less so for being accepted in their essence by conservative as well as liberal and labor parties in most of the countries concerned.

The extent of the change—the extent to which there are now fewer servants in the houses of the rich and more bathtubs in the dwellings of the poor—becomes evident if one compares the present-day position of industrial workers, as well as of farmers, in the high- and middle-income North Atlantic countries (that is, those with more than $350 per capita income for the average of 1952-1954) with what their conditions were in the 1890's or as recently as during the Great Depression of 1933. The social and economic change that has occurred during these last sixty years seems quite comparable in speed and extent to many of those major changes that we found occurring in our historical cases.

The political aspects of the fundamental change include the widespread acceptance of free labor unions and collective bargaining in industry; the emergence of stable and effective organizations representing farming interests; a general shift toward a greater extent of openly avowed interest group or "pressure group" politics; and an increase in effective political mass participation, either directly through voting, or indirectly through active or tacit support of interest groups.

Together, these changes have brought with them a change in centuries-old habits of social deference and obedience, of passive acceptance of economic and political inferiority, of long-inherited inequalities of opportunity. All these are now being challenged. In many other parts of the world this challenge has been accompanied by revolutions, civil wars, and the rise of dictatorships. But it is characteristic of the high-income countries in the North Atlantic area—and only to a much lesser extent of the middle-income countries, and even less of the low-income ones—that this challenge has been met and contained by methods of peaceful change. Here the characteristically "Western" way of life has consisted in a peculiar combination of relatively high income, constitutionalism, and reforms, which thus far has made it possible for this period of rapid social change to be peacefully "negotiated" in both senses of the word. This process of relatively rapid but negotiated social change is itself an aspect of the way of life characteristic of the economically strongest, as well as the politically most powerful, of the North Atlantic countries.

No other break with the recent past seems to be of sufficient magnitude to make for a distinctive way of life. Even if atomic energy for peaceful uses should develop its expected potential, this would not generate a major change in political and social values or habits of behavior within our meaning. It would have mainly economic consequences that would magnify existing trends, but which would probably not change political behavior radically. (It might well help, however, to spread the way of life enjoyed by the high-income countries to their less wealthy neighbors within the North Atlantic area.)

On the whole, we do find that a distinctive way of life characterizes the North Atlantic area except for Spain and Portugal, with Italy in a somewhat doubtful position.

4. *Core Areas and their Capabilities.* One of our findings which challenges a prevailing notion is that a balance of power,

designed to prevent any one unit from becoming much stronger than the others, did not have to be maintained among the members of a large union or federation.[30] Instead, the development of a strong core, or nucleus, seemed to promote integration if the core area had certain capabilities. One was the capacity to act— a function of size, power, economic strength, and administrative efficiency. The other was ability to respond to the other units involved.[31] These core areas were larger, stronger, more advanced political units around which integration developed. By "advanced" we mean politically, administratively, economically, and educationally, without any implication of superiority in moral or aesthetic values. Furthermore, not only the existing capabilities, but the growth in those capabilities, seemed important.[32]

By almost any measure, the United States today is the "core area" for the North Atlantic area, and since the United States and Canada form a long-integrated security-community, we may also refer to the United States–Canada as a core area. While there are also cores within sub-areas of the North Atlantic area, they are never quite so predominant within their sub-areas as the United States is for the North Atlantic as a whole. The first capability—the ability to act—is present in the United States, but the second capability—to respond—is decidedly less apparent as a reliable habit. While the Marshall Plan and NATO are examples of significant and generous United States responses, its immigration policy and some of its trade policies (such as the recent tariff on Swiss watch movements) are conspicuous examples to the contrary. Because of the wide discrepancy in foreign-policy views between political leaders at any one time (Senator Bricker and Secretary of State Dulles, for example), the response is apt to be discontinuous and unreliable. Recurring isolationism is still a danger.

It is worth stressing that in our historical cases it was not only the core areas that had to have high capabilities in order for amalgamation to succeed. Generally, it was not true that amal-

---

[30] See Chapter II, Section A, 1.
[31] See Chapter II, Section A, 2, E.   [32] See Chapter II, Section A, 2.

gamation came to pass because the government of the participating units had become weaker or more inefficient, and men
had been forced to turn away from these increasingly incapable
organizations to the building of a larger and less decrepit common government. Rather, amalgamation occurred after a substantial increase in the capabilities of some or all the participating units.[33] A thorough study would reveal which of the North
Atlantic countries meet this qualification today, but the core
area is probably the most important.

On the whole, the power to act and the ability to respond is
generally high in the core area, and has improved vastly since
the beginning of the second World War, as compared with the
interwar period. Yet the degree and speed of responsiveness required for success may well be increasing as more international
organizations are formed or proposed.

5. *Superior Economic Growth.* Another of these conditions we
found to be a markedly superior economic growth, either as
measured against the recent past of the area to be integrated,
or as against neighboring areas. This did not have to be present
in all participating units prior to integration, but it had to be
present in at least the core area.[34] Conversely, prolonged economic decline or stagnation, leading to economic conditions
comparing unfavorably with those in neighboring areas, was
found to be a disintegrative condition.[35]

In the North Atlantic area, there is no doubt about the
superior economic growth of the core, whether it is considered
to be the United States or the United States and Canada together.
Economic growth of the area as a whole also seems adequate to
fulfill this condition. Rate of growth, rather than absolute growth,
is more significant for comparisons. And to follow our historical
findings, this should be growth of a type that allows a markedly
higher level of living than before, or at least enough to provide
the expectation of a continually higher level in the future.

Because of war damage, comparisons beginning with the immediate postwar years would not be very illuminating. Some of

---

[33] See Chapter II, Section A, 2, E.
[34] See Chapter II, Section C, 2.   [35] See Chapter II, Section D.

the countries that were badly destroyed could hardly help but show the greatest growth rate, and this rate would not give so much promise of continuing as would a rate based upon a steadier trend. We shall compare, therefore, 1954 with 1937, and we shall use industrial production figures (since we have no comparable figures on gross national product).

We then find that Canada has shown the largest growth (127%), followed by the United States (107%). The others ranged from 93% down to 8%, all showing at least some gain.[36] (Finland, Iceland, Portugal, Spain, and Switzerland are not included because comparable figures were not available for them.) Since a good deal of industrial production goes into armaments, the actual levels of living may be compared with somewhat greater reliability by using statistics of per capita private consumption—provided that we state the results in orders of magnitude rather than in precise figures. These show that the countries with "very rapid increases in standard of living" (45% to 50% in 1953 as compared with 1938) are the United States and Canada. The next highest group is 25% to 35%, and the only country in the North Atlantic area[37] to show even a slight decline is the Netherlands.[38] A different source, however, indicates that economic stagnation has characterized some aspects of life in Spain, Portugal, and Southern Italy more than other parts of the area.[39]

Turning to a contrast with leading neighbors, we find no reliably comparable figures on private consumption. Using gross national product, however, we find (for 1953 compared with 1937) an estimated rise of 62% for the U.S.S.R., 36% for Po-

[36] Computed from "General Indices of Industrial Production," in *General Statistics*, O.E.E.C., September 1955, p. 8. The figures are corrected for price level.

[37] Iceland, Luxembourg, Spain, and Switzerland are omitted because comparable figures are lacking.

[38] From *Trends in Economic Growth*, study made for the Joint Committee on the Economic Report, 83rd Congress, 2nd. Session, by the Legislative Reference Service of the Library of Congress, 1955, p. 64. The figures are corrected for price level.

[39] See *Economic Survey of Europe in 1953*, UN Economic Commission for Europe, Geneva, 1954, pp. 123-155.

land (1938 base), and 25% for Czechoslovakia, and a drop for East Germany (1938 base).[40]

All these figures indicate that in comparison with the recent past, and in comparison with the other units in the area, the United States and Canada form a nucleus that seems to meet the qualification of markedly superior economic growth. Furthermore, the North Atlantic area as a whole (with the exception noted) does seem to fulfill the requirement of economic growth compared with its recent past. And while it is not so clear a contrast, and though we cannot be sure because of incomplete figures, the North Atlantic area in general appears to show superior economic growth over that of its leading neighbors— those bordering it to the East. Even when compared with the U.S.S.R. and its allies in Europe, the North Atlantic growth rate holds up well for the period 1937-1953.

6. *Expectation of Joint Economic Reward.* We found that amalgamation was always preceded by widespread expectations of joint economic reward for the participating units.[41]

For many years certain groups of citizens in the United States and Europe have been pressing for union (amalgamation) of at least the democratic parts of the North Atlantic area, and their reasoning has been based partly upon economic gain expected from the great single market that would be created.[42] Some others feel that these gains might be realized just as well through closer ties leading toward a pluralistic security-community instead of a union—through an organization like the much broader General Agreement on Tariffs and Trade, soon to become the Organization for Trade Cooperation.

There are only scraps of quite tangential evidence about the expectations in the North Atlantic area, largely because North

[40] *Trends in Economic Growth* (*op. cit.*), p. 71.

[41] See Chapter II, Section C, 1.

[42] See, for example, Clarence Streit, *Union Now*, Postwar Edition, Harpers, 1949, p. 281; and "Atlantica's Economic Future—With and Without Union," in *Freedom and Union*, February 1955, p. 4. For a more specific statement, see Louis Domeratzky, "The Atlantic Area as an Economic Unit," in *Freedom and Union*, September 1950, pp. 6-10; *ibid.*, July-August 1950, pp. 6-14; *ibid.*, June 1950, pp. 6-11; and *ibid.*, February 1951, pp. 25-29.

Atlantic integration is not a leading issue anywhere, but especially not in Europe.

A careful investigation into the attitudes of a large sample of leading French businessmen was made in 1954 by the Institut d'Études Européennes.[43] It might be supposed that if economic gains were expected from North Atlantic integration, this would be expressed by businessmen. But, while they favored NATO by almost 10 to 1, almost 10 times as many chose "European" as a policy for France as against any other choice offered: "Atlantic," "European," or "National" policy alternatives. The investigators interpret this not as opposition to supranationalism, or to the United States (other evidence clearly refutes the latter), but to something else. The term "Atlantic," they feel, has been poisoned as a vision of the future by its current association with military planning, and thoughts of the military are very distasteful to the French. The investigators feel, therefore, that the preference for a European policy is a way of endorsing international solidarity without explicitly acknowledging the military priority. Businessmen concede the necessity of NATO at present, but they do not see the North Atlantic as the area for long-run organization. If and when NATO becomes more than a military organization, this attitude might conceivably change.

A different study, under different auspices, was carried on in West Germany through interviews with businessmen in the summer of 1954. This showed no indication that North Atlantic integration was an alternative being given any serious consideration in that country. When the European Defense Community proposal failed, the trend toward integration began to ebb; the Germans seemed to turn back into their own territory instead of toward a wider framework that was not presented to them as a clear alternative.[44]

We have found no public-opinion poll which throws light

[43] For an account of the preliminary findings, we are indebted to Professor Daniel Lerner, of the Massachusetts Institute of Technology, director of the project, New York, 1956.

[44] For information on this point, we are indebted to Professor Gabriel Almond of Princeton University, who conducted the study reported in *World Politics*, viii, 2, January 1956, pp. 157-186.

directly on this point. The nearest to it was a question put to a representative cross-section of Americans concerning (among other questions about world organization) a union of democratic nations.[45] Of those who favored this alternative, about two-thirds said (among their various reasons for favoring it) that a union of democratic countries "would solve a good many of the economic problems now existing between us."[46] Other polls cover either Western European integration or a portion of it such as the European Coal and Steel Community.[47] Apart from the cross-section type of poll, there are surveys of opinions of particular groups, but again these do not probe into expectations regarding integration of the North Atlantic area, or even regarding NATO. For example, interviews with 900 United States business leaders were held in the Spring of 1954 by the National Opinion Research Center. A third of the executives "said they had changed their attitude toward tariffs during or since the second World War, and more than three-quarters of those who had changed said they had shifted toward a freer trade policy."[48] An earlier example of the trend is found in a *Fortune* poll of business executives in 1939 which showed that only about 19% thought tariffs should be lowered, while in 1954 some 38% thought so.[49] If a desire for lower tariffs indicates an expectation of gain from integration (though not necessarily the amalgamated type), then a trend could probably be discerned if enough

[45] About 6% of the persons interviewed selected the following answer from among six alternatives: "In addition to continuing with the United Nations, we should also unite with the friendly democratic countries into one government in which each member nation would in effect become a state, somewhat like the different states in this country."—Elmo Roper, "American Attitudes on World Organization," *Public Opinion Quarterly*, vol. 17 (1953-1954), no. 4, p. 408.

[46] *ibid.*, p. 417.

[47] See, for example, *Public Opinion in Western Europe: Attitudes Towards Political, Economic, and Military Integration*, Reactions Analysis Staff, Office of the (U.S.) High Commissioner for Germany, January 1953; and "Les Français devant les premières réalisations européennes," *Réalités*, September 1954, p. 20; also the issue of *Sondages*, 1955, no. 2, devoted to the European Coal and Steel Community.

[48] This survey was done under the auspices of the Center for International Studies at the Massachusetts Institute of Technology, and the results were summarized in *Fortune*, April 1955, p. 107.

[49] *idem.*

pieces of this kind of evidence were available. It would not apply specifically to integration of the North Atlantic area, however, and this is one of the aspects of the problem which needs a great deal more research.

On the whole, we see no real evidence that the expectation of economic gain from an Atlantic federation, or even from pluralistic integration, is widespread in the sense of mass feeling. We are even doubtful that the leadership in each country has any expectations as yet. They do not, in the matter of economic benefits, seem to go beyond a policy of freer trade.

7. *Wide Range of Mutual Transactions.* It turned out to be essential for amalgamation (and helpful for pluralism) to have a multiplicity of ranges of communication and transactions between the units involved, and also a fairly wide range of different functions and services, together with the organizations to carry them out.[50] In contemporary terms, this would be shown by all sorts of interactions—written and spoken messages, face-to-face contact, and dealings such as trade—and in addition by the work of international organizations, governmental and nongovernmental.

It seems clear that these interactions and institutions are much greater today than they were a hundred years ago, but this is true not only of the North Atlantic area but of most of the world. Considerable research would be needed before we could say with assurance that the network of interaction is really dense enough to be favorable to integration in the near future. The density would have to be so much higher today than a hundred years ago, to keep up with the increased number of politically relevant people, that assessment becomes difficult. A combination of research and informed political judgment is necessary. Some of this kind of research has been undertaken—the flow of mail and flow of trade. The first was mentioned earlier,[51] in the discussion of mutual responsiveness. The mail figures, however, revealed a threat to future interaction, as they showed a trend toward increasing self-preoccupation in practically all

50 See Chapter II, Section C, 4.   51 See Section B, 2, above.

important countries of the area during the past 40 years. In the United States, the trend has been noticeable even longer: the ratio of domestic to foreign mail was about 25 to 1 in 1880, about 28 to 1 in 1928, and about 65 to 1 in 1951.[52] The same trend of self-preoccupation is indicated by the ratio of United States domestic national income to total foreign trade. It was about 5 to 1 in 1879, about 7 to 1 in 1913, and about 12 to 1 in 1950.[53]

On the other hand, the existing network of international trade is the most striking evidence we have of real economic ties within the North Atlantic area. If we calculate for each country in the area the top two countries to which it exports and the top two countries from which it imports, we find that the flow is to and from other countries within the North Atlantic area almost exclusively.[54] The ties are much stronger among North Atlantic countries than with outside areas, as far as exports and imports are concerned.

There are a few clues, among the countries involved, to the kind of interaction which comes from international reading of each other's publications, listening to each other's radio programs, or viewing each other's moving pictures and television shows. One part of this flow of information has been studied carefully over a sample period of time; it shows the clear preference that the United States and Western Europe give to each other. In terms of volume of foreign news columns in each other's newspapers, a recent survey showed that correspondents, news services, and editors (as well as readers) are directing more

---

[52] Unpublished studies at the Center for Research on World Political Institutions; and Karl W. Deutsch, "Shifts in the Balance of Communication Flows: A Problem of Measurement in International Relations," *Public Opinion Quarterly*, xx, 1, Spring 1956, pp. 143-160.

[53] *idem.*

[54] In 1954 there were only six exceptions out of the 80 possible relationships: Australia received the United Kingdom's largest percentage of exports and the Union of South Africa its second largest; Brazil accounted for the second largest percentage of imports of the United States; the U.S.S.R. received Finland's second largest percentage of both exports and imports; and Angola (a colony) received Portugal's second largest percentage of exports. These relationships were compiled from the *United Nations Yearbook of International Trade Statistics, 1954,* 1955.

attention mutually to those areas than to other parts of the world, except where a specific crisis (like the Korean War) is involved.[55] But is it not surprising to find that "the average reader reads very little of the foreign news in his favorite newspaper."[56] Furthermore, "of the 1,780 daily newspapers in the United States the *Times* is the only one where domestic news has to fight for space in the paper; in the other 1,779 just the opposite is true (borderline exception: *The Christian Science Monitor*)."[57] A survey of U.S. foreign correspondents showed that the only countries "adequately" covered for the United States reader were Canada, Great Britain, France, West Germany, Italy, and Japan.[58] This is another indication of the greater attention paid generally to the leading countries of the North Atlantic area as compared with others.

When we come to the finding that a fairly wide range of different common functions and services is essential, with the organizations to carry them out, we find very little covering the area as a whole, but a great many organizations which cover only parts of the area. Probably the only organization to which all 19 countries belong is the unobtrusive but efficient Universal Postal Union, which covers the world with a membership of 93 "countries." All 19 North Atlantic area countries except West Germany belong to the United Nations, though Finland and Spain are newcomers. Fifteen of the 19 belong to the General Agreement on Tariffs and Trade (soon to become the Organization for Trade Cooperation). All except two of the 19 countries belong to some operating international organization covering primarily the Western European or North Atlantic area, and to which several other countries in the area belong; Finland and Spain are

---

[55] This survey covered the United States, India, and eight countries of Western Europe: Belgium, France, Italy, the Netherlands, Sweden, Switzerland, the United Kingdom, and West Germany—*The Flow of the News: A Study by the International Press Institute*, Zürich, 1953, pp. 69, 105, 107, 222, 251, and 254.

[56] *ibid.*, p. 9.

[57] Russell F. Anderson, "News from Nowhere," *Saturday Review of Literature*, 17 November 1951, p. 80.

[58] *ibid.*, p. 81. See also Jacques Kayser, *One Week's News: Comparative Study of 17 Major Dailies for a Seven-Day Period*, UNESCO, 1953, p. 93.

the exceptions. The Council of Europe includes 12 of the 19, and the Saar as well. NATO also includes 12 of the countries, though not the same ones. The Organization for European Economic Cooperation and the European Payments Union each include 15 of the countries. Six contiguous countries of Western Europe make up the most supranational of any organization in the world today—the European Coal and Steel Community.

The North Atlantic countries also share common membership in many functional organizations. Of the 85 existing active functional organizations in the world,[59] two are merely bilateral—the International Joint Commission, for example, between the United States and Canada. Of the 83 multilateral functional organizations, 8 have a membership made up entirely from among North Atlantic countries; the Central Commission for the Navigation of the Rhine, for example, is made up of the United States, United Kingdom, France, Belgium, the Netherlands, Switzerland, and West Germany. 52 have 3 or more North Atlantic members and one or more from outside that area; the Intergovernmental Committee for European Migration is an example, having 24 members, of whom 13 are in the North Atlantic area. (This leaves 23 that have either no members, or less than 3 members, from the North Atlantic area.) This means that of the 83 multilateral organizations, 60 perform functions internationally with 3 or more North Atlantic area countries participating, and in most cases the number of those countries is much higher. Of the several hundred international nongovernmental organizations in existence, it is safe to say that the great bulk of them have members from every country in the North Atlantic area.

All these organizations taken together, governmental and nongovernmental, cover a very wide range of interactions and they involve directly quite a wide variety of persons in every country of the area.

[59] There is no complete list, but the *Yearbook of International Organizations* has the nearest to it. Its editors eliminated 457 international governmental organizations as being inactive and listed 92 as active. Of these, we consider 85 to be functional organizations, and our classification is based upon this group.—*Yearbook of International Organizations, 1954-1955*, Union of International Associations, Brussels, 1954, pp. 133-227.

On the basis of very incomplete evidence, we feel that interaction of the type discussed here is quite high for the North Atlantic area and that it may well be growing. This growth may offset or overcome to some extent the threatening tendency toward greater national self-preoccupation which we have already noticed. Furthermore, we see no strong reason why the North Atlantic area is too large to handle quite a wide range of interactions, with the corresponding organizations. Although it is clear that there will not be so wide a range of interactions between Canada and Austria as there is between France and Belgium, there may well be a linkage working in matters of this sort: Canada may not interact much with Austria, but it does with Britain, which in turn interacts with Austria.

8. *Broadening of Elites.* A more clearcut conclusion is indicated by our finding that another essential condition for amalgamation (and a helpful one for pluralism) was a broadening of the political, social, or economic elites, both as to recruitment from more of the social strata and as to maintenance of continuing connections with those strata.[60]

Democracy has continually spread since the periods when amalgamation was achieved in our historical cases. The franchise has broadened greatly, and in a democracy this usually means the recruitment of political elites from a wide variety of social strata. (It might seem that if the political base has already been broadened as much as possible, there would be no further chance of broadening the elite, but this is not necessarily the case in many countries.) Democracy also discourages the elite from breaking connections with the strata from which it came.[61] It is not necessary to document the fact that labor has risen steadily in politics and government. Education, too, has become so nearly universal that college and university students now come from a much broader range of classes. As governments increased in size, their bureaucracies increased in size and the governmental elite also had to be enlarged.

---

[60] See Chapter II, Section C, 2, last paragraph.

[61] For a discussion of some tendencies toward growing social stratification even in a democracy, see C. Wright Mills, *The Power Elite*, Oxford, 1956.

These generalizations may not apply to all countries in the North Atlantic area, but certainly they apply to all the major ones as measured either by power or leadership.

A caution is in order here, however. It may be that if the elite is broadened beyond a certain point, it will hinder more than help toward amalgamation in the modern day. If it should reach a point where overwhelming mass consent were needed, amalgamation might be more difficult than it was formerly.

9. *Links of Social Communication.* The presence of unbroken links of social communication between the political units concerned and between the relevant social strata within those units was another of the conditions in this category. These links provided effective channels of communication both horizontally and vertically, and they involved both persons and organizations.[62]

We have no clear picture of this condition in the North Atlantic area. It may be that the Catholic and Protestant churches are more of a force in this direction now than they were a hundred years or even 20 years ago, because they are not so likely to have their international links disrupted by war between countries of the Western world. War today is less likely among most of the countries in the North Atlantic area than it has been in the past. This fact may give not only the churches, but other cross-national institutions that used to be shattered by periodic wars, a chance to solidify their links. The whole pattern needs investigation: the strength not only of the church links but of international nongovernmental organizations of all sorts; the impact of student exchange and labor-exchange trips; the nature of personal relationships between certain groups of people, such as the industrialists of the Ruhr and Lorraine; and the influence of groups such as the Swiss bankers as a link between business leaders of certain countries. The College of Europe, up to October 1955, had graduated students from 16 countries, of which 14 were in the North Atlantic area; about 20% were employed in European organizations, public or private,

---

[62] See Chapter II, Section C, 2.

but most of the others returned to their own countries after an educational experience which may well have rendered them more effective as links of social communication.[63]

Political parties might be considered a possible link across national borders. The first thing to be said about this is that in the North Atlantic area there is no such thing as a truly international party cutting across many of the national boundaries. But it should also be said that, while several of the North Atlantic countries have a leading Catholic party and a leading non-Catholic or anticlerical party, no country is any longer unacceptable as a political partner to another merely because of its Catholic or Protestant character. Most countries have a leading liberal party and a leading conservative one. But the sharpness with which an ideology can be expressed depends so largely upon the number and influence of active parties in each country that the situation is far different where there are many (as in France) and where there are few (as in the United Kingdom). Furthermore, the Americans and British do not even have a religious basis for any of their party contrasts.

The most conspicuous contrast that would find rough counterparts in the party systems of almost all countries of the North Atlantic area is the liberal-conservative issue. To be sure, this is a very much oversimplified contrast, but it is still embodied in various countries in distinct parties, coalitions of parties, or wings or factions within parties. Countries with democratic institutions, however, are unlikely to be permanently liberal or permanently conservative. This major division between political parties thus may tend to weaken rather than reinforce the boundaries between countries. So might a development recently reported from the headquarters of the European Coal and Steel Community. A common Socialist policy-making process has been growing in the Common Assembly of that organization, where the Socialist deputies caucus before voting. An entire social-economic program seems to be emerging from this source.[64] Other

---

[63] Correspondence with College of Europe, Bruges, Belgium.

[64] Interview with M. Guy Mollet at Boulder, Colorado, September 1955, and letters from Professor Ernst Haas (University of California), January and February 1956, from Luxembourg.

party groups do the same thing to a considerable extent, and they have their own caucus rooms with secretary-general, files, and secretarial staff.

There are some signs of future cross-national party connections: "The beginnings of an international Christian Democratic movement, . . . the resurgence of world liberalism, neo-Fascist rumblings, the revival of the Socialist Second International, the gathering of latent forces among the erstwhile resistance movements, the first international party alignments at Strasbourg's Council of Europe—weak though all these attempts may still be, they can count on a certain response within different nations. These movements ought to be studied. . . ."[65] A more thorough understanding than we now have of the cross-national connections among political parties in the North Atlantic area would be highly desirable.

On the whole, the "unbroken links" do not seem to be very strong among most countries in the North Atlantic area. Until we learn more about present-day links, it remains only an impression that they seem weaker than they were among the American colonies or among the German states during the two decades before amalgamation; but they seem a little stronger than they were between Geneva and the Swiss Confederation in the early Sixteenth Century or between England and Scotland in the late Seventeenth.

10. *Greater Mobility of Persons.* The application is clear with regard to our finding that mobility of persons among the main units (at least in the politically relevant strata) may be essential for amalgamation and helpful for pluralism.[66]

The North Atlantic area is so far from reaching full-scale mobility of persons that we can only rate this condition as almost nil. Certain regions could qualify, such as England–Ireland with its nearly joint citizenship, and the Scandinavian countries with their common labor market; but the area as a whole could not. No matter how one defines "politically relevant" today, it

---

[65] Sigmund Neumann, "Toward a Comparative Study of Political Parties," in Sigmund Neumann, ed., *Modern Political Parties*, Chicago, 1956, p. 417.
[66] See Chapter II, Section C, 3.

seems clear that the North Atlantic area does not meet the test of mobility. Furthermore, the passing grade for the test has probably gone up, because so many more people are politically relevant now than formerly. Nor does it seem to us that circumstances in the twentieth century would make mobility any less essential than it was earlier, unless we assume that other means of communication are a modern substitute for personal contact, or else that numbers are offset by velocity. At most, it may be true that some of the most relevant persons now circulate with more velocity than their early predecessors, and therefore add up, in a sense, to a greater total number of persons.

What about people's attitudes toward the idea of free mobility? The very restrictive immigration laws in the United States are evidence of the negative attitude in the core area. The recent unsuccessful experience with the Italian coal miners in England shows one of the dangers of immigration of some kinds between certain countries in the North Atlantic area. A survey of polling data, for what these are worth, shows that very few questions have been asked directly on this point, and only one of them after 1950. In January 1946, only 5% of Americans wanted more immigrants from Europe to be permitted to come to the United States each year than had been allowed before the war; and 51% wanted to admit fewer or none.[67] Canadians were more hospitable, but even they were opposed when asked whether they would like to see a large number of immigrants from the European continent; 21% were in favor and 61% were opposed in April 1946. On the same date they showed their favoritism toward the British Isles, but still a bare majority opposed greater immigration even from that area, by a vote of 37% in favor and 45% against.[68]

[67] "Should we permit more persons from Europe to come to this country each year than we did before the war, should we keep the number about the same, or should we reduce the number?" More 5%; Same 32%; Fewer 37%; None at all 14%; No Opinion 12%.—American Institute of Public Opinion.

[68] "Would you like to see a large number of people from the European Continent migrate to Canada or not?" Favor 21%; Oppose 61%; Qualified 10%; Undecided 8%. "Would you like to see a large number of people

Perhaps because a "common labor market" sounded more acceptable, or perhaps because the question was asked in a slightly poorer country about a common labor market with two richer ones, or perhaps because the question was asked about the partners in a security-community, a poll in Norway offers quite a contrast. In March 1954, Norwegians were asked: "Do you think it would be advantageous or not if we had a common labour market in the Northern countries, so that Norwegians might without any restriction accept jobs in Sweden and Denmark and vice-versa?" 68% thought it would be advantageous, 32% thought not, and 36% did not know.[69] This poll, like the one on Canada and Britain, was taken inside a security-community, and in both cases the favorable percentage was higher than for areas outside the security-community. It would be relevant to know how Swedes and Danes would answer such a poll.

The only comparable question available for Europe as a whole seems to be a survey made in 1950 in twelve European countries on a somewhat different question: "Are you against or for allowing everyone to travel from one country to another without customs formalities, and allowing everyone who desires it to look for employment in our country?" For the composite of twelve countries, people were 71% in favor, 9% against, and 20% without opinion. The continental countries must have been overwhelmingly favorable, because the United Kingdom showed only 62% favorable and 24% unfavorable, with 14% having no opinion.[70]

It should be pointed out also that even where movement is entirely free, it sometimes goes unused. In Benelux, for example, "little or no movement has actually taken place, partly owing

---

from the British Isles migrate to Canada in the next few years or not?" Favor 37%; Oppose 45%; Qualified 10%; Undecided 8%.—Canadian Institute of Public Opinion.

[69] Survey 2-IV, Norwegian Gallup Institute, release of 27 March 1954.

[70] The countries were West Germany (including West Berlin), the United Kingdom, France, Italy, Holland, Belgium, Luxembourg, Switzerland, Norway, Denmark, Sweden, and the three Western Zones of Austria. The figures given are the mean of the national figures. This survey was made by the Eric Stern Institute, at the request of the European Movement.

to the persistence of unemployment in Belgium."[71] Economic factors of that sort are likely to keep mobility down between modern states, and "extensive transfers of manpower between European countries are unlikely to take place."[72]

Coming to the tourist level, where the visit is less than three months, real progress has been made in the North Atlantic area in abolishing visas. Among the 20 North Atlantic countries a comparison can be made in the total number of visas that would be required to travel into all these countries from all the others in March 1950 and in January 1955. This number has been reduced from 165 to 88. If four countries (the United States, Canada, Spain, and Portugal) are eliminated from the picture, no visas remain.[73] Tourist entry visas have been practically abolished in 5 years except for Portugal, Spain, the United States, and Canada.

On the whole, however, if free mobility of persons is necessary for amalgamation and helpful for pluralistic integration, this condition is far from being met today in the North Atlantic area and is a serious deterrent to further progress.

D ◈ SOME CONDITIONS THAT WERE HELPFUL BUT NONESSENTIAL FOR BOTH PLURALISTIC AND AMALGAMATED SECURITY-COMMUNITIES

Beside the ten conditions already discussed, we found four others that were helpful to both types of integration but not essential to either type.

11. *Reluctance to Wage "Fratricidal" War.* It may seem tautological to have found that a decline in the expectations of war, and an increasing reluctance to wage war between the units to be amalgamated, was an important step on the way to amalgama-

[71] Economic Commission for Europe, *Economic Survey of Europe Since the War*, Geneva, 1953, p. 221.

[72] *ibid.*, p. 162.

[73] Organization for European Economic Cooperation, *Tourism*, February 1955, p. 9, for 1955 figures. The 1950 figures are taken from *European-Atlantic Review*, Spring 1955, p. 29, but with the United States and Canada added on an imputed basis. No source for this 1950 table was found. Finland and Spain were obtained from their consulates.

tion in our historical cases.[74] If we knew how to promote this process to the point where the decline reached zero, we would have "solved" the problem of war, and nobody would care whether the result was amalgamation, pluralism, or neither. But we did find more specific aspects of the process: war had to become "somewhat less than respectable," and this had to be the case for at least one generation before amalgamation, and usually longer.[75] It had to be considered so unrespectable that it seemed fratricidal. Furthermore, we found that the outstanding issue leading to the emergence of a pluralistic security-community in the cases we studied was the increasing unattractiveness of war among the political units concerned.[76] War became unattractive either because it promised to be devastating and indecisive, or because it would bring on international complications that might engulf one or both sides, or because it was unpopular in all (or at least the strongest) of the countries involved.

It requires no essay, long or short, to point out that war is increasingly unpopular today, and for the reasons given—especially the first. Can there be any doubt that war has become less and less respectable as a means of settling disputes between countries in the North Atlantic area? This trend has greatly accelerated in the twentieth century, and especially since the end of the second World War. It is sometimes forgotten that until somewhere between a half-century and a century ago men in substantial numbers did not consider it vital, or even a sober possibility, to eliminate international war. And the declining enthusiasm with which war was undertaken in recent decades is an interesting indication: in the United Kingdom, 1854 as compared with 1914 and with 1939; in the United States, 1898 compared with 1917 and 1941; and in Germany, 1914 as compared with 1939. And in 1955: "To say that the people of West Germany have not reacted enthusiastically to the prospect of having a new army is to indulge in gross understatement."[77]

[74] See Chapter III, Section A.
[75] See Chapter III, Section A.   [76] See Chapter III, Section H.
[77] See Gordon A. Craig, "NATO and the New German Army," in William W. Kaufmann, ed., *Military Policy and National Security*, Princeton, 1956, p. 198.

In the North Atlantic area itself there are several countries between which war has not only become unrespectable but unthinkable. These are security-communities, or very nearly so, by definition. Examples are Norway–Sweden–Denmark, United States–Canada, United States–United Kingdom, and France–Belgium. Indeed the only serious problem in the area at the present time is Western Germany vis-à-vis other countries. While there is some reason to believe that war has now lost its respectability in the eyes of many West Germans, what little evidence we have is not entirely reassuring.[78] There is no way of knowing for certain how the influential elements in Germany feel about it, however, and testimony of observers conflicts. The Stresemann period seemed at the time to invite a rather safe prognosis of peace, but the outcome gives pause to any prophet. Even if the German problem is worked out, however, integration would not necessarily be achieved over the whole area, since by our definition this is a situation that *assures* for a "long" time *dependable* expectations of peaceful change.

In sum, the reluctance of countries in the North Atlantic area to wage war among each other is very high, with one possible exception, Germany, which at present is not at all clear.

12. *Outside Military Threat.* Where a foreign military threat existed, we found that its effects were transitory. Most often it provided an impetus toward temporary military alliances, while more permanent unions derived their main support from other factors. It has been possible to amalgamate in the absence of such a threat, and also the presence of such a threat did not always suffice to bring about amalgamation. At times, however, military threats fulfilled a helpful function if they induced the relatively privileged political units to become somewhat more generous in sharing their economic, political, or social privileges with potential partners in the new security-community. The ef-

---

[78] See, for example, the evidence from two poll questions taken in September 1954 and published in *Antworten*, by Erich Peter Neumann and Elisabeth Noelle, Verlag für Demoskopie, Allensbach am Bodensee, 1954, p. 137. Studies on neo-Nazism made by the Office of the (US) High Commissioner for Germany (HICOG) are also disturbing on this point.

fect, however, was hard to predict. Instead of inducing greater generosity, it sometimes had the opposite effect by amplifying a state of fear which actually reduced the responsiveness of the privileged units.[79]

The North Atlantic area certainly feels a military threat, and certainly that threat is foreign. It is also clear that the most "privileged" unit in the area (the United States), did rise to the occasion and take the "generous" alternative by fostering the Truman Doctrine, the Marshall Plan, and NATO. At the same time, this same sense of threat has made the United States less tolerant of dissenting voices among its friends—various types of neutrals such as India and Sweden, and other groups such as the German Social Democrats, certain British Laborites, and certain French neutralists.

Without knowing much more than we do about the feelings that at least the influential people in various North Atlantic countries have about the Soviet threat—whether it is real, whether it affects them imminently, and whether their own country, or a military alliance, or the establishment of a security-community, is the best means of defense—we can only say that the threat seems now to be considered serious. As the threat waxes and wanes, however, feelings about it have their ups and downs. To that extent it is somewhat unreliable as a condition helpful to integration, even where it does not actually hamper integration processes by promoting rigidities through fear.

13. *Strong Economic Ties.* It turned out that strong economic ties among the units to be integrated were not essential, though they were helpful, to integration of either type.[80]

We have already noted that the countries of the North Atlantic area are finding their best customers almost invariably among themselves.[81] On the other hand, the relative weight of their mutual trade, as compared with the total volume of their economic activities at home and abroad, has not increased significantly, compared with the state of affairs about 1890 or 1914. In an earlier period—the first half of the nineteenth century—

[79] See Chapter II, Section B.
[80] See Chapter II, Section B.   [81] See Section C, 7, above.

international economic interdependence had increased conspicuously. In terms of the relative share of foreign trade in total national incomes, it may have reached its peak somewhere about 1860 to 1870. Between 1870 and 1914, however, when domestic national incomes grew faster than international trade, the economic historian Werner Sombart formulated his "law of the declining importance of foreign trade."[82] This has been the situation generally since 1914.[83]

In sum, we can say only that while the economic ties are generally stronger among countries in the North Atlantic area than they are between countries within the area and those outside, it would require more research to say whether these ties are really close or whether they are becoming any closer.

14. *Ethnic and Linguistic Assimilation.* The term "ethnic" frequently denotes membership in a people. It implies a sense of kinship based on some expectations of intermarriage among families; common patterns of culture; and effective mutual habits of social communication, including a common language. In a narrower sense, as used in this study, a common language is not essential for the existence of a people. Members of one Swiss people speak four languages, and speakers of one English language belong to many peoples. Thus ethnic and language groups are distinguished from each other. They overlap but need not coincide. Accordingly, ethnic groups and language groups are referred to side by side in our study. Nationalism, based largely upon ethnic and language distinctions, is still a great force. Yet it is worth noting that integration—even by amalgamation[84]— has taken place in the past without ethnic and linguistic assimilation of the populations concerned. We found no upper limit on the number of such groups that could be integrated.

[82] See Werner Sombart, *Die deutsche Volkswirtschaft im 19. Jahrhundert,* 3rd edn., Berlin, Bondi, 1913, pp. 368-376, 528. Cf. Albert O. Hirschman, *National Power and the Structure of Foreign Trade,* University of California Press, 1945, pp. 146-151.
[83] In 1870-1913, for example, imports constituted a larger share of British national income than they did after 1945, but since imports had become more precarious in the latter period, the problem of procuring them was likely to receive more attention.
[84] See Chapter II, Section B.

There is no doubt that the number of ethnic and linguistic groups in the North Atlantic area is larger than in any of our historical cases. These great ethnic and linguistic differences within the North Atlantic area today prompt the question: Are nationalistic conflicts increasing or decreasing in the mid-twentieth century within the North Atlantic area? As far as the states themselves are concerned, we would judge that it has been decreasing somewhat since 1945. And as far as minority groups *within* states are concerned, these appear not to be at all dangerous. The revival of Gaelic and of Welsh does not seriously affect either the United Kingdom–Irish relationship or the United Kingdom internally. From the viewpoint of security, other instances of political activity among ethnic or language groups in the North Atlantic area since the first World War have remained of minor importance: the Alsatians in France, the Flemings in Belgium, the Austrians (South Tyrolese) in Italy, and the French in Canada. Most of the area seems to have settled down in this respect, and only at its fringes, in Algiers and Cyprus, do we meet exceptions.

Finally, the only evidence we see of greater assimilation in recent years is the growing use of English as a second language throughout most of Western Europe. English is already the primary language of about half the people in the North Atlantic area, and is becoming the second language of much of the other half.

In sum, we see very little evidence of ethnic or linguistic assimilation in the North Atlantic area. And we feel that while it is not necessary for much of this to take place in order to achieve integration, its absence is bound to be a deterrent which would have to be overcome by more progress toward fulfillment of other conditions.

E ◇ STATE OF INTEGRATION IN SUB–AREAS OF THE NORTH ATLANTIC

In this book we are not discussing the question of regionalism, interesting and important as that is. We have not applied our findings to the well-known problems of Western European integration, or to the familiar question whether a tightly organized Western Europe would promote or retard the later integration of a larger area.

In a very rough way, however, we can see which region has the highest ratings in terms of the various conditions we found to be important for integration, and then see which countries can be added to that core region with more and more loss of integrative possibilities. It gives us a crude idea of the direction and the size of steps that might most logically be taken outward from the core. It does not, however, take into account present movements that are well advanced (such as Western European integration) or organizations already set up (such as the European Coal and Steel Community, the Council of Europe, or the Nordic Council).

Using both a rough quantitative and qualitative judgment, we come out with the core area (United States and Canada) far ahead of other sizeable regions in terms of the conditions surrounding integration. All 14 of the conditions are to be found in the relationship between these two countries, and most of them to a high degree. If the United Kingdom and Ireland are added, only the condition we have called "mobility of persons" is missing, and most of the other conditions are much weaker than between the United States and Canada. Having crossed the ocean barrier, we next cross the language barrier (dropping the condition we have called "ethnic and linguistic assimilation") and find that the Scandinavian countries and Benelux can be added with only a slight reduction in the number and intensity of integrative conditions. When we move to a fourth level, quite a drop occurs by adding West Germany, France, Austria, and Switzerland. Another drop occurs if Italy is added. Finally, the longest drop of all occurs when Spain and Portugal are added.

It is no reflection upon either our findings or United States foreign policy to note that the two are in conflict on this point. We are looking only at the possibilities of integration, while United States foreign policy (in supporting both Western European integration and NATO) is looking mainly at the possibilities of defense against Communism. The task of forming a security-community is different from that of defending an area against outside attack. Although of course integration is one way of achieving a tight community for defense purposes, its main object is *internal* peace.

◈

To summarize: of the 14 conditions we considered helpful or essential for integration, we found that 8 are currently high for the whole North Atlantic area generally. Two of the low 6 conditions seem not to be essential to forming either a pluralistic or amalgamated security-community. But one of the low 6 is "responsiveness," a condition which may be essential for a security-community of either type.

We do not wish to base any predictions on this sort of evidence. The most we can do is to indicate what might be done about moving somewhat closer to integration in the North Atlantic area as a whole. We shall do this by suggesting some implications that our findings have for policy.

CHAPTER V

◇◇◇

Policy Implications for the North Atlantic Area

◇◇◇

When matters of policy are raised, the first question to ask is: "Policy for whom?" We propose to apply our findings from the standpoint of those who would like to promote integration of the North Atlantic area. We could state them almost as well from the opposite standpoint, of those who would like to deter integration. But it is clear from the assumptions and definitions presented at the outset[1] that we are studying integration as a means of eliminating war that has been *proven* effective over certain areas in the past. While we did not find, from our studies, that further large-scale integration would necessarily be feasible in the near future, we certainly did not lose confidence in that approach as compared with any other that we have heard of.

Perhaps we should add a reminder about our definitions. Integration (the achievement of a security-community) is of two kinds—where the governments of two or more political units are merged, and where they are not merged. The first we call amalgamated and the second pluralistic; we do not conclude that one of these is inherently "better" than the other. We do not know of any third method of eliminating war that has proved successful in the long run. We should also add that in this chapter we are discussing the North Atlantic area as a whole, and not the regions within it.

A ◈ POLICY GOALS

After assessing the situation in the North Atlantic area in Chapter IV, we can see the evidence for our statement early in that chapter that pluralism is probably the more promising approach to integration at the present time, leading perhaps to later amalgamation. Not only does the historical evidence

[1] See Chapter I, Section A.

indicate that this might be the case, but the application of specific pieces of that evidence shows that by no means all the conditions essential to amalgamation are near fulfillment; some of them are apparently a long way from it. It is true that one of the two conditions essential to a pluralistic security-community—responsiveness—has been attained only to a low degree, but this element seems more nearly within reach than some of the missing elements that would be needed for amalgamation. Therefore a pluralistic security-community is apt to be easier to achieve.

If it is also true, as our historical studies indicate, that pluralistic security-communities are apt to be somewhat more stable than the amalgamated type, and that they are at least as effective as amalgamated ones in keeping the peace, then we are justified at this stage in considering pluralism as the major and most general policy goal to be sought. Furthermore, there is some historical evidence that the pursuit of this goal does not seem to preclude later amalgamation, while the pursuit of amalgamation first may well preclude the attainment of pluralism.[2] And while progress toward integration of both kinds can be made gradually along the same pathway, the pluralistic approach has an extra safety feature. It allows a period of testing to make sure that we really have a security-community before national self-defense is tapered off too far. Countries need not disarm suddenly, or even merge their armed forces, until integration is assured. As the prospect of war becomes gradually more remote, they can withdraw their troops from their common borders, unit by unit, while still retaining troops for more general disposition. Or, more likely in the modern setting, they could transfer defense expenditures from the making of end-products (such as weapons) to intermediate products which can be shifted between peaceful and military uses (such as commercial aircraft, strategic machine tools, and atomic power plants).

In this connection, one of our historical findings suggests that common institutions for policing and coercion (a feature of amalgamated security-communities) tend to appear only at a

2 See Chapter III, Sections D and E, 2, last paragraph.

late stage in the amalgamation process, while the noncoercive approaches are more frequent in the earlier stages.[3] This indicates that promoters of amalgamation should not try to build such institutions as a strong international police force until they judge the North Atlantic area to be already well advanced toward amalgamation. Otherwise, it would seem more promising to concentrate on the development of noncoercive institutions— those which would be most helpful in strengthening the sense of community among the countries concerned. "The Welfare of the individual in society should be recognized as an end in itself and the purpose of all organization, national or international. But the direct effort to promote it may also prove the speediest road to general and enduring peace."[4]

In addition to these two general goals, there are five less general policy goals that emerged from our survey of the situation in the North Atlantic area. They were selected on the basis of two attributes—they are important and they are farther from being achieved than some of the others.

1. *More Responsiveness.* A problem of first importance is the increasing of mutual responsiveness among the countries of the North Atlantic area. We conclude that the area rates rather low in this requirement, compared with what is probably needed for integration even of the pluralistic type. But we found that since the second World War there is some evidence of a trend toward greater responsiveness, at least on the part of the major countries.[5]

Basically, it seems clear that responsiveness between nations can be increased by certain obvious but difficult means—more information about one another, more attention to that information, more joint operations, and more actual contact. We cannot go into a discussion of the whole process of social learning that should be speeded up if progress is to be made along this line. But obviously one of the prime requisites is the willingness of

---

[3] See Chapter II, Section A, 1.
[4] P. E. Corbett, *The Individual and World Society*, Center for Research on World Political Institutions, Princeton University, pub. no. 2, 1953, p. 59.
[5] See Chapter IV, Section B, 2.

people to listen to each other. There still remains an understandable reluctance to do this in any formal way, because to listen implies the possibility of being persuaded; and to be open to persuasion implies the possibility of losing part of a nation's freedom of decision, since there is an expectation that persuasion should be effective at least some of the time.

More concretely, however, some of this reluctance to listen has been overcome in recent years. There has been a great deal of consultation over allocation of expenses, over manpower, over manufacturing contracts, over leadership, and over broad strategy and operating procedure among members of the North Atlantic Treaty Organization. The annual NATO budget review is an unprecedented performance. Members bring in figures covering the economic situation of the country, as well as specific figures on their NATO and non-NATO expenditures and budget. The officials are questioned and cross-questioned on their statements and a thorough analysis is made. Final decisions are made by unanimity, so that various countries obviously make concessions—a very high form of responsiveness. Yet this is not enough. In one recent period of ten days two events occurred that illustrate this point. The Foreign Minister of Norway, Mr. Halvard Lange, was quoted in a responsible newspaper as having said that the great powers must "change their habits of consultation" where smaller members were concerned.[6] He referred to United States decisions that had been characterized by Secretary Dulles as coming close to war, to British refusal to discuss the Cyprus question in NATO, and to French disinclination to talk about the North African problem in NATO. Ten days later the statement issued at the end of the Eden–Eisenhower conferences in Washington said: "We reaffirm that the North Atlantic Treaty is essential to our common security. We regard this association as far more than a military alliance. We welcome the increasing range of consultation in the Council on political and other problems."[7] Institutional devices for making consultation easier and

---

[6] *New York Times*, 23 January 1956, p. 3.

[7] *New York Times*, 2 February 1956, p. 4. This last statement did not necessarily mean that consultation would be broadened to include more of the

more frequent could be multiplied; some of these will be mentioned later.

Another of our findings from the historical cases gives emphasis to this point. We found that for responsiveness there had to be a considerable amount of established political habits, as well as functioning political institutions, favoring mutual communication and consultation. To be effective, these habits and institutions had to insure that messages from other governments would not merely be received, but that this would happen speedily, that they would also be understood, and that they would be given real weight in the process of decision-making.[8] Nothing short of a perceptive study of the decision-making process in the Foreign Offices of at least the major North Atlantic countries would give us real insight into this problem. The main requirement would seem to be a receptive and responsive attitude on the part of the higher officials, backed by an understanding public. Contributing to such a tremendous accomplishment are smaller, almost mechanical, matters that can be more easily dealt with than those involving official attitudes and public opinion. These matters cluster around administrative structures and around the communications within those structures. An example of what we mean is brought out in a recent study of one sector of the French policy-making process. This points out that even when one country perceives clearly another country's different interpretation of the international scene, the differences "sometimes are spoken of in terms of 'clashes of national interests,' which implies a monolithic, immutable nature to state interaction on the basis of which shifts in action cannot easily be forecast and can hardly be explained."[9] Fortunately, in the United States we seem to be more and more aware of the need for

---

members. However, within a month there was a meeting of the large and small countries of NATO which was unprecedented for its openness.

[8] See Chapter II, Section E.

[9] Edgar S. Furniss, Jr., *The Office of the Premier in French Foreign Policy-Making: An Application of Decision-Making Analysis*, Foreign Policy Analysis Project, pub. no. 5, Princeton University, 1954, p. 58. See also pp. 48-49, 56-57, and 59.

studying this process of quick and accurate responsiveness to the international situation.[10]

2. *Greater Capabilities.* The ability to act and to respond we find generally high in the core area (United States and Canada), but we are not sure how high it is in certain other parts of the North Atlantic area.[11] The policy should be to improve responsiveness of the core area and to see that other political units in the area maintain their strength and their responsiveness. This involves both political and economic strength, so that the political instability of the French government, for example, should not be a matter of indifference to those who would promote North Atlantic integration any more than economic instability should be. Since we found that a substantial increase in the capabilities of some or all the units involved will promote amalgamation, there should be an effort to build up not just the core area, but as many of the countries in the whole area as possible. There is a common interest, perceived or not, in seeing that other countries in the area do not suffer serious economic decline—quite apart from the potentially infectious nature of such a setback.

Economic assistance is one way to do this. Military assistance is another, not only because it lightens the burdens of defense against possible aggression but also because, as in the case of France, it helps to lighten the burden of sometimes rebellious colonies. Political support in the United Nations on such issues as colonialism is another way of increasing the capabilities of a country such as France. It is difficult to do this, however, without violating what is usually called domestic jurisdiction. For example, it may be that a colonial situation is almost hopeless, as in Indochina; in that case it might have been best to persuade the French, in the interest of maintaining their maximum strength, to share responsibility in the area. If NATO as an organization, or the United States individually, had taken the

10 See *The Administration of Foreign Affairs and Overseas Operations,* Brookings Institution, Washington, D.C., 1951, esp. p. 12. See also Daniel S. Cheever and H. Field Haviland, Jr., *American Foreign Policy and the Separation of Powers,* Harvard, 1952.

11 See Chapter IV, Section C, 4.

responsibility for defending Indochina, it would have called for a liberal attitude by France toward the concept of domestic jurisdiction.

There is another reason why capabilities may have to be increased within the countries of the North Atlantic area if there should be a rising tide of mass expectation of more governmental services. Such a tide would probably mean also a greater mass participation in politics. This might have two kinds of result. The independence of small countries might be imperiled because their limited capabilities to act might fall short of the claims put upon them. And large countries might be imperiled because of overtaxing the limited capabilities of their governments to perceive and respond to the rising volume of claims that might confront them. If this happened, both small and large countries might be thrown into a crisis at the same time. The governments of small countries would be jeopardized by their lack of power to act, and those of large countries or federations would be jeopardized by their lack of ability to pay enough attention to claims and to respond to them. If this should happen, it would be difficult for the North Atlantic area either to remain in its present political form (separate countries) or to move toward one or more amalgamated governments. Some or all of the area would then suffer from a kind of *immobilisme*.

3. *Greater Range of Mutual Transactions.* Even though the present range of mutual transactions seems quite high and the corresponding institutions rather numerous,[12] one of the main policy goals in the North Atlantic area should be to increase that range. For purposes of integration, the range could hardly be too broad nor the number of transactions too high.

Increasing trade is perhaps the first feasible step, through bilateral or multilateral agreements or even customs unions. Yet we must not overemphasize the economic side: in the judgment of a distinguished economist, "to accept as obviously true the notion that the bonds of allegiance must necessarily be largely economic in character to be strong, or to accept unhesitatingly

[12] See Chapter IV, Section C, 7.

that where the economic entanglements are artificially or naturally strong the political affections will also necessarily become strong, is to reject whatever lessons past experience has for us in this field."[13] Actually, the helpfulness of economic ties may lie largely in the extent to which they function as a form of communication and as visible sources of reward.

Increased exchange of information and ideas should also be promoted. It would be foolhardy to predict that, however mutually unpalatable foreign information and ideas might be, integration would be advanced by their greater exchange. A more accurate way to put it is that integration could hardly be achieved *without* a greater exchange of this sort.

Much the same reasoning applies to the free mobility of persons, which we shall discuss later.[14]

4. *More and Stronger Links of Social Communication.* Although we know little about the "unbroken links" between North Atlantic countries, we concluded in Chapter IV that on the whole they do not seem to be very strong. We can say with more conviction that integration would be promoted if these links could be both increased and strengthened.

It seems obvious to say that all forms of closer communication should be increased if this goal is to be attained. This common-sense approach is supported somewhat by indications from a current piece of research. It will be recalled that the historical cases showed these links to be persons and institutions that had strong connections both horizontally across the boundaries of political units and vertically within those units. When the Institut d'Études Européennes conducted its interviews with French businessmen in 1954,[15] it found that those doing no export business at all supported the proposed European Defense Community in a ratio of 2 to 1; those who did some export, but less than half their total volume of business, supported the

---

[13] Jacob Viner, *The Customs Union Issue,* Carnegie Endowment for International Peace, New York, 1950, p. 105.

[14] Section 5 below.

[15] Preliminary findings communicated by Professor Daniel Lerner, who directed the project.

European Defense Community by 3 to 1; and those whose exporting business was over half their total volume supported the European Defense Community by 6 to 1. The investigators interpret this striking difference not in economic terms, but in terms of exposure to all the major channels of international contact and communication. An "index of foreign exposure" was made and applied. Then it was found that those who rated high in the index of foreign exposure (horizontal) also tended to be more highly exposed to the flow of messages and events in their own national network (vertical). These men, with their horizontal and vertical connections, seem to be one example of the potential "unbroken links" which our studies indicate are so valuable for integration. Other examples could undoubtedly be uncovered, and others eliminated, by further research.

5. *Greater Mobility of Persons.* Freedom of movement across national borders we found to be lacking in the North Atlantic area, generally to such a degree as to be a serious deterrent to further progress in the direction of even a pluralistic security-community.[16]

It is not enough to have a policy goal of simply letting the bars down. That might well be the ultimate goal, but sense of community could be retarded instead of advanced if immigration were opened too completely or too suddenly. Free mobility is the ultimate in direct contact among persons, and direct contact entails risks. Something should be said about that problem, since to avoid the worst dangers should be a part of the policy goal. In spite of the fact that contact is probably the most efficient and permanent method of gaining knowledge about human actions and values, the risks are great. It has often been pointed out that animosities may develop or favorable images may be destroyed by contact. Yet our findings incline us strongly to believe that, where countries in the North Atlantic area are concerned, this risk is unavoidable if we are ever to know whether the threshold of integration can be crossed in the contemporary world. If closer contact causes at first withdrawal into

[16] See Chapter IV, Section C, 10.

oneself, this may be a step that is necessary before inhibitions can be later relaxed.[17]

The problem seems to be, then, largely one of assuring the least possible strain during the early period of contact. Since it would be working against the current to try to keep down the number and intimacy of contacts, it would seem wise to provide for whatever strains can be foreseen. Political judgment would have to be exercised with real sensitivity to make sure that the degree of internationalism being practiced did not exceed the capacity for handling it. For example, when Italian workers are needed in Germany,[18] the European Coal and Steel Community would do well to see that the influx is timed properly, that it does not cause displacement of any significant groups of Germans from the more desirable jobs or the better housing, and that in general the newcomers do not bid too seriously for the scarce economic and social valuables. By the same token, decent living conditions would have to be made available to the immigrants themselves. Much of this, though certainly not all, could be handled by deliberate planning. In short, the risks involved should be foreseen but should not be allowed to slow down any more than absolutely necessary a policy of increasing the exchange of persons, goods, and ideas among the North Atlantic countries.

Another possible approach would be to increase first those types of international mobility, such as travel and study, that involve a minimum of competition or deprivations in the receiving country. This could be done in part by reducing or eliminating the remaining visa requirements in the North Atlantic area. Free mobility with the right to settle, and to compete in the labor market or in other economic activities, could be gradually increased at a later stage.

[17] See the suggestive notion of "self-reference effect" put forth by Harold Lasswell in *The World Revolution of Our Time: A Framework for Basic Policy Research*, Stanford, 1951, p. 32. See also Ralph Linton, "Nativistic Movements," *American Anthropologist*, xlv, no. 2, April-June 1943, pp. 230-240.

[18] An agreement was signed in 1955. *See Manchester Guardian Weekly*, 29 December 1955, p. 7.

B ◈ POLICY AS TO METHODS

Our historical case studies yielded a few valuable clues concerning the ways in which the issue of integration became acute, the nature of leadership in the integration movement, and the types of appeal and methods used in promoting integration. Some of these may have considerable meaning for policy-makers today.

1. *Integration as an Issue.* To learn some of the ways in which the issue of integration became acute in the past may help in observing the process in the North Atlantic area, and in deciding how and whether to avoid or to seek such a sharpening of the issue.

A. We found that the issue of integration became acute during a double assault on the habits of behavior of people in the area about to be integrated. They were emerging into a new "way of life," and this way of life was being challenged from outside: men were made aware of the extent to which the new way had already developed and of the extent to which they had already become attached to it. In addition, it helped if a new generation was coming into political power at the time. But the first two conditions were more important.[19]

While we identified a distinctive way of life in most of the North Atlantic area, it was not a newly-emerging one except in two ways: widespread acceptance by national governments of substantial responsibility for economic welfare, and the new realization that wars are almost certain to be totally destructive for all parties to any conflict. It is debatable, however, whether the latter realization actually affects the habits of most people in the area, or affects only the consciousness of leaders and thinkers.

As for the challenge, that has been present to a varying degree since 1945 in the form of the Soviet Union, but the same sort of challenge was also present from about 1935 onward in the form of Germany. It can safely be said that the non-Soviet, non-Nazi values in the distinctive way of life were better appreciated

---

[19] See Chapter III, Section D, first four paragraphs.

because of these challenges. In a sense, there is today a double challenge: both Soviet Communism in particular and atomic weapons in general. The challenge may well have affected popular feeling about national sovereignty more than has been revealed, but either deeper research than we have seen so far, or more political experiments, would be required in order to find out. This is one good reason why experiments with such organizations as the European Coal and Steel Community should not only be launched but should also be carefully studied as they operate.

B. In undertaking political experiments at the international level, we should be warned by history that local political issues were always dominant in the early stages of amalgamation or integration movements. The issue arose mainly when people demanded greater capabilities, greater performance, and greater responsiveness from their governments than those governments were able to provide. Integration of either kind was first considered as a means to furthering these ends, and not as an end in itself.[20]

At first glance, this conclusion seems to conflict with our finding that amalgamation came about not because governments had become weaker or more inefficient, but instead after a substantial increase in capabilities.[21] There is no conflict, however. The point is that in the *early* stages the issue of amalgamation or integration was made acute by governmental weaknesses, but integration (either amalgamated or pluralistic) actually did not take place until capabilities had increased. In other words, integration from strength is more to be expected than integration from weakness, although weakness is sometimes more likely to raise the issue of integration in the first place. People are not apt to demand a larger political unit simply because their own country is failing to perform well enough those services that it is basically able to perform; they are more likely to do this after the government has put its house in order and has the self-confidence from which to negotiate with other governments.

20 See Chapter III, Section D, early portions.
21 See Chapter II, Section A, 2, E.

It may well be that the North Atlantic area (as well as some other parts of the world) is passing through the early stage rapidly, at least with regard to the most important single function of a government—self-preservation, or national defense. We should not assume, however, that the area is anywhere nearly past the point where local issues are not of prime importance. While it may be impossible for the national government to supply defense properly, it can still supply most other services that are expected.

The lesson here is threefold for those who wish to promote integration. Every country in the area has an interest in seeing that the capabilities of every other country do not fall too far below demands in the eyes of its own citizens. And no national politician can neglect, or appear to neglect, domestic issues in favor of international issues, no matter how well he knows that the latter may be prerequisite to the long-run solution of the former. For example, if a French premier wants to be effective in helping to extend the powers of The Six to an atomic energy pool, he will first make sure that inflation in France is given real attention. Even further than this, politicians must tie international issues to the satisfaction of domestic needs insofar as possible if they are to promote integration. That is, the international policy must have a payoff in terms of demands already existing on the domestic scene. Robert Schuman advertised the proposed European Coal and Steel Community not alone on grounds that it would make war between France and Germany "not only unthinkable, but in actual fact impossible";[22] it would also leave the owner of a business "free to organize his business, to draw profits from his own personal skill," and "in no case will the workers' standard of living have to be lowered; this is an absolute rule." But more than this: "The Authority will see that . . . production is expanded while prices are kept at the lowest levels."[23] In the North Atlantic area, as elsewhere, the judgment of the politician may do more to find ways of tying

[22] *New York Times*, 11 May 1950, p. 11.

[23] Robert Schuman, speaking to the Consultative Assembly of the Council of Europe, 10 August 1950, app. II of *The Council of Europe and the Schuman Plan*, Council of Europe, Strasbourg, 1952, pp. 25, 28, and 23.

international issues to domestic demands than the skill of the research man.

c. Another finding was closely related to this last: that the issue of amalgamation played only a minor role at the outset of an integration movement. Rather, a functional approach was used, whether it led to amalgamation or pluralism.[24]

This indicates that today also campaigns for amalgamation may be much less effective than campaigns for pluralism. With the latter, the preservation of national sovereignty can be stressed. There is no doubt that the appeal of national sovereignty is very strong today, even though it may be weaker than it once was. When a major country joins an international organization, it hopes to have a large part in its policy, if not to dominate it. One pat example of this is the result of a poll in 1943, when Americans were asked about an international police force. Seventy-seven percent favored creating a worldwide force; but when those in favor were queried as to the size of such a force, the number favoring one that could police any country (including the United States), and would be large enough to do so effectively, fell to 14%.[25] More recently, the same sort of phenomenon was demonstrated in a German poll. When West Germans were asked, in September 1955, whether they believed that the European countries could as a practical matter form a United States, 59% answered yes and 17% no. When they were asked whether they would vote for such a thing, they were even more positive (68% yes and 7% no). But when they were asked whether a European Parliament should have the last word on important questions that also concerned Germany, 41% thought the German Parliament should have the last word, and only 33% the European Parliament; 10% said "it depends" and the other 16% said they did not know. A generally similar vote was recorded when people were asked whether the European Parlia-

[24] See Chapter III, Section D.

[25] This and other polls on the subject are analyzed in *An International Police Force and Public Opinion*, by William Buchanan, Herbert E. Krugman, and R. W. Van Wagenen, Center for Research on World Political Institutions, Princeton University, pub. no. 3, 1954.

ment's decisions should be binding on Germany, or only if the German Parliament agreed to be bound.[26] In other words, the Germans were in favor of a confederation perhaps, but not a federation.

This finding does not mean, of course, that those who advocate and work toward amalgamation of the North Atlantic area are either useless or detrimental. At the least, they help to protect those people who hold a less extreme position on this issue from being attacked for extremism. And at the most, they may be right in judging that times have changed so radically that amalgamation is a much less extreme proposal than it would have looked a few years ago.

2. *Leadership.* Concerning the leadership of integration movements, we learned three noteworthy things from our historical studies.

A. We found that in the early stages of integration movements the leadership was typically furnished, not by any single social class, but by a cross-class coalition, and that such a coalition usually united some of the "most outside of the insiders" in a political alliance with the "most inside of the outsiders."[27]

To apply this insight to the contemporary North Atlantic area would first of all require a careful sociological definition of "insiders" and "outsiders" today. This should be followed by a study of the backgrounds of the leaders of the Atlantic Union movement, as well as of leaders who favor integration without union. Since this has not been done, the most that can be said here is that the movement certainly has some "insiders" among its leadership, but that they are not numerous. The movement has not yet become a major issue anywhere, especially in Europe. Therefore it is difficult to know what a person signing a document such as the Declaration of Atlantic Unity[28] is actually

---

[26] *Der Europa-Rat (II)*, study no. 220 of the Institut für Demoskopie, Allensbach am Bodensee, mimeographed, 1955, pp. 1, 3, 5, and 6.

[27] See Chapter III, Section D.

[28] This declaration, with 244 signers from eight countries, urges closer integration of NATO countries as quickly as possible, although it does not call for federation. It was published in March 1955 by a group of citizens

willing to do if he comes into a position of governmental responsibility. Guy Mollet, for example, is a signer who subsequently
became premier of France. While he is known to be actively
pan-European, he has yet to demonstrate whether he will find
a strong pan-Atlantic policy consistent or feasible. There are
also others who were insiders in the governmental sense at one
time and who signed after they left office—such as former President Harry S. Truman. Still others are active supporters and
also highly active in politics—such as Senator Estes Kefauver of
Tennessee.

In policy terms, the leadership of the movement would probably do well to make sure that future leaders represented various
social classes. It would seem especially wise to bring in genuine
leaders of new and rising social groups that seem to be in the
process of exerting greater influence in politics—such as labor,
white collar employees, scientists and technicians, suburbanites,
and in some countries farmers. Just which groups are in fact
likely to exercise increasing influence in politics in particular
countries is often a matter of known sociological and political
trends and it is a not infrequent subject of research.[29]

B. The second thing we learned about leadership is more directly relevant to policy. It is the finding that integration was
promoted in its early stages by political coalitions (and occasionally even by involuntary cooperation) between conservatives and
liberals or radicals. Leaders could and did differ widely in their
values and their political philosophies, provided only that they
could work together, or at least somehow cumulate their contributions.[30]

Those who claim to lead in the early movement toward in-

---

closely associated with the Atlantic Union Committee. It is the only list
available of persons on both sides of the Atlantic who strongly support North
Atlantic integration. While strong supporters, not all the signers are active
in this cause.

[29] For example, on the growing importance of the suburbanites and other
groups on the vote in American politics, see Samuel Lubell, *The Future of
American Politics*, Harpers, 1951. See also Louis Harris, *Is There a Republican Majority?*, Harpers, 1954.

[30] See Chapter III, Section D.

tegration of the North Atlantic area are indeed drawn from both the moderate Right and Left in all the large countries of the area. The radicals of the extreme Left and extreme Right are the only political leaders who are firmly against it. But in the United States and Canada, the liberals (as this vague term is generally understood in the United States) are more numerous and more prominent, while in most of the main European countries the weight seems to be more on the conservative side. There is a reason, however, why the American leadership is somewhat weighted on the liberal side. The traditionally liberal party is out of office, and the Republicans in Congress are waiting for Administration policy before committing themselves on paper, so as not to embarrass their party. At any rate, we have no evidence from either side of the Atlantic that the pro- and anti-integration issue (to the extent that it exists) breaks down along liberal–conservative lines.

The only policy suggestion on this point is that the movement needs more Republican support in the United States—perhaps a revival of the Vandenberg tradition—and generally more support from liberal and socialist elements in Europe. A practical way to bring this about might be to decide what the most salient issues are for American conservatives and for European liberals and socialists, respectively, and to link these specific interests with the program of integration. For example, if it should turn out that conservatives were intensely preoccupied with problems of national security, they might come to see North Atlantic federation as a means to overcome the unavoidable deficiency in manpower of any one country alone. Likewise, if European socialists should turn out to be most preoccupied with social security, they might under certain conditions come to consider North Atlantic federation as a means to a possible North Atlantic social security system on a federal-state basis.

c. Active and direct popular support played only a minor role in the early stages of the integration movements that we studied.[31] However, there were in the early stages two special sources of

---

[31] See Chapter III, Section D.

opposition: certain rural groups (peasants and farmers) and privileged groups. Yet neither of them, we found, exercised decisive influence in the long run.[32] It is not surprising that we also found the proponents of integration often making concessions to these rural groups. Where this was not done, the long-run prospects of integration usually were distinctly unfavorable.[33] In short, the peasants and farmers seemed to be the hardest group to convince, and yet they needed to be convinced for long-run success. Making concessions to the privileged groups was standard procedure. By "privileged groups" we mean those classes (or sometimes regions) which exercised special influence, such as the aristocracy. But making these concessions seemed to have only a small, though distinct, effect on the ultimate outcome of the integration movement.[34]

On the contemporary scene, do we have rough equivalents of these two groups? The modern peasant or farmer in France is in some ways different from his nineteenth-century counterpart in Germany and Italy, but he may still be just as different from his urban co-nationals today as he was in the nineteenth century. We would need to know more about changes in the pattern of land ownership and about differences in attitude between owners and workers in at least the major countries. The rural population is a much smaller proportion of the total in the North Atlantic area than it was about a hundred years ago. Yet that population may be influential far beyond what its numbers would indicate in matters of this sort—somewhat as the political influence of American farmers has been increased by the disproportionately large representation of rural areas in Congress. Peasants and farmers have not yet been directly affected in a serious way by steps toward European integration, and a test might come if the projected "vegetable pool" for the freer interchange of European agricultural products were actively promoted.[35] As for the "privileged classes," the changes from the nineteenth century have been massive. In any case, for political purposes the

[32] See Chapter III, Section F.
[33] See Chapter III, Section F.　　[34] See Chapter III, Section F.
[35] See S. L. Mansholt, "Toward European Integration: Beginnings in Agriculture," *Foreign Affairs*, October 1952, pp. 106-113.

main thing is to know which groups feel that they would lose substantially by integration. This is a problem which calls for a combination of objective research and skilled political judgment.

There has been no such study with regard to North Atlantic integration as an issue except for the 1953 Roper poll cited earlier. It showed, for the United States only, that there was no significant difference of opinion concerning a union of democratic nations (closest to North Atlantic integration) between the various economic classes, age groups, educational levels, political party preference, or geographic groups.[36] Even more indirect and doubtful evidence comes from another poll. This tested sentiment for and against Western European union in September 1952. It showed little variation between groups, though there was some indication that support for both integration in general and for amalgamation in particular was greater among the better educated and the economically and professionally better situated.[37] There is not, however, enough information of even this tangential sort upon which to base policy recommendations at present.

In order to assess the strength and location of their adversaries, leaders of integration movements in their early stages will naturally, if they have the facilities for doing so, inquire into the attitudes of people who think they would lose by North Atlantic integration. But, in view of our findings, they might look with special care into attitudes in the rural areas. It may be that the only reason success has correlated with active peasant and farmer support so closely in the past is that by the time those areas had concurred, all others were already in support. If that is not the

[36] *Survey of American Public's Attitudes Toward Certain Kinds of World Cooperation as a Means to Peace*, August 1953, by the firm of Elmo Roper, pp. 79-85. This represents the details of the poll that was summarized as Elmo Roper, "American Attitudes on World Organization," *Public Opinion Quarterly*, Winter 1953-1954, pp. 405-442.

[37] Office of the (U.S.) High Commission for Germany, *Public Opinion in Western Europe*, 1953, pp. 11-14 and 187 and 190. The poll was conducted in Great Britain, France, Italy, the Netherlands, and West Germany and covered both West European "union" in general and a West European government in particular.

case, however, there may be special advantage in concentrating upon the rural areas even today. Intelligent politicians will also be ready to make concessions without giving away the essence of their policy. There are devices for doing this in the modern world, even though the problem with regard to rural areas is a complicated one.[38] For example, in the United States many problems of agriculture have been successfully dealt with by federal rather than local institutions in recent years; price supports are a case in point.

Finally, while promoters of an integration movement should not be surprised to find only slight support among the masses in the early stages, this should not deter them from starting early to gain that support, because we shall see later that for eventual success broad popular participation has been crucially important.

3. *Major Appeals.* Among the various appeals used for spreading the idea of integration in the cases we studied, there were three that turned out to be especially important, and a fourth that is of particular interest because it was, surprisingly, unimportant.

A. The appeal for more individual rights and liberties, or for more rights and liberties for groups, was the most decisive one that appeared, and the appeal for greater equality was nearly as decisive.[39] These can be discussed together. It may not be so obvious that appeals should be made today along these same lines. Has this appeal become less potent in view of the fact that rights and liberties (including equality) were substantially achieved during the nineteenth century in the North Atlantic area? Or has the definition of rights, liberties, and equality altered in the twentieth century? We think the latter is the case.

In the eighteenth and nineteenth centuries these terms were understood in their classical political sense—such matters as protection against arbitrary treatment by authority, especially procedural rights in connection with arrest and punishment, and

---

[38] See the chapter on "L'Organisation des Marchés Agricoles Européens," pp. 217-232 in Dotation Carnegie, *L'Integration Economique de L'Europe,* 1953.

[39] See Chapter III, Section E, 1.

freedom of speech and assembly. But over the past few decades, and especially since the opening of the twentieth century, the list of "human rights" has grown considerably, at least in the Western world. We pointed out this break with the past when we discussed the distinctive "way of life" in the North Atlantic area.[40] In particular, many economic and social expectations about basic standards of food, housing, employment, and educational opportunity have moved from the private into the public sphere.

Thus liberties are becoming merged with opportunities, and social and economic rights are becoming political. Legislation dealing with these expectations is gradually tending to develop them into political rights, and the fundamentals of this legislation are now accepted by all major political parties in the North Atlantic area except the Communists. The wide international support for the United Nations Declaration of Human Rights, and the debate about the contents of a proposed Convention on Human Rights, are both evidence of this continuing process. The very fact that several countries feel strongly that such a Convention should contain guaranteed economic rights is an indication; and this was the essence of the argument about it in the United Nations.[41]

It is in terms of these newly emerging rights and liberties that we find substantial groups in all North Atlantic countries whose needs and expectations are still a long way from fulfillment. The politicians in each country often know best who these people are. If integration is to appeal to these groups, it will have to be conceived and presented as a further advance toward greater rights and liberties and toward the greater measure of equality

[40] See Chapter IV, Section C, 3.

[41] It is widely held that there is a real difference between political rights on the one hand and economic and social rights on the other, and therefore the United States (among others) has held out against a single Convention embodying both sets. See Mrs. Eleanor Roosevelt's reasoning in the United Nations on this point. *UN Gen. Assembly, Off. Records, Plenary Meetings,* 6th Session, 1951-1952, 374th meeting, 4 Feb. 1952, p. 504. More recently, the United States Government has gone farther and opposed conventions on either subject, even failing to ratify the Genocide Convention after 50 other countries had done so.

that comes with them. On the other hand, taking political rights in their classic eighteenth- and nineteenth-century sense, there are few if any major groups in the North Atlantic area that feel especially abused.[42]

B. Appealing to the development, strengthening, or defense of a distinctive way of life was found to be quite effective in the past.[43] This appeal is already used widely by the proponents of North Atlantic integration, and it appears to be a sound one. We have already mentioned the "way of life" common to most of the North Atlantic area and also the double challenge to it from Soviet Communism and from the danger of atomic arms.[44] All we need to add here is that as the issue of integration comes to the forefront because of the challenge to a distinctive way of life, it would be effective policy to put this situation in the form of an appeal for closer association—not simply military, but also political. This might be especially effective if people were made more aware of the speed and scope of the changes that have been occurring in the area during the last few decades. Since the Atlantic area is clearly the nucleus of strength against Communism and is also clearly a part of "western civilization," this appeal could also emphasize the need for tightening the bonds within this nucleus as a means of defending western civilization in general.

C. The appeal that deserves special mention because, surprisingly, it did not turn out to be an effective one in the cases we studied, is the appeal that greater power would result from amalgamation.[45] This refers to total national power for the amalgamated unit that would be greater than the power which could be mustered by adding all the units together if they remained separate. It also refers to power as an end in itself, or

---

[42] Spain and Portugal may be exceptions, although even this is not certain. Algerians are clearly an exception, and the North–South Irish question (particularly as it applies to the Catholic counties of North Ireland) may be another. But the French Canadians, certainly a major group, are quite well settled into a generally satisfactory situation.

[43] See Chapter III, Section E, 1.

[44] See Section B, 1, A, above.

[45] See Chapter III, Section E, 1.

at least to power that is stressed more prominently than the goals which it is supposed to serve.

Sometimes this appeal may be discerned in United States support of NATO, even though amalgamation is not involved and the rationale is that we are building up the area as a means of being able to negotiate from strength. Unless the objects of negotiation are carefully specified and quite stable, this kind of appeal can come very close to suggesting power as an end in itself. Those who promote North Atlantic integration might do well to stress power as a means toward more rights and liberties, toward greater equality, and toward the defense of a distinctive way of life. It may be much more important, even, to gain closer unity on the special values in the "way of life" being defended than to emphasize the drive for greater power to defend that way of life.

4. *Methods of Spreading.* Among the various political methods used to promote integration in the more advanced stages of a movement, four have special interest for us in terms of current application.

A. The most decisive method was to bring about strong and direct popular participation in an amalgamation movement or (still later) in the operation of amalgamated institutions.[46] (The first part of this finding could also be applied to pluralistic movements.)

In the mid-twentieth century, the policy implied by this finding is clear because of the even greater need in mature democracies for interesting masses of people in any successful political movement. But how can the leaders of the movement do this?

One way is to work, not only with the people directly, but also directly with decision-makers. In the United States, the Atlantic Union Committee, which includes a number of influential persons, has been instrumental in having a resolution introduced in Congress. This calls for a United States invitation to NATO countries to explore at a conference of political delegates "to what extent their peoples might further unite within

---

[46] See Chapter III, Section E, 2.

the framework of the United Nations, and agree to form, federally or otherwise, a defense, economic and political union."[47] As of February 1956, there were 17 Senators and 72 Congressmen listed as sponsors, and another 156 Congressmen had expressed their support of the resolution.[48] Yet no political party has adopted the program in its platform, either in the United States or elsewhere. Indeed the United States Secretary of State does not favor the resolution in its present form, advising instead the use of existing organizations in Western Europe and the Atlantic area for promoting the increased unity which the State Department strongly favors.[49]

The movement cannot be said to have a mass appeal as yet. Even the organizations of private citizens which have been built up to help promote the nonmilitary aspects of NATO are extremely cautious. The Atlantic Treaty Association, made up of national citizens' organizations (such as The American Council on NATO and the Belgian NATO Committee) met for the first time in June 1955. It approved a resolution expressing "the hope that the forthcoming Atlantic parliamentary conference may pave the way for meetings of Atlantic parliamentarians at regular intervals in the interest of the Atlantic Community." But in doing so, it discussed and deleted some wording which would have implied approval of the idea that such meetings might lead to the creation of a Consultative Assembly for NATO similar to that of the Council of Europe.[50]

Earlier we pointed out that expectation of joint economic reward seemed to be a condition helpful to pluralism and essential to amalgamation.[51] There is a corollary to this that also arises from our historical cases: that the fulfillment of *all* those

[47] S.C.R. 12, 84th Congress, 1st Session. It continued actively before the 2nd Session.

[48] Interview with Mr. Walden Moore, former Executive Secretary of the Atlantic Union Committee, in New York.

[49] See letter from Secretary of State John Foster Dulles to Senator Estes Kefauver, dated 22 August 1955, published in *Freedom and Union*, vol. 10, no. 9, October 1955, p. 3.

[50] Atlantic Treaty Association, "Minutes of the First Assembly," mimeographed, p. 14 and p. 12.

[51] See Chapter II, Section C, 1.

expectations was not necessary for either type of integration. At the least, however, a tangible "down payment" was needed.[52]

If a policy is adopted of increasing direct popular support by raising expectations of gain, there is a natural fear that if those expectations are not fulfilled the movement will fail. If our finding can be applied here, it seems to mean that both promoters and opponents of integration have good reason to worry somewhat less about the dangers of frustrated expectation than they are inclined to do. We do not mean to say that expectations would not have to have any relation to the probabilities, and that planners could neglect to estimate the impact of economic gain and loss. But we do mean that it might be equally important for planners to estimate in detail the network of expectations within the North Atlantic area. They would do well to learn all they possibly can about the actual extent and nature of expectations in each country—the structure of those expectations among political, social, and economic classes, and the comparative expectations as between countries. If expectations were found to be higher than probabilities, policymakers would not have to feel completely discouraged by lack of "realism" in their plans, so long as the gap between expectation and fulfillment did not become too large.

It is important to avoid "gross deception"[53] through exaggerated promises, without becoming bogged down in endless discussion of all the pros and cons. Perhaps "it is as much the fact of working toward a convincing goal as the realization of the goal itself which improves attitudes and morale."[54] But we do not agree that it is "doubtful if a full clarification of the advantages and disadvantages of economic integration or a careful planning of the various steps by which such an integration

[52] See Chapter II, Section C, 1.

[53] "It would be a gross deception of the public to think that what would happen, if we were united with Europe, would be an immediate increase of well-being for everybody."—D. W. Brogan, "The Idea of European Union," *Eighth Montague Burton Lecture on International Relations*, University of Leeds, 1949, p. 10.

[54] Theodore Geiger and H. van B. Cleveland, *Making Western Europe Defensible*, National Planning Association, Washington, D.C., Planning Pamphlet no. 74, August 1951, p. 30.

may be approached will promote progress in this direction. The theory that a reconciliation of interests can more easily be achieved if all the economic consequences of alternative actions have been forecast is probably not a very realistic one. Great changes in the relations between countries may perhaps occur more easily if undertaken as a leap in the dark."[55] Promoters of the movement may take their choice of tactics, but they must not inflate their promises beyond the possibility of at least some partial fulfillment.

B. It may seem a paradox to find that the next most effective method of promoting an amalgamation movement was to use the pluralistic approach, usually coupled with specific promises to respect the independence and sovereignty of the political units concerned.[56] To emphasize over-all amalgamation was generally more of a burden than a help to the movement.[57] We have already discussed a related finding—that the issue of amalgamation played only a minor role at the outset of an integration movement. This carried through into the later stages of the movement also.

If a sudden jump to amalgamation is highly improbable, and if it is unwise to stress amalgamation as a goal but wise instead to emphasize national sovereignty, what room is left for progress toward amalgamation? It seems to us that functionalism offers perhaps the best intermediate ground for approaching either pluralism or amalgamation. A functional organization does effect partial amalgamation in a very small way by delegating some governmental functions from the participating units on a low or high level of decision-making.[58] And functionalism does not make a point of impinging upon national sovereignty. A good example today at a low level is provided by the Universal Postal Union, where decisions in this international organization are made and put into effect on certain postal matters without prior reference

[55] Ingvar Svennilson, "Problems of Economic Integration," in Arthur W. Macmahon, ed., *Federalism: Mature and Emergent*, Doubleday, 1955, p. 458.
[56] See Chapter III, Section E, 2.
[57] See Chapter III, Section E, 2, last paragraph.
[58] See Chapter III, Section B.

to the member governments. An example at a higher level is afforded by the European Coal and Steel Community, where the decisions taken without prior formal reference to member governments are of a more far-reaching sort because the function handled is more controversial and more important. We are not making the familiar distinction between political and nonpolitical functions, because this breaks down under observation. We follow general usage, however, by calling a functional arrangement one which has an operating body of some kind to carry out the function and which has no single political superior governing its actions.

What light did our historical studies throw upon this functional approach? We found that, if they were carefully limited, functional organizations with a few members might well be used as an approach to either kind of integration. Amalgamation could be approached functionally, step by step, and this method also seemed less hazardous than an attempt at immediate all-out amalgamation. But there seemed to be no evidence that functionalism, as such, would make any major contribution to the success or failure of an integration movement.[59] This means that functionalism seems a safer approach to integration than a more ambitious one like sudden federalism, but it also means that functionalism is no guarantee of eventual success.

Policy implications are numerous. Promoters of integration need not try to avoid functionalism in the belief that it gets in the way of later over-all amalgamation. Again, we find that campaigning for over-all amalgamation may well be less effective than campaigning for specific functional organizations. Functionalism should not be regarded as a broad highway leading toward amalgamation, although we are not prepared to say the same about pluralism.

Since it is within the power of governments today in the North Atlantic area to strengthen or weaken functional arrangements, to create new ones and to abolish old ones, this is a field where the future can be influenced to quite some extent.

[59] See Chapter III, Section B.

In particular, NATO—as a limited functional organization—could be strengthened greatly.[60]

Finally, the fact that small functional organizations had not been a hindrance to later amalgamation of a larger area helps to answer one of the leading questions of international organization—whether regional organizations hamper the later development of more nearly universal organizations. Our findings suggest that they are more likely to help than to hinder. This arises from historical experience with core areas;[61] those cores were not regional international organizations, but they were even tighter, so that the point is even more clear. An example is the amalgamation first of England, and then of England and Wales, and then of England–Wales and Scotland.

The main value of functional organizations today may well be in their side-effects, especially in forming habits of communication and responsiveness of the kind we discussed earlier. Obviously such organizations also help to increase the "range of different common functions and services, with the organizations to carry them out" which we discussed earlier.[62] For example, a study group of the Royal Institute of International Affairs cites the opinion of some observers that it may be optimistic to think that "NATO will learn to do one job by doing another." Yet the study group itself concludes: "In fact, the experience of the organization so far suggests that it is not too optimistic. Such are the ramifications of defense policy in the modern State that governments which really cooperate intimately in defense matters will be automatically led to cooperation in political and economic matters."[63]

Another judgment would be that functional organizations of a nonmilitary type are likely to be more effective in promoting integration. They are likely to appear more as sources of reward than as means for distributing burdens.

[60] We shall say more about this in Section B, 4, D, below.
[61] See Chapter III, Section A, fourth paragraph.
[62] See Chapter IV, Section C, 7.
[63] *Atlantic Alliance: NATO's Role in the Free World*, Report by a Study Group of the Royal Institute of International Affairs, London, 1952, p. 100.

c. If, as we have just implied, the pluralistic approach is more promising at the present time, another of our findings creates quite a problem for those who are now promoting amalgamation. We found that the task of eliminating rival plans at a later stage became crucial for promoters of an integration movement. In addition to acquiring broad support and overcoming apathy and opposition, leaders of those movements had to get people to make up their minds. They had to make the integration issue paramount in politics. They had to link the remaining urgent local pressures and issues to it, and they had to present eventually the practical approach to integration in terms of a single political plan, eliminating all competing approaches to it.[64]

What course of action does this leave for current proponents of amalgamation? Unless they want to take a chance that the interim step of pluralism can be shortened greatly or even jumped, they may feel that they are jeopardizing the whole integration movement by promoting the idea of federation (amalgamation). We think there is a way out of their dilemma—one which, indeed, some of the main proponents of North Atlantic integration are taking. Instead of opposing those who are working for limited integration (in the popular sense; pluralistic integration in our sense), they might concentrate on opposing rival programs which are far more clearly a hindrance to North Atlantic integration. Two of these are isolationism and an alliance limited strictly to military functions. By showing the inadequacy of these nonintegration programs for making progress toward the elimination of war, they might at least throw the spotlight upon integration plans of either one type or the other. Little needs to be said these days about isolationism, but we do have something more to say about military alliances.

D. In fact, another significant finding was that a military alliance turned out to be a relatively poor pathway toward amalgamation,[65] and presumably also toward pluralism. Closely related to this, we found evidence that the presence of excessive

---

[64] See Chapter III, Section F, end.   [65] See Chapter III, Section E, 2.

military commitments—excessive in the sense that they were felt at the time to bring considerably more burdens than rewards— had a disintegrative effect.[66]

These findings tell us to beware of considering NATO as a purely military alliance, and to be sure that rewards like security and prestige balance as nearly as possible such burdens as taxation and the military draft. They support the policy of those who would strengthen the political, economic, and social features of the Organization. Clearly NATO is chiefly a military organization, built in the first place to counter an outside military threat. But if our finding is valid, and if policy-makers are working toward integration, they should be looking beyond the glare of the Soviet headlights and into the dark area behind, at a future time when the Soviet threat may not furnish the cohesive force which it did in 1949. They should look within NATO for signs of binding forces that may have appeared since the organization began. Planners might find that they could move ahead more vigorously if they dropped what may be a tacit assumption that both the danger of an East–West war and the opportunity for integrating the North Atlantic area will disappear at the same moment.

Meanwhile, NATO calls for intimate cooperation. One close observer found in 1954 that "it is in the process of building up an adequate defense that subtle encroachments on national sovereignty have been occurring."[67] Although this observer believes that "no very great progress has been made, rapid progress in the political sphere was not to be expected." To illustrate the beginning that has been made, he points out that "national authorities have submitted to independent reviews of their capabilities and of at least some of their plans, and . . . national policy has undoubtedly felt the influence of allied activities in many subtle ways."[68] When each country has to bring its national accounts before the other members of the organization and subject itself to cross-questioning and analysis at the annual

---

[66] See Chapter II, Section D, third and fourth paragraphs.
[67] J. D. Warne, *N.A.T.O. and Its Prospects*, Praeger, 1954, p. 49.
[68] *idem.*

review, freedom of action is considerably limited. The political and economic interdependence of the members becomes constantly greater as requirements and capabilities are reconciled in the broad areas of production, manpower, and finance.[69]

An interest in building up the political and economic side of NATO has not been entirely lacking from the very start, to judge from pronouncements of government officials. Lester Pearson, for example, made the point for Canada at the signing ceremony: "This Treaty, though born of fear and frustration, must however lead to positive social, economic and political achievements if it is to live."[70] Interest in following up this line of policy has been considerable, though secondary to the military side. Not only does the American press give this impression clearly, but there is tangible evidence. A special consultant, Dr. H. J. Reinink, of the Netherlands, was appointed in 1954 to study the possibilities of cultural cooperation among the members. A working group in Labour Mobility has already reported. And the so-called Pearson Committee to consider the further strengthening of the North Atlantic community, and especially the implementation of Article 2,[71] has been in operation since 1952.

> Lord Ismay, the Secretary-General of NATO, wrote in his latest report that Article 2 "contains the fundamental goals of the Treaty—the attainment by the fourteen countries of 'conditions of stability and well-being' and 'strengthening of their free institutions.' The military effort, urgent as that is, represents one of the means, but not all, to achieve that end. Should the risk of aggression become less pressing

[69] For a clear description of the complexity of international programming within NATO, by one who was closely associated with the process, see George A. Lincoln and Associates, *Economics of National Security*, Prentice-Hall, 2nd. edn., 1954, chap. xx.

[70] U. S. Department of State, General Foreign Policy Series, no. 10, *The Signing of the North Atlantic Treaty*, Washington, D.C., 4 April 1949, p. 9.

[71] "The Parties will contribute toward the further development of peaceful and friendly international relations by strengthening their free institutions, by bringing about a better understanding of the principles upon which these institutions are founded, and by promoting conditions of stability and well-being. They will seek to eliminate conflict in their international economic policies and will encourage economic collaboration between any and all of them."—Article 2, in full.

than it is today, it may be discovered that Article 2 is the real battlefield. . . . We touch here one one of the profound reasons why so many of the peoples of the member countries show moderate interest in NATO. They are ready to accept the Atlantic Alliance as a form of insurance policy against armed attack, but they are not yet prepared to recognize it as a means of achieving progress in more fruitful fields of human endeavor. It is up to the Council to correct this error. . . . The work will be slow, uphill and often frustrating. But it is worth any effort. . . ."[72]

Apart from the appointment in May 1956 of a distinguished three-man commission[73] to make recommendations on greater NATO activity in non-military fields, there has thus far been little tangible progress within NATO to report. Earlier Lord Ismay himself had written: "In the social field . . . the extension of transatlantic cooperation seemed unlikely and, in fact, the Council have not found it possible to make any headway."[74] Nevertheless, the Lisbon Declaration of 1952 is still one of the organization's main guides, and it stated that the "members of the Council look forward to the time when the main energies of their association can be less concentrated on defence and more fully devoted to cooperation in other fields. . . ."[75] This is present United States policy as indicated by Secretary of State Dulles in his New York speech and subsequent news conference on this subject in late April[76] and implied by President Eisenhower when he said in his Baylor University address that "it is idle to talk of community of interest with them [liberty-loving people in other lands] in measures for defense, without recognizing community of interest with them in that which is to be defended."[77] By June, the three-man committee mentioned earlier had drafted

[72] *NATO: The First Five Years, 1949-1954*, Utrecht, 1954, p. 159.
[73] Halvard M. Lange, Gaetano Martino, and Lester B. Pearson, the Foreign Ministers of Norway, Italy, and Canada.
[74] *ibid.*, p. 153.
[75] The Declaration appears in *Department of State Bulletin*, vol. xxvi, no. 663, 10 March 1952, p. 368.
[76] See *New York Times*, 24 April 1956, p. 14, and 25 April 1956, p. 10.
[77] *New York Times*, 26 May 1956, p. 6.

a questionnaire to be sent to each of the Foreign Ministers of the member countries. This is said to contain a question exploring the extent to which the members would be willing to be guided by a majority view within the Council of Ministers in developing national policies.[78] Answers to this and to the economic and social questions on the list may throw considerable light upon the conviction behind the statements of U.S. officials and others—a conviction which will have to be strong if progress is to be made toward integration.

There are signs of progress in that direction from quarters that are pushing NATO from the outside. This, too, is slow. Their main achievement so far has been to convene a meeting of members of parliament from NATO countries which met in July 1955 at Paris. Of the 175 parliamentarians attending from all fifteen NATO countries, a few were established leaders, but most were not, including the United States delegation of six Congressmen. This meeting recommended an Atlantic Parliamentary Assembly and set up a continuing committee looking toward the possibility of an official consultative assembly for NATO; this could either be appointed from among parliamentarians, like the Consultative Assembly of the Council of Europe, or it could eventually be an elected body.[79]

Several other concrete suggestions have been made.[80] The Ministerial meetings of the North Atlantic Council itself might be used for wider and deeper discussion of nonmilitary matters. More of this is taking place, according to Lester Pearson, Ca-

---

[78] See *New York Times*, 22 June 1956, pp. 1 and 3.

[79] There are dangers in having such a body, especially if it is an elected one, unless its duties are clear and significant. A survey was recently conducted by the *Rheinischer Merkur* among West German delegates to the three existing international consultative assemblies. The objective was to learn whether they favored a change from the appointment of assembly delegates to a system of direct election. While an overwhelming majority favored such a change, one contrary opinion is of particular interest: Herr Gerstenmaier (C.D.U.) President of the Bundestag, felt that as long as an elected body had no specific duties and sphere of competence, its election would only confound hopes and disillusion the public about the idea of closer European union.—*Rheinischer Merkur*, Köln, 16 December 1955, p. 4.

[80] These are outlined by Norman Padelford in "Political Cooperation in the North Atlantic Community," *International Organization*, IX, 3, August 1955, at pp. 358-362.

nadian Minister of External Affairs: "In so far as political prog-ress is concerned, we have made a great deal of progress. . . . I remember Mr. Spaak . . . commenting on the better atmosphere we were developing in the council in the sense that the discus-sions were . . . becoming more and more like cabinet discussions and less and less like formal international meetings."[81] The sub-ministerial meetings of the permanent representatives on the NATO Council might also broaden and deepen their discussions. Another method would be to hold periodic conferences of the NATO countries in the way that the Organization of American States holds periodic Inter-American Conferences. The Consulta-tive Assembly mentioned above is, however, the most far-reach-ing suggestion yet made. And there are various reasons why some of the governments are opposed to setting up a large delibera-tive organ; these reasons hinge largely upon the need for main-taining secrecy in the defense aspect of the discussions. This is another instance where short-run security considerations clash to some extent with progress toward long-run integration.

Our findings tend to support the view that "Those responsible for guiding NATO affairs should explore practical additional ways of furthering cooperation within the association in the non-military realms. . . ."[82] A former United States representative on the NATO Council has put this point well: "If measures to ease the economic strain caused by the defense buildup are within the realm of national action only, then NATO has created pres-sures which it can do nothing to relieve. In the long run this will accentuate the political difficulties, since public opinion is less likely to accept the burdens imposed by NATO defense plans if there is no collective effort among the Treaty partners them-selves to cushion the impact of the burden and deal with the economic and social problems."[83]

Although several countries in the North Atlantic area are not

[81] Extracts from Minutes of Standing Committee on External Affairs, House of Commons, 24 May 1955, pp. 541-542.

[82] Padelford, loc. cit., p. 364.

[83] Charles M. Spofford, "NATO's Growing Pains," Foreign Affairs, xxxi, 1, October 1952, p. 99.

members of NATO,[84] we consider it possible to foster greater responsiveness among NATO countries without too great a risk of losing some responsiveness between the NATO and the non-NATO countries.

C ◈ MAJOR GAPS IN KNOWLEDGE

Our studies of the strategy of integration left us strongly impressed with the importance of political innovation and invention. We found that many of the central institutions of amalgamated security-communities were highly original and improbable at the time they were adopted.[85] This has implications for both policy and research. Policy-makers might do well to shift the burden of proof a little more onto those who see too much danger in experiments with new means of gaining responsiveness and too much danger in putting into institutional form whatever can be gained. Researchers might give priority to contemporary questions of political integration. A great deal could be done also by studying more historical cases in order to check the findings from our small sample.

There is, however, a task of greater urgency in the international organization field. We have enough clues from history now to follow up our findings with some efficiency on the contemporary scene. A half-dozen of these questions, or clusters of questions, seem to us to rank high on the list.

1. What are the current images held concerning "Atlantic unity"? How salient are they in people's minds? Are they focused on amalgamation, or on pluralism? How are they related to images of national sovereignty?

2. Which groups, in which North Atlantic countries, are holding these images, and with what favorable or unfavorable attitudes? The following information is needed: which groups believe they would gain from integration, and which believe they would lose; how people's expectations are related to their knowl-

---

[84] These are Austria, Finland, Ireland, Sweden, Switzerland, and Spain. The last, we have found, is not a prime candidate for successful integration into the area anyhow.

[85] See Chapter III, Section G.

edge; and how these images and attitudes are related to the amounts and kinds of communication that people have received from other North Atlantic countries.

3. What types of dominant values have to be compatible among the units to be integrated in order to achieve (a) an amalgamated and (b) a pluralistic security-community? What is a minimum list of such values that would be required before people over a given area would consider that they were living jointly an acceptable "way of life"?

4. What are the sub-areas, within the North Atlantic area, where the network of international communication is strongest, and what are those where it is weakest? Which sub-areas have changed the most in either direction? It is especially important to know what groups form the main personal links between countries.

5. How seriously do people in the North Atlantic area regard the threat of the Soviet Union as a threat to their safety? Which groups do so, and in which countries? To whom do they look for protection—their country, other countries, or an international organization? If they support NATO, is protection against the Soviet Union their only motive for doing so?

6. What concrete steps might soon be taken to increase the sense of community among some or all North Atlantic countries, so as to provide a series of small but tangible successes leading toward eventual integration of the entire area?

A. Assuming, from the evidence of our historical studies, that certain increases in communication among North Atlantic countries would tend toward integrating the area, there may be particularly strategic forms and topics of communication that could be identified. The relative importance of news flows, travel, mail, educational interchange, and the like, could be assessed.

B. The present levels of communication flow in the North Atlantic area could be compared with the levels in situations where integration has been achieved or where it now exists. A study of specific steps that might be taken to foster an increase in that communication could include, for example, an inquiry into the advantages and costs of an Atlantic postal union which would, on the present model of the United States–Canada and the United Kingdom–Canada, carry all first-class mail at domestic rates. The advantages and costs of extending this idea to other classes of mail could also be investigated.

c. Those institutions and arrangements—national or supranational—should be identified which have been most effective in recent times in promoting consultation, cooperation, and responsiveness among any of the North Atlantic countries. What have been the common characteristics, if any, of those institutions and arrangements? In particular, what has been the effect so far of the European Coal and Steel Community upon sense of community within its area?

d. The effectiveness of arrangements to facilitate freer mobility of persons among any North Atlantic countries should be examined. What would be the advantages and costs of extending such arrangements? For example, the United States and Canada, the United Kingdom and Ireland, and the Scandinavian countries have special relationships in this field, running in different cases along a scale from freedom of tourist travel to something close to joint citizenship. There might be particular advantages and particular costs in extending special mobility to particular groups—priests and ministers, judges, teachers, editors, students, or certain government officials.

e. Much might be learned from the experience of particular legal and administrative inventions in this general field. For example, as in England and Scotland after 1608, what would be the advantages and costs if two or more countries arranged to grant joint citizenship to all persons born in those countries after a certain date? Or what would be the practical effects of a "full faith and credit" clause among participating countries, along the lines of the one contained in the United States Constitution and the Articles of Confederation?

These are some of the gaps in our knowledge which should be filled if a policy of moving toward a security-community for the North Atlantic area is to be advanced.

CHAPTER VI

◇◇◇

Conclusions

◇◇◇

A study like this cannot end with a short, neat prescription for policy. At this stage we can only summarize, with selection and perspective, some of the main points that are dealt with in the body of the book. These points are covered primarily in terms of our historical findings, and in a form preliminary to the full study. We offer here no final conclusions; they could not be made with the evidence from the limited number of cases we studied. Rather, we are writing in terms of indications and probabilities.

We found that the North Atlantic area, although it is far from integrated, seems already to have moved a long way toward becoming so. It rates high in eight of the fourteen conditions that we found either essential or helpful to integration. Only two countries, Spain and Portugal, seem to offer at this time striking disabilities for integration with the rest of the area. As for the other countries as a whole, they still rate low in the remaining six conditions that seem important for integration; and one of these conditions may be essential to either amalgamation or pluralism. This is the matter of responsiveness of governments, elites, and electorates of each country to the messages and needs of the other governments and peoples in the area. Since the second World War, however, mutual responsiveness in the North Atlantic area seems on the whole to have increased.

Within the area, a number of countries have already achieved pluralistic integration with each other, notably the United States and Canada. Together with the United Kingdom and Ireland, they form a group of four countries among whom the largest number of conditions favoring integration seem fulfilled already, so that one might think of them as a potential North Atlantic nucleus.

What policies seem most likely to promote integration?

The most effective approach seems to be that of pluralism, whether or not the ultimate object is amalgamation. This policy concentrates upon increasing the machinery and traditions of mutual consultation, communication, and cooperation. It seeks to eliminate all expectations of warfare among the North Atlantic countries, together with all specific preparations for it. Historically, such pluralistic integration has proved easier to attain, easier to preserve, and just about as effective as amalgamation in eliminating war within the area integrated. Moreover, we found that the pathway toward pluralistic integration was essentially the same as that toward amalgamation, at least for a long distance along the path. Whatever promoted pluralism also facilitated amalgamation, and sometimes factors that hindered the one also hindered the other. To pursue pluralism would not preclude eventual amalgamation, but an attempt at abrupt amalgamation might well postpone for a considerable time even pluralistic integration.

An increase in the responsiveness of governments and political elites to the needs and desires of other countries in the area seems to be extremely important for integration. Such responsiveness requires increased attention, fuller and more accurate understanding, and more rapid and effective action. A policy aimed at increasing responsiveness among the North Atlantic countries would have to include four overlapping goals. First of all, it would require an increase in the capabilities of the governments concerned in the fields of administration, policy formation, decision-making, and action. We found that weaker governments did not lead to stronger supranational institutions, but that stronger and more capable governments did. Second, increasing responsiveness would require a greater range and volume of communication and other transactions between the countries concerned, and particularly an increase in the transactions associated with rewards and expectations of reward. Third, such a policy would require the strengthening of the social groups, institutions, and organizations that function as unbroken links of social communication between the participating countries, and to increase their influence and popularity within each country. Finally, such a policy would have to aim at increasing greatly the mobility of persons throughout the area.

The most promising general method for moving toward these goals seems to be more and better communication. This would involve not only a greater exchange of goods, persons, and ideas, but also more institutions for carrying on consultations between governments and, where possible, for making joint decisions. It would also involve providing appropriate legal and institutional safeguards, such as those needed when the mobility of persons is increased. These safeguards, however, should not prevent imaginative experimentation with hybrid political institutions.

Among the most specific methods for promoting integration, some proved far more decisive than others. Those we found to be outstanding were the stress upon pluralism and the preservation of national sovereignty, and the emphasis upon domestic issues in each participating country. Most people in the past have tended to regard integration as a means to achieving some object of domestic politics. Beyond security from war among their respective countries, they sought political institutions—separate or common—that would assure them a better life in peacetime.

Political coalitions cutting across class lines were usually more effective than class movements in promoting integration. These coalitions would typically unite members of rising social groups and classes with those members of the established elite who were more favorable than the bulk of their peers to political and social change. Successful integration movements usually gained support from both conservatives and liberals. Often these movements were initially opposed by privileged elements and by the rural population, and skill in making compromises with these groups was important for eventual success. Broad public support for integration movements tended to come only at a later stage of the movement, but eventually it became crucial. With today's mass participation in politics, broad support is perhaps even more crucial.

The most effective appeal for integration has been—and probably would be now—the promise that it would result in greater individual rights and liberties, and in greater equality. In modern terms this would mean not only the classic political rights of the eighteenth and nineteenth century tradition, but also particularly the social and economic rights to greater opportunity and welfare which by now have to a large extent become political rights as well. This consideration confirms the importance of another major appeal—the expectation of economic gains. It was sufficient (even for amalgamation) if such expectations were fulfilled in part rather than completely, provided that a substantial portion of this fulfillment came at an early stage. Another effective appeal was the call to defend a way of life which appeared to be under attack but which was already becoming recognized as distinctive and desirable.

In contrast to all these, the appeal that power, as an end in itself, would be increased by integration often seemed to have little effect. Military alliances seemed to be relatively poor pathways toward amalgamation, as well as toward pluralistic integration. In and by themselves, such alliances did not seem to be very helpful. To be effective, they had to be associated with nonmilitary steps. Similarly, foreign military threats were often helpful to integration, but were not essential. This indicates that opportunities to integrate the North Atlantic area do not necessarily depend upon the continuation of a Soviet military threat, although that threat does seem to have helped toward greater unity.

In more concrete and current terms, our findings indicate the need for two general policies. One is to experiment with functional organizations within the North Atlantic area, such as the European Coal and Steel Community and the proposed European Atomic Energy Agency (EURATOM). Such experiments might help the participating governments and peoples to develop firmer habits of responsiveness, and also to gain experience concerning the capacities and limitations of such organizations. These experiments continue outside NATO, and could even prosper in the eventuality that NATO might for some reason decline as a binding force in the North Atlantic area.

The other promising policy seems to be preservation and further development of the chief international organization in the North Atlantic area—NATO. The most progressive steps would seem to be more and more toward the economic and social potentialities of this unique organization, and toward the greater political possibilities that might come from new organs of consultation and decision which could be built into it. There may well be a real opportunity in the near future to make NATO much more than a military alliance and, without alienating any nonmembers within the area, to move at least some of its member countries closer toward integration. This may be one of the most effective ways to advance the development of political community in the North Atlantic area, and to contribute to the eventual abolition of war.

APPENDIX

◇◇

An Example of One Type of Research Method Used: Flows of Trade and Mail Among 15 North Atlantic Countries

◇◇

One of the methods we used was a rather crude quantitative analysis of the flows of some kinds of transactions between the countries of the area studied, and the changes in these flows with the passing of time. None of these statistics are conclusive in themselves. But in their sampling of the activities of millions of people over the lifetime of over two generations, they seemed to offer food for thought.

Trade. Our findings show considerable change in the distribution of trade between fifteen countries within the North Atlantic area. These are all the countries within the area as we have defined it except Austria, Luxembourg, Portugal, and Spain. Austria, although one of our cases, has not been included, since in this case the statistics before and after 1918 are not comparable. For each country, the most important flows of exports and imports to other countries were calculated. A flow between any two countries was considered sufficiently important to be represented in our summary if it held either first or second *rank* in the imports or exports, respectively, of at least one of them. That is, the figures showed a *percentage share* in the exports or imports, respectively, of each country.

Taken together, these representations of first and second ranking trade flows show the asymmetry of much of the international trade in the North Atlantic area. It is rare for two countries to be linked closely by import and export flows which rank first in the North Atlantic trade for both of them. The United States and Britain in 1880, and the United States and Canada in 1928 and in 1952, furnish examples for this type of link.

The most frequent type of link we found, however, was asymmetrical, with a large country holding first or second place in the relevant foreign trade of many small ones, but with each of the latter only taking a minor share of the foreign trade of their larger partner. Certain large countries thus stand out, somewhat like stars in the sociograms used by social scientists, such as J. L. Moreno, to measure the popularity of individuals in a small group. In our trade picture for the North Atlantic area, the "star countries" seem to have changed over time: if Britain seemed still dominant in 1880 and 1913, it had to share first place with Germany in 1928 and 1937. By 1952 the main concentration of high ranking trade channels for the area had become centered on the United States, perhaps for the first time in history.

In terms of these flows very few European countries appear closely linked by trade to their neighbors. Most links, rather, seem to go across the sea: from the continental countries to Britain, and after the second World War to the United States. Italy, Germany, and France have remarkably few high-ranking trade channels to link them to each other, and the relative economic isolation of France from its European neighbors seems to have grown from 1880 to 1952.

Continental Western Europe, in particular, did not seem to form any obvious economic unit in terms of the flow of trade in 1952, on the eve of establishment of the European Coal and Steel Community. Rather, many of the main trade flows of its major countries continued to lead to the English-speaking world.

Mail. We also calculated the flow of mail among the same fifteen countries for three of the same years—1913, 1928, and 1939—and for 1949, the latest year for which data could be obtained.

Again, when the percentage share of each flow in the total North Atlantic mail of each country is considered, the main ties are not among the large countries of continental Western Europe, but rather between those and the English-speaking world. However, the links of postal correspondence among the Europeans are relatively stronger than are those of trade. The picture of a

growing isolation of France from Germany and Italy seems con-
firmed, and so is the picture of growing bonds between Britain
and Ireland. Finally, the changing centers of communication between 1913 and 1949 confirm the changing "star" pattern of
North Atlantic trade. Here the focus shifts from Germany in
1913 to Britain and Germany in 1928 and 1937, and at last
the United States appears on a level with these two countries
in 1949.

◈

To follow up these impressions and their implications would
require much additional research. The data could be made more
complete. The actual trade and mail flows could be evaluated
against the theoretical flows that could be expected from the
mere geographic proximity and size of population of the countries involved. Trade and mail flows within the North Atlantic
area could be contrasted for each country with corresponding
flows to countries in other areas, such as Latin America, Asia,
Africa, or Eastern Europe. Flows of other transactions, such as
travel, migration, or the dissemination of views, could be added.
Most important, perhaps, trade and mail data for 1954, 1955, or
1956 would be needed to indicate more recent trends.

Until then, no excessive reliance should be placed on the
limited data here collected. But until it should be modified by
better evidence, a lingering image may remain: the relative fragmentation of continental Western Europe, and its contrast to
the remarkable density of the web of transactions in the North
Atlantic area as a whole.

INDEX

pected, 202, from amalgamation, 49; growth, 51, 58, 67, rate of, 139-141, superior, 139; levels, 18; life, regulation of, 23; stagnation, 63, 139; strength, 138; ties, 44, 67, 145, 157, 157-58, limits of, 168-69, or gains, 49, 58

Economic Commission for Europe, 140n, 154n
economics, 127
economies, nationalized, 127
economists, 124
Ecuador, 15
Eden–Eisenhower conferences, 165
education, 36, 91, 138, 197
educational opportunity, 182
Eisenmann, Louis, 43n
Eisenhower, Dwight D., 165, 193
Eisenhower, Milton, 119n
election, direct, to international bodies, 194n
electorates, 199
elite, 27, 58, 63, 78, 91, 114, 201; broadening of, 52, 58; closure of, 63
elites, 40, 41, 45, 56, 58, 63, 84, 88, 93, 148, 199; merging of colonial, 76; political, 32; recruitment of political, 148
emotional, 62
employment, 136, 182
end-products, military, 163
enforcement, 5, 8, 26
enfranchisement, 132; of women, 132
England, 12, 18, 28, 29, 35, 38, 44, 47, 49, 51, 89, 99, 102, 106, 110, 189, see also United Kingdom; amalgamation of 72, 82; economic growth, 51; Ireland, 27, 30, 79, 82, 103, 108, 110, 151; Northern Ireland, 82, 108, 110; Scotland, 29, 76, 78, 81, 82, 87, 102, 104, 106, 110, 151; unification, 18, 23; Union of 1707 with Scotland, 72; Wales, 29, 76, 81, 82, 102, 103, 104, 106, 110; Wales, amalgamation, 72, 189; Wales–Scotland, amalgamation, 72
English, 36, 52, 99, 107; Irish relations between 1889 and 1914, 36; Irish union, 103; language, 158-59; Scottish, 71; Welsh union, 76
Englishmen, 57, 63, 74
English parliament, 71
English Protestant sects, 52

English-speaking Canadians, 56
English-speaking countries, 206
Episcopal Church, 47
equal access, 45
equality, 50, 184, 202; appeal of, 181-82; political appeal of, 98, 100
Eric Stern Institute, 153n
Eschenburg, Theodor, 52n
essential, 72; see conditions
estates (organized social classes), 87
ethnic group, 62; defined, 158
Europe, 10, 48, 131, 141, 142, 176, 178; agricultural pool, proposed, 131, 179; atomic energy pool, proposed, 131; Big, 117; Central and Western, 15; Council of, 117, 147, 160; Council of, Consultative Assembly, 174n, 194; Eastern, 15; Little, 117; Statute of, 127; Western, 120, 145, 159, 185; Western, attitudes toward integration, 143n; Western, continental, 206-07; Western, integration, 143
European, 10, 128
European Atomic Energy Agency (EURATOM), 202
European Coal and Steel Community, 143, 160, 171, 173, 174, 188, 198, 202; Common Assembly, 150, 206, ECSC, 131, 147, 150
European Defense Community (EDC), 142, 169-70
European federation, attitudes on, 175-76
European government, West, 180n
European immigrants, attitudes toward, 152
European Movement, 153n
European Parliament, 175
European Payments Union, 147
"European" policy, 142
European union, Western, 180, 180n
exchange, labor, 149; of ideas, 130; of persons, goods and ideas, 171; students, 149
expansionism, 126
expansion of territory, 24
expectations, 46, 58, 62, 67, 72-73, 110, 139, 141-44, 154, 165, 182, 196; decline in, 72; economic, 186-87; economic and social, 182; of living standards, 42; of loss from integration, 180; of warfare, 200; non-economic, 50; partly fulfilled, 202

predictability, predictions, 36, 56-58, 67, 129

prenationalistic sentiments, 19

preoccupation, with domestic politics, 119, *see also* self-preoccupation

Preradovich, Nikolaus von, 53n

pressure, 83, 112, 195; adventitious, 96; groups, 84, 93, 136, 137; local, 113; transient, *see* burdens

prestige, 55, 60; through NATO, 191

previous administrative and/or dynastic union, 44

priest, 93

privileged, classes, 110, 112; country, 130; elements, 201; groups, nationalities, etc., 62, 99, 105, 156-57, 179; groups, resistance of, 111; political units, 45; regions or units, 111

privilege, privileges, 45-46, 62, 71, 99-101, 103, 106; appeal of, 100-01; of the clergy, 103; sharing of, 156-57

probability, 11, 17, 25, 86, 100, 103-04, 114, 186

procedure, 8

pro-clericals vs. anti-clericals, 76

production, 192

professional groups, 107

programs (for federal union), 102

promoters, of amalgamation or integration, 95, 101, 114, 184

propaganda, 101, 105, 125

Protestant, 33, 46-47, 56, 64, 73, 74, 99, 150; and Catholics, 46-47, 77; Dissenters, 103; North Irish, 99, 103; opponents, 77

Prussia, Prussian, 27n, 28, 29, 38, 39, 40n, 44n, 47, 51, 52n, 55, 75, 89, 102, 113; economic growth, 51; elite, 53, 53n; increase in capabilities before 1871, 39, 50; leadership, 92, 94; Polish minority, 44n; responsiveness to Hanoverian needs, 40n

Pryde, George S., 49n

public, increase of, 92

public opinion, 32, 74, 166, 195; in American colonies, 74; in Norway, 75; Sweden, 75-76; Swiss cantons, 74

"quantitative" comparisons, 98

quantitative statements, 81n

race problem, 47

radicals, 76, 79, 89-90, 177

Radowitz, Joseph Maria von, 89

railroad, 43

ranges of transactions, *see* transactions

rate of change, 42

rate of claims and burdens upon central governments, 42

rate of growth, 24

Rath, John R., 60n

reason, rational, 134

Redlich, Joseph, 43n, 77n

reform, reforms, 63, 79, 94, 113, 131, 137; attitudes toward, 78-79

reformation, 76, 78

regionalism, 159-60, 189

regions, 132; outlying or underprivileged, 63; privileged or favored, 99

Reinink, H. J., 192

religion, 124; depoliticized, 125

research, desirable, 58, 130, 139, 149, 151, 166, 170, 173, 177, 180, 196-98, 207; foreign, references to, 23

Reservatrechte, 71n

reserves, 96

resources, 25, 35, 42, 90, 96, 119

respect, balance of, 55, 71

responsibility for welfare, 136

responsiveness, x, 25, 27, 36, 40-41, 61, 66, 87, 119-20, 129-33, 138-39, 144, 157, 161, 163-63, 173, 189, 198-200, between NATO and non-NATO countries, 196; among NATO countries, 196; capabilities for, 40; of England to Ireland, 36-37; of Prussia to Hanoverians, 40n; of United States, 138; within NATO, 194-96

reunion, 16, 55

revolutions, 96, 137; American, 19; French, 45n; of 1848, 45n

rewards, 71, 169, 189, 191; at early state, 202; balance of, 55, 71; joint, 81, 185-86; joint, expected, 141-44; timing of, 71, 202

Rhineland, 52

Richmond, Va., 107

rights, 36, 50, 99, 182, 184; individual, 100, 202; individual, appeal of, 100; to oppose government, 124; to organize, 124; of peasants, 114; political, 36, 181-83; to settle, 171; social and economic, 181-83, 202

Right, extreme, 178, moderate, 178

risks, of sudden amalgamation, 82

Risorgimento, 79n, 106n

etc.; international, asymmetry of, 205; Italian states, 44; policy, 143-44; privileges, 45

traditions, 37, 91, 93; democratic, 134-35; national, 132; Western, 134

traffic loads, 41

transactions, 58, 68, 116; associated with rewards, 200; balance of, 54-56, 70-71; domestic vs. foreign, 23, 120, 157-58; flows in North Atlantic area, 205-07; growth in, 148; linkage of, 148; ranges of, 189, 200, *see also* communication, intermarriage, mail, migration, trade, travel, etc.; ranges of, multiplicity, 58, 67, 144-48; ranges of, new, 70, 189; ratio between foreign and domestic, 120

transition, 33, 71, 76; to integration, 33-35

transportation, 12, 22, 43, 121

Transylvania, 15-16

travel, 130, 154, 171, 197; speed of, 11; tourist, 198

Treaty of Integrity in 1907, 35

Treaty of Washington, 64

Treitschke, Heinrich von, 88n

troops, foreign, legal status of, 128-29

Truman, Harry S, 177; Doctrine, 157

trust, 57, 129

Tudors, 55, 78

Tunis, 131

Turkey, Turkish, 9, 18, 117; challenge, 99; rule, in Hungary, 77

Ulster, 16, 18, 64, 108

unanimity, 165

underprivileged groups, 62

understanding, 57, 67, 119, 200

unification, of the American colonies after 1765, 18; of England and Scotland, 18, 23; of England and Wales, 18, 23, 55; movement, 7, 58, *see* amalgamation movement, integration movement; *see also* England, Germany, Italy

uniformities, 14

union, unions, 7, 19, 27, 45, 47, 87, 112; of crowns, 73, 80-81, 87; customs union, 41; as political issue, 47, 93-94, 112-13

union, Austria–Bohemia–Hungary, 81; Belgium–Netherlands, 1815-1830, 63; cases of, 15-16, 24; of democratic nations, 143, 180; dynastic, 18; England–Ireland, 1801, 16, 18, 24-25; England–Ireland, breakup, 16; England–Scotland, 1707, 16, 23-24, 44-45, 189; England–Scotland, 73, 114; England–Wales, 17, 18, 24; between England and Wales, 45, 53; Finland–Sweden, 15; Finland–Russia, 15; of NATO countries, 184-85; Newfoundland–Canada, 23; Norway–Sweden, 17-18, 24-25, 44, 81, 88; Poland–Lithuania, 15; Poland–Ukraine, 15; political, of Catholics and Protestants, 125; political, cases of secession from, 15-16, 24

Union of South Africa, 16; trade, 145n

uniqueness, 4, 13

unitary government, state, etc., 113, *see also* centralization

United Kingdom–Ireland, 159, 199; mail flow, 207

United Kingdom–Netherlands, 29

United Kingdom, *see also* Britain, England; Great Britain, 10, 25, 28, 60, 117, 128, 131, 146-47, 150, 160; attitudes to war, 155, foreign mail, 207; Gaelic and Welsh revivals, 159; imports, 158n; income, 134; news flow, 146n; opinion data, 153n; Parliament, 41-42, 45; trade, 145n, 206

United Nations, 143, 146, 182, 185; Declaration of Human Rights, 182; Economic Commission for Europe, 140n, 154n

United Nations Relief and Rehabilitation Administration (UNRRA), 131

U.S.S.R., 140-41; trade, 145n; as threat or challenge, 157, 172-73, 183, 191

U.S.S.R. and Soviet-dominated Europe, income, 133-34

United States, 5-7, 10, 15-16, 25-26, 28-30, 39, 47, 49, 61, 71, 72, 79, 80, 89, 106, 110, 116, 120, 121, 127, 128, 130, 131, 142, 143, 147, 157, 154n, 165, 167, 178, 182n, 184, 194

United States, administration policy, 178; assistance to Greece, 131; attitudes, on international police, 175; attitudes, to war, 155; attitudes, on world organization, 143n, 180; attraction of, 67; Civil War, 87n, 107; Confederate Army, deserters, 108; as core area, 138; domestic income vs.